Enter the Undead Author

The Fairleigh Dickinson University Press Series in Law, Culture, and the Humanities

Series Editor:
Caroline Joan "Kay" S. Picart, M.Phil. (Cantab), Ph.D., J.D., Esquire Attorney at Law; Adjunct Professor, FAMU College of Law; former English & HUM professor, FSU

The Fairleigh Dickinson University Press Series in Law, Culture, and the Humanities publishes scholarly works in which the field of Law intersects with, among others, Film, Criminology, Sociology, Communication, Critical/Cultural Studies, Literature, History, Philosophy, and the Humanities.

On the Web at http://www.fdu.edu/fdupress

Publications

George Pate, *Enter the Undead Author: Intellectual Property, the Ideology of Authorship, and Performance Practices since the 1960s* (2019)
Victor Li, *Nixon in New York: How Wall Street Helped Richard Nixon Win the White House* (2017)
Marouf A. Hasian, Jr., *Kafkaesque Laws, Nisour Square, and the Trials of the Former Blackwater Guards* (2017)
Michaela Stockey-Bridge, *The Lure of Hope: On the Transnational Surrogacy Trail from Australia to India* (2017)
Ted Laros, *Literature and the Law in South Africa, 1910-2010: The Long Walk to Artistic Freedom* (2017)
Peter Robson and Johnny Rodger, *The Spaces of Justice: The Architecture of the Scottish Court* (2017)
Doran Larson, *Witness in the Era of Mass Incarceration: Discovering the Ethical Prison* (2017)
Raymond J. McKoski, *Judges in Street Clothes: Acting Ethically Off-the-Bench* (2017)
H. Lowell Brown, *The American Constitutional Tradition: Colonial Charters, Covenants, and Revolutionary State Constitutions 1578 – 1786* (2017)
Arua Oko Omaka, *The Biafran Humanitarian Crisis, 1967-1970: International Human Rights and Joint Church Aid* (2016)
Marouf A. Hasian, Jr., *Representing Ebola: Culture, Law, and Public Discourse about the 2013–2015 West Africa Ebola Outbreak* (2016)
Jacqueline O'Connor, *Law and Sexuality in Tennessee Williams's America* (2016)
Caroline Joan "Kay" S. Picart, Michael Hviid Jacobsen, and Cecil E. Greek, *Framing Law and Crime: An Interdisciplinary Anthology* (2016)
Caroline Joan "Kay" S. Picart, *Law In and As Culture: Intellectual Property, Minority Rights, and the Rights of Indigenous Peoples* (2016)

Enter the Undead Author

Intellectual Property, the Ideology of Authorship, and Performance Practices since the 1960s

George Pate

FAIRLEIGH DICKINSON UNIVERSITY PRESS
Vancouver • Madison • Teaneck • Wroxton

Published by Fairleigh Dickinson University Press
Copublished by The Rowman & Littlefield Publishing Group, Inc.
4501 Forbes Boulevard, Suite 200, Lanham, Maryland 20706
www.rowman.com

6 Tinworth Street, London SE11 5AL

Fairleigh Dickinson University Press gratefully acknowledges the support received for scholarly publishing from the Friends of FDU Press.

British Library Cataloguing in Publication Information Available

Library of Congress Cataloging-in-Publication Data

ISBN: 978-1-68393-158-4 (cloth : alk. paper)
ISBN: 978-1-68393-159-1 (electronic)

∞™ The paper used in this publication meets the minimum requirements of American National Standard for Information Sciences Permanence of Paper for Printed Library Materials, ANSI/NISO Z39.48-1992.

Printed in the United States of America

Contents

Preface

Two personal experiences generated the seed of an idea that would become this project. The first occurred when I was still an undergraduate. A cease and desist letter from a prominent playwright's representation very nearly closed a theater company with which I regularly worked and that I considered an artistic home. The issue was a casting decision with which the author took issue regarding the race of the actor playing a particular character. The theater company in question (if I am being coy, it is only out of respect for the privacy of friends) had to close down the rest of the run just after the production opened and well short of the planned length of the run. The results were refunds, lost potential revenue, loss of investment for rights, sets, costumes, and actor and director salaries. As a not-for-profit company already surviving by the skin of its teeth year after year, the blow was devastating and would have been fatal if not for the tremendous outpouring of community support. Once the initial anger over this case subsided, I found myself asking questions about how it served a writer to limit the exposure of his own work. As an undergraduate with an English major, I also immediately noticed the discrepancy between this very real, seemingly unbridled authorial power on one hand and, on the other hand, the purported death of the author—a concept treated as a settled theoretical question in my studies. I carried these questions about authorship and power with me through the rest of my academic career.

The second significant personal moment in developing my ideas about these questions came some years later when I was working as a stand-up comedian in Chicago's alt-comedy scene. The issue of joke stealing reached its climactic point during this time, with public confrontations between famous comedians accusing one another of theft, sometimes even interrupting each other's sets in vicious attacks. Rumors swirled around the comedy community that some of these confrontations had even become physical. The issue permeated to my lowly level of comedians being paid less than minimum wage to tell jokes in smoky bars in the suburban hinterlands of the far northern reaches of the Red Line. My friends were on constant alert for joke thieves and bristled at even a perceived slight, a joke too similar to their own, someone activating the same joke-writing convention that they (not to mention everyone else) had used. I noticed that audiences, though, could hear essentially the same joke from two different comedians in the same evening and react entirely differently based on the performance quality. In fact, it seemed to me that audiences, after shows, were much more likely to remember performance style than particular jokes. I also knew that comedy had a long history of circulating material and routines. So I added to my old questions about authorship and power the issues of authenticity and originality.

As I began to explore these issues, a single concept repeatedly asserted itself as the thing that linked these cases and the questions they raised: intellectual property. Not just intellectual property *law*, but the very concept of owning the immaterial fruits of intellectual and creative labor. Far beyond a means for protecting and encouraging creative practice, the idea of intellectual property continually interpellates creative practices as, at their core, varieties of the capitalist mode of production. The artists and critics who make use of and hail intellectual property protections, in doing so, reproduce capitalist ideology even as they espouse anticapitalist rhetoric. This book explores and unpacks this central tension: the artist who claims progressive or even revolutionary political and social goals while simultaneously engaging in reproducing the dominant ideology through his production practices and celebration of intellectual property protections. The explanation goes far beyond mere hypocrisy; it involves a complex matrix of incentives, hierarchies, and self-effacing assumptions about common sense and value.

I owe the existence of this book to more people than I can possibly mention, but I would like to take a moment to directly thank as many as I sensibly can. Marla Carlson and David Saltz not only helped enormously with the earliest work that would become this project, but they also shaped me as a scholar and as a person. Enormous thanks also goes to Fran Teague, Oliver Gerland, Ric Knowles, Scott Magelssen, and anyone else I'm forgetting who read and responded to any part of this over the years. I am also forever indebted to Caroline Picart and everyone else at Fairleigh Dickinson University Press. As I was revising this, I was invited to attend the Yale Conference on Copyright and Collaboration in the Theater by Derek Miller and Brent Salter. The conversations were invigorating and challenging and in many ways directly contributed to the final form of this book. There were far too many participants to name everyone individually, but special thanks are due to Oren Bracha for his insight and patience. Speaking of insight and patience, I offer my endless gratitude to my wife, Libby Ricardo, who not only has read more draft pages in this process than anyone over the last half decade but has also provided emotional and moral support throughout. This book would not exist without her, and I look forward to the opportunity to return the favor.

Introduction

In 1984, the American Repertory Theater staged a production of Samuel Beckett's *Endgame* that would become legendary for the controversy it caused.[1] Director JoAnne Akalaitis decided to set the play in a burned-out subway station. Beckett's script, however, calls for a "bare interior" with two windows, a door, two ashbins, and an armchair.[2] Beckett's American publisher, Grove Press, attempted to force ART to shut down the production because, Grove Press claimed, the change in setting and addition of music deviated from the script and therefore violated their contract.[3] Martin Garbus, the lawyer representing Beckett and Grove Press, sent a cease and desist letter demanding the production be stopped. In this letter, Garbus tells Robert Orchard, then-executive director of ART, "your play is not Beckett's. It distorts the meaning of the play. After having your production described to him, Samuel Beckett says 'this has nothing to do with my play. You cannot do this. It should be stopped.'"[4] After some negotiations among Akalaitis, Grove Press, and Beckett, the author and publisher agreed to let the production continue with the concession that the following note from Beckett be included in the program:

> Any production of *Endgame* which ignores my stage directions is completely unacceptable to me. My play requires an empty room and two small windows. The American Repertory Theater production which dismisses my direction is a complete parody of the play as conceived by me. Anybody who cares for the work couldn't fail to be disgusted by this.[5]

Beckett here does not just express his distaste for the production, although distaste certainly seems to figure into his comments. Instead, he attempts to invalidate the performance altogether, to use his authorial position to mark the production as aberrant, as not-*Endgame*, and to suggest that to like the production is to dislike or, worse, to fail to understand Beckett. Similar to the language in the cease and desist notice, this statement attempts to sever the link between Beckett and the performance without relinquishing ownership. When *Endgame* ceases to be Beckett's, it must be stopped. The ART *Endgame* case has as much to do with property as with artistic integrity.

On some level, Beckett's insistence on ownership sits a bit at odds with his image as an artist known for his disdain of popular success. More broadly, his strong-handed enforcement of that ownership seems at odds with the concept of the death of the author, the idea that the author behind a work disappears as that work enters into an ever-circulating discourse. The author was declared dead in the 1960s, yet here is that dead author responding with legal force to a director's creative practice, a practice in many ways activated by the author's own alleged demise. The author has, in a sense, become undead. Or, perhaps more likely, the author never really died in the first place. Even as the concept of the death of the author was gaining ground among critics, scholars, and artists, the United States passed a new copyright law in 1976 that reaffirmed and even expanded upon the ownership rights of actual, living authors, and a number of incidents such as the ART *Endgame* controversy demonstrated an even greater growth in the extralegal power of authors to limit the use and in some cases even interpretation of their work. In other words, just as the author was declared theoretically dead, his power and influence were expanding. So broad was this expansion of powers, I argue, that authorship became the default mode of cultural production for all creative fields. In other words, the model of authorship that rose in response to the death of the author became the normative case against which all other models of cultural production were judged. In no field does the default to authorship have a greater or more immediate impact than in theater and performance.

Two questions regarding authorship and theater guide my research. First, what role does authorship play in theater and performance since the 1960s? Following Artaud's call for "no more masterpieces," innovative theater artists in the second half of the twentieth century often define themselves by their rejection of textual authority, so exploring the pressures authorship exerts on theater in this period provides important insight about the way theater defines itself in relation to and in distinction from other modes of cultural production. A number of court cases, legal articles, scholarly books, essays, and collections have examined the growing dissonance between postmodern theoretical reconsiderations of art and authorship on one hand and legal and institutional stagnancy on the other. My second question, then, asks what unique challenges theater and performance present in this growing body of research about the relationships among theory, the law, cultural assumptions about the law, and cultural production. Though the precise effects of this relationship vary among the different theater and performance genres I examine, a major theme appears repeatedly. Theater practitioners and performers rhetorically embrace postmodern concepts such as the death of the author or espouse anticapitalist ideological commitments while simultaneously engaging with modes of production ultimately aligned with an author-centric, hierarchical, neoliberal ideology. I will argue that these conflicts result not from hypocrisy but from something much more complex: a series of contradictions and paradoxes built into the cultural construction of authorship that provide a place for resistant ideologies in order to keep them in check. The history of theater in the United States from the 1960s to the present is full of performance practices moving away from or rhetorically resisting a textual basis, so understanding how authorship in turn resists its own decentralization is crucial to understanding this period in theater and performance history. My examination of this history has led me to two conclusions that I will advance throughout this book. The first is that the ideology of authorship often exerts greater actual regulatory force than the law itself. The second is that one cannot embrace the aesthetic values of authorship and its attendant legal protections without being complicit in reproducing neoliberal ideology.

AUTHORS AS OWNERS, INDIVIDUALS, AND ORIGINATORS

Understanding the impact of authorship rests on having a solid foundational definition of the author. The author is a broad cultural construction, a contested term with a long and complex history and one that means different things in different contexts. A lawyer might, for instance, have a very different idea of what it means for one to be an author than a playwright. For present purposes, I will define authorship as a cultural construction consisting of three attributes that appear across discourses and disciplines regarding creative production: ownership, individuality, and originality. I focus on these attributes both because of their centrality to the ideology of authorship and because each causes unique problems when applied to theater and performance. These attributes also figure strongly in legal scholarship on the author. In his study of the relationship among Romantic authorship, copyright law, and ideology, legal scholar Oren Bracha identifies individuality, ownership, and originality as the three features of authorship most prominent among narratives of authorship's contested role in the development of policy and, more importantly, in extralegal conceptions of intellectual property.[6] These three features may not constitute an exhaustive account of authorship, but they point to the most significant sites of conflict and points of inquiry especially in terms of late twentieth-century cultural production. I should also note at this point that by authorship I do not necessarily mean literary production. I use the term authorship to point to a particular relationship between cultural producer and cultural product. By author I do not mean writer but instead an owner of an original cultural product the originality of which is intimately tied to that owner's unique individuality. In this sense, one could author a painting, a work of music, or a performance. It is to this three-pronged relationship between producer and product that American institutions and cultural assumptions default. When I refer to a figure such as Edward Albee as an author, I am specifically referring to his functioning within this tripartite identity of authorship as owner, individual, and originator. When I refer to him as a playwright, I am specifically referring to his practice of writing plays.

The idea that authors possess or should possess intrinsic ownership rights to the works they create both validates the author aesthetically and supports her ability to profit from her creations. Ownership is a matter of control, of an ability, backed by the law, to limit others' abilities to access and use something. Mark Rose sees this ability as central to the idea of authorship, contending that "the distinguishing characteristic of the modern author . . . is proprietorship; the author is conceived as the originator and therefore the owner of a special kind of commodity, the work."[7] Rose argues that the modern concept of an author places less emphasis on creativity than on ownership, that the creation of the work is secondary in importance to the author-owner's exclusive ability to control and profit from it. Bracha echoes Rose's emphasis on the work as a "special kind of commodity," pointing out that the work can assume multiple forms and survive multiple processes, such as adaptation or translation, with its essential identity intact, at least for legal and commercial purposes.[8] An author is not just an owner, then, but a special kind of owner with a broad set of powers to control even certain references to her property. Theater, particularly text-based theater, presents a challenge to this notion of authorship as ownership because all text-based theater involves at least two distinct works—the play text and the performance—with, arguably, separate creators. The figure of the author-owner who controls and is in turn responsible for the work in all its forms and transformations leaves no room for other artists in text-based theater to make claims to ownership or even to creativity. The author-owner construction vests the playwright with all the commercial and aesthetic power and potentially leaves other theater artists out in the cold. While other art forms experience this tension when dealing in derivative works such as adaptations or translations, theater presents a special case because it deals with this on a daily basis. Every play performance is, in some sense, a derivative work. None of this is to say that ownership is somehow foreign to or incommensurable with theater per se, only to point out that the literary model of the author-owner who exerts total control over all meaning, circulation, and use of a work becomes much more complex when applied to any collaborative theater or performance practice. Text-based theater especially complicates authorial ownership because of the necessary transformation of the original work and because of the multiplicity of creators who collaborate on a production.

Individuality functions as both aesthetic validation and a prerequisite for market participation; Rose compares authors' individual identities to product brands.[9] The concept of the author as individual has strong ties to Romanticism, with its images of authors set against the world, unappreciated in their time, even bolstered in their artistry by their retreat from society. Martha Woodmansee argues that the emphasis on the author's individuality is a historically limited, contingent phenomenon. She points out that "as late as the 1750s in Germany the writer was still being represented as just one of the numerous craftsmen involved in the production of a book—not superior to, but on a par with other craftsmen."[10] Individual authorship, then, not only fetishizes isolation but also places authors (writers) at the top of a hierarchy of cultural production.[11] By comparing the rhetoric of individual genius with the continued and even increasing reality of collective and collaborative writing in both creative practice and the corporate world, Woodmansee suggests that the ideal of individualism enshrined in the cultural construction of authorship obscures the complex reality of collaboration that defines most cultural production. Though he does not specifically address theater, Rose addresses the problem of reconciling individual genius to a collaborative production apparatus, arguing that the rhetoric of individual genius "elides the role of the publisher—or, in the case of films, of the studio or producer—in cultural production."[12] The collaboration of multiple individuals as well as the combining of different disciplines both constitute key features of most theatrical practice, so the ideal of individualism can cause problems in any theatrical production model. The innovative theaters of the 1960s to the present create an even greater problem for individualistic authorship because of the premium many of these theaters placed on collaboration even at the level of creating the text.

Originality builds on individuality. If authors must be singular, discrete individuals, then originality functions as the demand that each individual distinguish herself from every other in order to keep everyone separate and competitive. The rhetoric of authorship demands ex nihilo creation of new works that could only be created by a particular artist's unique voice, obscuring, as Rose points out, "the fact that cultural production is always a matter of appropriation and transformation."[13] Bracha cites originality as the clearest exemplar of the complicated relationship between Romantic authorship and copyright law. He shows that at the same time originality was becoming more important rhetorically, it was losing its standing as a prerequisite for legal protection.[14] In other words, the originality threshold works must meet to qualify for copyright protection is technically quite low, but the demand for originality still exerts powerful rhetorical force in legal and extralegal arguments. Intellectual property cases call on originality in a way that other property cases do not because intellectual or intangible property is more susceptible to copying. Most tangible products cannot be easily duplicated; multiples have to be produced. I cannot, in other words, simply place your apple on a copy machine and have an apple to sell. I have to grow my own or steal your actual, physical apple.[15] If I put your short story on a copy machine, though, I walk away with a copy of your short story that I can then copy and distribute endless times without changing its identity. Because they are more susceptible to copying, then, intangible goods in general offer institutional and aesthetic challenges to the concept of originality. Theater and performance complicate the matter of originality even further by adding embodied goods—performances—to the equation. In addition, theater practitioners as a matter of routine produce performances of texts that have been performed countless times before, yet those performances are not necessarily derivative of other performances of the same text. A performance's originality, in fact, may be most recognizable in comparison to other performances of the same material. The originality of a new production of *Hamlet* must be determined by looking at its relationship to other productions of *Hamlet*, a process of comparison that recognizes the play is not original even while understanding how it is. Again, theater strains the tenability of the original/derivative dichotomy, then, because a performance of a play is, by default, simultaneously an original work and a derivative work.

This picture of the cultural and ideological construction of Authorship in the late twentieth century owes an enormous debt to and helps to reproduce neoliberalism. David Harvey, one of the leading scholars on neoliberalism, says that "Neoliberalism is in the first instance a theory of political economic practices that proposes that human well-being can best be advanced by liberating individual entrepreneurial freedoms and skills within an institutional framework characterized by strong private property rights, free markets, and free trade."[16] Harvey goes on to argue that neoliberalism becomes, in the last few decades of the twentieth century and into the present, an all-encompassing ethic in which all other ethical systems become subsumed to the logic of the marketplace and all cultural, political, and social interactions come to be understood in terms of the market and with the assumption that ensuring the greatest possible freedom and power to the individual is the ultimate good in all cases.[17] In other words, neoliberalism claims to herald the end of politics to be replaced by competition and individual self-interest in all arenas shaping social and cultural change. Harvey points out that creating widespread consent to the ideas of neoliberalism means placing neoliberalism's assumptions as deeply held but not deeply thought-about notions of how things work, and that such placement must occur across a wide variety of cultural channels.[18] Authorship maps neatly onto neoliberalism, with its veneration of the individual and its distrust of collaboration. Although the playwrights considered in this book often, in the content of their work, rail against neoliberalism or at least its associated ideas and policies, they embrace and reproduce its assumptions about production and exchange when it comes to their professional practices and their roles as authors.

I focus on these three aspects of authorship—ownership, individuality, and originality—because each reveals something about the relationship at the heart of my research between the innovative performance practices and established ideological structures. Each of these three in some way gets at late twentieth-century authorship's complex dual allegiances to Romanticism and neoliberalism. Take individuality as an illustrative example. Individuality is a key aspect of Romantic authorship. It valorizes the genius removed from society, recollecting experiences in tranquility, to quote Wordsworth, untouched by corrupting society, free to plumb the depths of his own nature. Individuality also serves neoliberalism because the virtue of competition at the heart of neoliberal ideology valorizes self-interest above all else. Thus, the very aspect of Romanticism that scorns market value in favor of rhetorics of freedom, transcendence, and isolation is the same aspect that renders it so amenable to neoliberal ideology. I am painting in broad strokes here, but this is the general pattern of authorship's function in interpellating Romantic or other countercultural or revolutionary thought within a dominant neoliberal ideology, a pattern that will appear in the case studies throughout my arguments. This process is complex and less one-sided than it may seem.

I argue that authorship as I have defined it functions as a kind of default mode of cultural production. I want to make clear that when I refer to institutional or cultural defaults to authorship along these lines of originality, ownership, and individuality, I do not mean that authorship inscribes its assumptions onto other art forms. Default does not mean dominant or all-encompassing. Defaults are starting points, the assumed parameters applied to all members of a given class unless explicitly modified. Like the default settings on a word processor, institutional and legal defaults to authorship do not mean all instances of cultural production are necessarily subsumed under the model of authorship. My word processor does not force me to leave an extra ten-point space after every paragraph; it just does so unless I tell it otherwise. And sometimes, even after I have told it otherwise. Repeatedly. The cases I study reflect the frustrations of a stubborn default setting, of a system reluctant to accept that its most basic assumptions may not fit all cases. The point is not to show how authorship overwrites other modes of cultural production, but to show how institutions and cultural assumptions tend toward assuming other modes of cultural productions function under the same basic settings as authorship and to show the problems that assumption causes. The default to authorship does not reign in all theater- or performance-related issues from the 1960s to the present, but I want to explore the often adverse effects it has had in the cases I examine.

INTELLECTUAL PROPERTY

No discussion of the relationship between the ideals of Romantic authorship and the practicalities of cultural production can proceed without looking to copyright law because, as Rose puts it, "no institutional embodiment of the author-work relation . . . is more fundamental than copyright, which not only makes possible the profitable manufacture and distribution of books, films, and other commodities but also, by endowing it with legal reality, helps to produce and affirm the very identity of the author as author."[19] Eric E. Johnson makes a similar case; intangible goods create special problems because there is "nothing you can do to stop other people from using or enjoying a copyable work. (Unless, of course, there's a law.)"[20] In other words, the intangible work can only function as a commodity given some kind of external norm, convention, or statute prescribing rules for its circulation. Since the identity of the author depends so greatly on a relationship to the work, understanding the laws that actuate and regulate the work's dissemination as a marketable good proves vital to examining authorship. I hesitate even to use the term "intellectual property," as it threatens to conflate and oversimplify several distinct branches of the law. Accounts of intellectual property law often clump together four different legal concepts: copyright, trademark, patent, and right of publicity. Of these four, I will primarily deal with copyright and, to a lesser extent, right of publicity. Copyright most clearly impacts my questions about authorship and performance. Copyright has evolved from a right to print copies to a more broad set of powers to control the reproduction, dissemination, transformation, and even, in some cases, interpretation of the extensive work.[21] This study will often show the effects of copyright's evolution on performance practices. Right of publicity, which protects public figures from having their likenesses or personalities used for promotion or endorsement purposes without securing consent from or financially compensating that public figure, primarily affects performance in the ways it provides legal definitions of such elusive concepts as personality and artistic style.[22] Trademark, dealing with businesses' rights to protect images associated with their products, and patent, granting exclusive rights to use certain processes and inventions, have little impact on performance. As Johnson points out, each of the four branches of law that often fall under the umbrella of intellectual property has its own set of justifications and assumptions and each deals with a distinct type of market, so treating them as one unit causes problems.[23] These different branches get conflated for an understandable reason, however: all deal with the problem of treating intangible goods as property. The real problem then is not so much with the term "intellectual property" as it is with the phrase "intellectual property *law*." The former points to the idea that intangibles such as arrangements of words or images removed from their physical instantiations can function as property while the latter perilously suggests that there exists a single, overarching branch of the law that can deal with all such property in the same way. A better term for many of the works I will discuss, then, might be the broader legal term "intangible property," of which intellectual property is a species. I have elected to stick with "intellectual property," however, both for the sake of familiarity and for the associations it suggests between the product and the creative process.

Because the many essays from law journals I consult throughout this book come from a discourse operating under very different conventions from my own, I offer some notes on my approach to the question of the law. Many of the legal scholars and scholars from other fields who talk about legal issues do so in terms of the law itself. In other words, they study matters such as legislation and court opinions to explore how the law is working. Their arguments have to do with matters of law. In a legal case, a matter of law is the question of how the law applies to the case as opposed to a matter of fact, which is a question of the facts of a case. A question of whether copying a joke is illegal is a matter of law; a question of whether someone copied a joke from someone else is a matter of fact. My arguments in this book are fundamentally not about matters of law in the legal sense of the phrase, even when dealing with the law, for two important reasons. First, one of my major claims is that it is very often not the law itself that informs decisions made or actions taken in the name of the law. Instead, assumptions about the law and more deeply about the "common sense" underlying the law—assumptions that contribute to the cultural construction of authorship—often exert influence in excess of the law itself. This influence can take several forms. It can appear in the self-enforcement of conventions or norms among creative communities, norms with tighter restrictions than the law itself but that cite the law as their exegesis. This influence also exerts real regulatory power when parties with greater power to litigate force other parties to concede even when the law might be on the side of the weaker party. Second, a major part of my point in this book is to argue that these cases show institutional, cultural, and social defaults to the values of ownership, individuality, and originality. So when I say that a legal case privileges individualism, for instance, it is not to say that the law is wrong or being applied incorrectly. As a matter of law, the law is doing what it is supposed to do. My point is to show that "doing what it is supposed to do" means privileging individualism over collaboration in these cases. In other words, my argument is fundamentally not a legal argument, but an ideological argument about the law itself and its relation to other cultural forces.

THE PROBLEM OF IDEOLOGY

The associations among authorship, theater, and other cultural forces necessarily raise ideological questions because they draw attention to the influence of both state institutions and widespread assumptions about creative practices as well as to the challenges those practices provide or fail to provide to dominant modes of production. I use the word "ideology" then, to refer to assumptions that erase themselves as assumptions and instead purport to be self-evident or common sense. Much of my thinking on ideology starts with the work of Antonio Gramsci and Louis Althusser. From Gramsci I take the idea of cultural hegemony as the means by which a dominant class maintains support from a suppressed class by successfully ingraining the moral and intellectual beliefs that best serve the interests of the dominant class as "common sense" for all classes.[24] Common sense—basic assumptions about reason, logic, and morality—is therefore contingent and ideologically loaded. Cultural hegemony functions largely through what Althusser calls "ideological state apparatuses," those social, cultural, and legal institutions that help reproduce dominant ideologies.[25] Althusser argues that these institutions promote certain ideological values under the auspices of what they claim are politically neutral, common sense, or universal virtues. The law, for example, often claims to serve the people and protect their intrinsic rights to freedom and safety, when in actuality, he argues, it inscribes onto the public those values that best serve the dominant class. In terms of the present study, the idea of intellectual property promises to protect artists, but it also inevitably reproduces capitalist values. Althusser also argues that while they may function differently, "all ideological state apparatuses contribute to the same result: the reproduction of the relations of production, i.e. of capitalist relations of exploitation."[26] While Althusser importantly points to the ways in which cultural and social institutions reproduce ideological assumptions, his arguments tend to be unidirectional. The (always capitalist) state always inscribes its ideological assumptions onto passive subjects. Terry Eagleton offers a more flexible definition of ideology as a "motivated mystification," a definition that conveys the false neutrality of common sense and universal virtues without resorting to the determinism of Althusser's ideological state apparatuses.[27]

Authorship, as I have defined it, serves as a tool for reproducing the assumptions underlying neoliberalism as common sense through the channels of cultural production. Each of authorship's three key features in some way serves the particular kind of "common sense" necessary to support neoliberalism. Ownership, the right of a private individual or entity to limit the use of a good or resource and ability to profit from leasing that right, perhaps most obviously supports a capitalist ideology because it is the basis for exchange and trade. It may even feel obvious that a writer should exercise such control and privileges over the fruits of her labor, but the idea that a particular arrangement of words can count as property to be owned and limited in this way actually represents a relatively recent development, one that had to overcome a great deal of skepticism from Western legal and institutional forces. Also, that feeling of the natural relationship between creation and ownership is an example of ideologically loaded common sense. Ownership as an aspect of authorship, then, not only supports but expands the scope of ideological assumptions about property by fostering the ability to treat intangibles as property.[28] Individualism bolsters both the ideal of competition at the heart of neoliberalism and the American mythology of the self-made man. The image of the author as a sole creator whose necessary isolation maintains the purity of her unique genius discourages collaboration, implicitly equating the need to collaborate with a weak or incomplete individual talent. The praise of individualism as part of a narrative of pulling oneself up by one's own bootstraps sows suspicion of collectivity. Originality functions ideologically in close concert with ownership. In order for something to have value, to be worth excluding others from using it, it must offer something not already available to the market. Furthermore, when someone creates and owns a work, he can only exclude others from using it if he can prevent others from copying it. So originality is not a politically or economically neutral virtue of artistry, the purely aesthetic celebration of unique voices or points of view, but instead also functions as a crucial support for a competitive, individualistic trade and market system.

The narrative of ideology, authorship, and performance is not a story about either literature or capitalism imposing foreign values onto theater. The point is that in the 1960s, the most self-consciously innovative theaters intentionally moved away from the dominance of the text and toward a performance-centric aesthetic and ethics. But the strength of authorship as default mode of cultural production complicated efforts to reject authorship, and the more theater and performance genres denied the author's central significance the more emphatically authorship asserted itself as the "natural" or "correct" mode of cultural production. When I say that the ideology of authorship exerts more practical regulatory force than the law, I simply mean that assumptions about authorship as the default mode of production influence the behaviors and production practices of theater artists to a greater extent than the law does. Even in radically reinventing theatrical practice, then, theaters, playwrights, and performers often reproduced the ideologies supporting the very models of production and exchange that they rhetorically opposed in their works and elsewhere.[29] The end result was an ever more emphatic, reactionary insistence on originality, individuality, and ownership as the natural default conditions of all cultural production, even in fields previously amenable to collaboration and free circulation of material such as the musical and stand-up comedy.

THE DEATH AND RETURN OF THE AUTHOR

These reactionary restatements of authorship as the common sense mode of production happen in the 1960s in no small part due to pronouncements of the author's death by Roland Barthes and Michel Foucault.[30] Roland Barthes argues in his 1967 essay "The Death of the Author" that authors have always been dead, erasing themselves into oblivion at the moment of writing because committing thought to language requires an instantaneous entry into the endless exchange of symbols, a system without origins and therefore without originators or authors. Barthes further argues that our notion of the author results from the rise of humanism and reaches its apex and logical conclusion under capitalism because of its praise of individualism, the idea that each social actor rises or falls within a society according to her own innate abilities. Foucault pursues a slightly different tactic in his 1969 lecture "What Is an Author?" He replaces questions about the author and her intentions with questions about the ways in which the idea of the author functions within particular discourses. In other words, whereas Barthes simply dismisses the author as a casualty of language as an endless exchange lacking a center, Foucault seeks to interrogate the uses and implications of the idea of the author itself as a discursive tool. In both cases, though, the message is clear: the author, the real historical person whose intentions and individual genius set the limits for the proliferation and exchange of meanings, no longer exists, no longer can exist, is dead. And many of the innovative theater practitioners who come up in this study—the Open Theatre and the Wooster Group, to name two—start from this assumption, suggesting that the death of the author fits into a larger cultural trend of questioning any centralized authority holding the final word on truth and meaning. But many of the cases in this study will also show that killing the author off is not so simple in the theater because of the continuing legal presence of a particular author. Authors and their estates have the power, both legal and extralegal, to inflict very real, practical consequences on those who take for granted their figurative death, and these consequences take effect in theater more often than in other modes of cultural production. Thomas Pynchon is not going to show up at your door with a cease and desist because he thinks you misinterpreted *Gravity's Rainbow*. Edward Albee might do—and in fact has done—the same over *The Goat*. Much of the story of theatrical and performance practice since the 1960s arises from authors' insistence that the author is not dead. Theater is the perfect site to examine how the death of the author plays out in practical terms because the author keeps coming back with a vengeance.[31]

AUTHORSHIP, DISCOURSE, AND CHANGE

Theater is not, of course, the only site of disparities among discourse, theory, and practice regarding the death of the author. A fairly large body of scholarship has emerged over the last two decades or so dealing with such disparities and coming to a number of different conclusions. Several major threads of argument have emerged about the relationship among theories of authorship, creative practice, and institutional limits such as the law or publishing industry norms. The first of these threads suggests that copyright law has strayed from its purpose of protecting artists and ensuring their ability to operate on fair terms in the market and has instead come to support the interests of large corporations at the expense of individual artists' rights. Lawrence Lessig is perhaps the most well-known advocate of this theory, arguing that by allowing the expansion of corporations' ownership rights to intangible property the law is gradually chipping away at processes of exchange and influence that have long been the basis of creativity and innovation.[32] Siva Vaidhyanathan makes a similar argument, asserting that copyright laws do not only benevolently offer protection to artists but also "expose and depend on American ethical assumptions and cultural habits."[33] And Kembrew McLeod went so far as to legally secure a trademark to the phrase "freedom of expression" as a kind of symbolic protest, showing how trademark law infringes on the freedom of expression by allowing McLeod to limit others' use of the phrase embodying the idea itself.[34] According to these arguments and many others of their kind, copyright law comes to discourage the very innovation it was intended to protect by vesting a small number of powerful individuals and corporations with an overly broad ability to control uses of and references to common cultural material.

If the above arguments call for a return to a more noble form of copyright serving its purpose of protecting artists' ability to profit from their works, then a second line of arguments goes even further, suggesting that copyright law needs to adapt to major paradigmatic changes in assumptions about cultural production such as the death of the author. In other words, these arguments suggest that copyright needs not to return to its roots but to step into cultural theory's present. Martha Woodmansee and Peter Jaszi edited a collection of essays largely espousing some version of this view, and their introduction and the essays they contributed provide this line of argument with its manifesto.[35] Woodmansee argues that modern copyright law erroneously treats as universal a certain set of assumptions about authorship.[36] She points out that authorship has functioned under other sets of assumptions in the past and thereby undermines the alleged universality of the contemporary model of authorship instantiated in current copyright law. Furthermore, she argues not only that these assumptions are not universal but that they are now outdated, reflecting an understanding of cultural production that no longer obtains. The law, in her view, needs to adapt to the radical theoretical and practical changes regarding the practice of writing. Peter Jaszi takes this argument even further by suggesting that contemporary copyright law forcefully inscribes a Romantic concept of authorship onto contemporary practice whether it fits or not.[37] Rose takes this argument in a slightly different direction. He argues that while copyright no longer reflects the realities of cultural production and should change, the situation is not necessarily a crisis and will only slowly resolve itself over time. He suggests that the cultural reluctance to abandon authorship results from an understanding that changing copyright would mean acknowledging and accepting a paradigmatic shift in understandings of artistic merit and market value.[38] In any case, these arguments all see copyright's adapting to postmodern and poststructural theories as a desirable goal.

The most outspoken opponent of this line of reasoning is David Saunders. Saunders consistently decries the arguments of Woodmansee, Jaszi, Rose, and others, arguing against what he calls the "pressure to subordinate positive law to the direction of aesthetics."[39] Saunders also suggests that legal decisions are in no way beholden to shifts in philosophy or aesthetics, demanding only "legal answers" to "legal problems."[40] Mark Lemley makes a similar case, suggesting that not only should the law not adjust to current aesthetic theories, but that it never had any real relationship to aesthetic theories such as Romantic authorship in the first place.[41] Both arguments dismiss aesthetic theories as empty and at their worst frivolous, purely rhetorical constructs fine for discourse about creative works but completely out of place in serious discussions of the real business of the law.[42] According to these arguments, then, the law has nothing to do with authorship and functions as a completely independent entity. That the law fails to adapt to changing creative practices is not the law's problem.

In a sense, I position myself outside of the question of whether the law should adapt to changing theories and practices of cultural production. My present purpose, rather, is to examine the law's ideological underpinnings and scope of influence. In other words, one major aim of my study is to take a step back from the question of whether and how contemporary law and aesthetics should correct the rift between themselves and instead reexamine that rift itself. I also want to make clear that I do not see the law's ideological influence as unilateral, total, or deterministic. In some cases an apparent incommensurability between the law and a particular aesthetic is merely rhetorical, a divide between practices of cultural production and widespread assumptions and arguments about the law rather than between those practices and the law itself. In other cases, the law may seem to inscribe or demand certain values such as individuality when in fact it only defaults to those values but can accommodate others such as collaboration. And for almost every case in which the law seems inflexible, unable to deal with revolutionary artistic practice, there is another showing the exact opposite. Again, I intend to show that ideas about the law, even when they exceed the scope of or even directly contradict the law, exert enormous ideological and practical influence. The relationship between art and the law in the late twentieth and early twenty-first centuries is both more complex and less contradictory than many arguments on both sides suggest, and my project seeks to chart the intersections as well as the points of divergence and make sense of both.

A great deal has been written about the role or function of the author in both law journals and literary studies. Far less has been written about authorship in theater scholarship. But the figure of the author haunts theatrical practices and culture with both aesthetic and highly practical consequences, especially in the period of the 1960s to the present. I have already hinted at some of the issues this relationship raises, but I would like to refocus on the central questions before moving from the literary and legal discourse to the theater scholarship. Theater complicates the issue of authorship as a model of cultural production because its production apparatus includes many more agents with their own financial and creative interests in the project than does literary production. In literature, the story runs that the author writes a work that is then disseminated to the public, although of course editors and publishers complicate this to an extent. Theater complicates this narrative with its necessary intermediaries of directors, actors, and designers filtering the text from the author to the audience. And my reasons for looking at this relationship in the United States from the 1960s to the present have to do with radical changes in that period in both constructions of authorship and theatrical practices. Many theaters in this period moved toward the postdramatic, toward a rejection of the author's centrality to a production, further complicating the already fraught position of authorship within theater. Authorship's awkward mapping onto theater results partly, I propose, from the ideologically privileged position of authorship as the default mode of cultural production. By this I mean that cultural validation for artists in nonliterary fields often rests on comparisons to authorship.

Although relatively little theater scholarship has focused on the role of the author as a cultural institution and its effects on theater and performance practices per se, an interest in the broader issue of theater's relationship with social and cultural institutions, particularly the law, has blossomed over the last decade and a half and has picked up speed recently. Almost all of the scholarship in this area responds in some way to the work of Peggy Phelan, particularly her contention that performance's ephemerality and embodiedness render it immune to, outside of, or at least intrinsically resistant to market forces such as commodification.[43] Philip Auslander agrees with Phelan that because a live performance can be recorded but cannot itself be mechanically reproduced, performance itself cannot be copyrighted and therefore "escapes ownership, commodification, and other processes of regulation within a reproductive capitalist economy," but he argues that this escape in no way makes performance the privileged site of cultural resistance Phelan makes it out to be.[44] Furthermore, Auslander argues that "if performance persists only as spectatorial memory, then it persists in precisely the form in which it can be useful to the law that regulates the circulation of cultural objects as commodities."[45] Auslander's stance, then, is that performance may be nonreproducible and ephemeral and therefore function differently than other commodities, but it has no special claim to an intrinsic tendency to resist capitalist exchange models or other market forces. Oliver Gerland takes this argument a step further and points out that performances can, in fact, be owned and long have been. Performance's ephemerality, rather than resisting commodification, actually invites and supports it. He argues that claims such as Auslander's and Phelan's "create the mistaken impression that, because it is ephemeral, performance is somehow the opposite of a capitalist economy that circulates cultural objects," whereas performance's evanescence actually renders it attractive to market interests because its continual disappearance makes the work it communicates harder to steal.[46] Gerland sees performance then not as a slippery commodity that commercial forces either cannot reach or for which they carve out an approved and controllable if rhetorically aberrant space, but as the ideal commodity under twentieth-century capitalism and the contemporary copyright regime. Anthea Kraut reaches a similar conclusion. She points out that dance's complicated history with copyright and preference for internal and informal enforcement of property norms may seem to suggest that dance, because it is embodied performance, escapes commodification. The fact that norms even exist, however, and that dancers did engage in "stealing steps" suggests that these embodied actions have market value both to the dancers who steal steps and those who try to protect their original steps.[47] Most recently, Derek Miller has examined the history of the copyright performance in England, an often hastily produced performance of a play prior to publication designed to allow a playwright to retain performance rights. Miller most closely follows Auslander but gives more credit to Phelan's view of performance as naturally resistant to commodification, arguing that while performance may tend to resist commodification, forces such as copyright law can and do pull performance into a logic of commodification.[48]

Auslander's and Miller's arguments construct models of performance as ontologically incongruous with commodification and of a legal system that finds a way to draw performance into capitalist market relations. Auslander frames this process as evidence that the uniquely ephemeral ontology of performance among art forms provides it no special protections or privileges, legally or otherwise, whereas Miller sees the process as something of a forced transformation. My arguments explore the places where performance and commodification more comfortably converge. Many major cases in the development of copyright law involved plays and performances, leading performance itself to greatly influence the shape of modern copyright.[49] The relationship among authorship, copyright law, and performance is not always one of inscription, with copyright law overwriting performance's preexisting ephemerality and openness to exchange with tightly defined ontological boundaries, reproducibility, and market concepts such as monetary value and commodification. Sometimes the relationship is one of mutual influence and pressure.

My response to this complex discourse focuses around my three-pronged definition of authorship. Each of the following three chapters will focus on one of the three aspects of authorship I have identified and how it affects the practices of making theater in the second half of the twentieth century and into the twenty-first. Chapter 1 focuses on the author as owner. The cases in this chapter primarily come from the year 1984, in which three major playwrights either shut down or publicly derided productions of their own plays for deviating from the playwrights' intentions. Edward Albee shut down an all-male production of *Who's Afraid of Virginia Woolf?* in Texas. Samuel Beckett decried JoAnne Akalaitis's production of *Endgame* at the American Repertory Theater in Boston, only allowing it to be performed with a disclaimer in the program calling the production a complete parody of Beckett's play. And throughout the year, Arthur Miller engaged in a lengthy battle with the Wooster Group over the latter's use of Miller's *The Crucible* in their work *LSD: Just the High Points*, a conflict that eventually ended with Miller forcing the Wooster Group to close the show in early 1985. All three of these writers espouse staunchly anticommercial viewpoints, slightly differing versions of the idea that commercialism corrupts the purity of artistry. At the same time, their investment in the cultural construction of authorship, a concept paradoxically inextricable from commercialism, validates their practice of shutting down productions of their own works. In other words, while they decry commercial interests as corrupters of art, they bolster the underlying ideologies and cultural logic of commercialism not only by operating under an ideal of total ownership in which they own the works themselves as well as the work's presence in culture and society at large but also by devaluing the roles of other theater artists in order to maintain a theatrical hierarchy with a generically white, male author in the dominant role.

Chapter 2 focuses on the author as an individual. The ideal of individuality conflicts with the ideal of collaboration that infuses so much work in this period. I will first look at the spirit of collaboration and collectivity often celebrated as the heart of the radical theater movement of the 1960s including such groups as the Living Theatre and the Open Theatre. This collectivity is often cited as not only a radical change in theatrical practice, a movement away from hierarchical, text-based models of producing theater, but as an ideological challenge to the competitive capitalist ideology of the hegemony.

By looking more closely at the history of *The Serpent*—one of the most highly heralded examples of such collaboration—I will complicate the picture of its development and production as an example of collectivity. The production's history and the group's reflections on its legacy reveal a scenario in which authorship and individuality ultimately won out in both immediately practical and ideological terms. I will then turn to a genre of theater in which collaboration serves as the dominant norm rather than a new, radical, or countercultural development: the musical. Specifically, I will look at the case of *Thomson v. Larson* regarding the authorship of *Rent*. This case reveals an increasingly reactionary response against collectivity, a suspicion that collaboration somehow diminishes individual artistic merit and achievement, and a default to individual authorship within the legal system. In both cases, then, the default of individual authorship creates conflicts within collaborative practices in the theater, old and new, as well as asserts the continued dominance of a text-based, hierarchical model of cultural production whose closest ideological alliances are with the hegemony.

Chapter 3 focuses on the author as originator. I turn to stand-up comedy to examine authorship's demand for originality for a number of reasons. First, comedians occupy dual positions as authors and performers, so stand-up serves as a perfect site to investigate the conflict between these models of cultural production because comedians constantly navigate between the two. Second, stand-up comedians understand themselves as brands and products, so their relationship to the structures of commercialism and capitalism differs from many of the artists in the first two chapters who espouse anticommercial rhetorics while upholding capitalism's underlying assumptions through their practices. Authorship's position as default mode of cultural production creates problems in comedy not because of dissonance between rhetoric and practice but because of the way it overemphasizes comedians' roles as authors and undervalues their roles as performers. With regard to the more specific issue of originality within this conflict, stand-up from the late 1950s to the present—a period sometimes called the "persona" or "point-of-view" era of comedy—places unique demands for originality on comedians in roles as both writers and performers. The industry demands that comedians both write their own original material and develop their own unique performance styles to complement their writing. These modes of originality occasionally create a conflict of interest, as determining what counts as stealing, influence, or simply independent creation requires navigating the complex relationship between performance and authorship. The recent attention comedians, the press, and legal scholars have paid to joke stealing reveals a tendency to conflate performance-based and literary originalities, with the originality of content serving as a default for understanding what counts as an original and what a forgery. I argue that separating these two modes of originality and their corresponding concepts of stealing not only affords comedians as well as performers in other genres greater protection on a practical level, it also helps more clearly frame the sticky ideological issues in the relationship among authorship, performers, and commercialism.

These issues are both theoretical and practical in nature. The cases in the following chapters reveal something about the assumptions governing authorship, production, and creativity in the United States in the second half of the twentieth century. They also reveal that cultural assumptions about the law can have greater practical impact than either the letter or spirit of the law. At stake, then, is not just a question of the meanings generated by creative practices and the cultural construction of authorship. It is also a question of the practical limits restraining creative practice rights. I see the following cases not as symptoms of a problem to be solved, but as evidence of a cultural construction of authorship that has real practical effects. Most importantly, my goal is to show that these two questions, the theoretical and the practical, are inextricable. Understanding the ideological implications of authorship's position as the default mode of cultural production may ultimately provide the only means of opening up the space for other modes of creative practice to thrive.

NOTES

1. I have tried not to linger too long on the narrative of the ART *Endgame* controversy only because of how thoroughly other critics and scholars have already covered it. I use it here as the best-known exemplar of a much broader pattern that points to Authorship as the default mode of production. For the most thorough and thoughtful recent account of these events, see Natka Bianchini, "Bare Interiors, Chicken Wire Cages and Subway Stations—Re-Thinking Beckett's Response to the ART *Endgame* in Light of Earlier Productions," in *Samuel Beckett's Endgame*, ed. Mark S. Byron (New York: Rodopi, 2007), 121–44. See also Jonathan Kalb, *Beckett in Performance* (Cambridge: Cambridge University Press, 1989), 71–94.

2. Samuel Beckett, *Endgame and Act Without Words* (New York: Grove Press, 1958), 1.

3. Kalb, *Beckett in Performance*, 72.

4. Barney Rosset Papers, Beckett Collection, Box 3, Burns Library Special Collections, Boston College. The Estate of Samuel Beckett. Quoted in Bianchini, "Bare Interiors," 135.

5. Program for *Endgame* presented at ART, Cambridge, MA, 1984. Quoted in Kalb, *Beckett in Performance*, 79.

6. Oren Bracha, "The Ideology of Authorship Revisited: Authors, Markets, and Liberal Values in Early American Copyright," *Yale Law Journal* 118, no. 2 (2008): 192.

7. Mark Rose, *Authors and Owners: The Invention of Copyright* (Cambridge, MA: Harvard University Press, 1993), 1.

8. Bracha, "The Ideology of Authorship," 228.

9. Rose, *Authors and Owners*, 1. See also Jonathan E. Schroeder, "The Artist and the Brand," *European Journal of Marketing* 39, no. 11/12 (2005): 1291–305. Schroeder suggests that not only can a better understanding of art history improve understanding of how brands work, but also that art history can benefit from a marketing viewpoint, exploring how artists brand themselves. He argues that "Successful artists—those that manage to have their work widely exhibited, bought, and collected— may be seen as twin engines of branding knowledge, both as consummate image managers, and as managers of their own brand—the artist" (1293). The idea of the artist herself as the brand plays strongly into the rhetoric of authorship as the default mode of cultural production defined by ownership, individuality, and originality.

10. Martha Woodmansee, "On the Author Effect: Recovering Collectivity," in *The Construction of Authorship: Textual Appropriation in Law and Literature*, ed. Woodmansee and Peter Jaszi (Durham, NC: Duke University Press, 1994), 15.
11. Woodmansee, "Recovering Collectivity," 24–26.
12. Rose, *Authors and Owners*, 135.
13. Ibid., 135.
14. Bracha, "The Ideology of Authorship," 190.
15. See Eric E. Johnson, "Intellectual Property and the Incentive Fallacy," *Florida State University Law Review* 29 (2012): 628.
16. David Harvey, *A Brief History of Neoliberalism* (New York: Oxford University Press: 2007), 2.
17. Ibid., 2–3.
18. Ibid., 39–40.
19. Rose, *Authors and Owners*, 1–2.
20. Johnson, "The Incentive Fallacy," 628.
21. Bracha, "The Ideology of Authorship," 231.
22. For the standard legal treatise on the right of publicity, see J. Thomas McCarthy, *The Rights of Publicity and Privacy* (St. Paul, MN: West Group, 1999). McCarthy defines the right of publicity as "the inherent right of every human being to control the commercial use of his or her identity" (vii). For an excellent extended look at the development and impact of the right of publicity, especially its mutually supportive relationship with capitalist ideologies, see Jane M. Gaines, *Contested Culture: The Image, the Voice, and the Law* (Chapel Hill: The University of North Carolina Press, 1991).
23. Johnson, "The Incentive Fallacy," 626.
24. Antonio Gramsci, *Selections from Cultural Writings*, ed. David Forgacs and Geoffrey Nowell-Smith, trans. William Boelhower (Cambridge, MA: Harvard University Press, 1985), 420–21.
25. Louis Althusser, "Ideology and Ideological State Apparatuses (Notes towards an Investigation)," in *Lenin and Philosophy and Other Essays*, trans. Ben Brewster (New York: Monthly Review Press, 1971), 127–88.
26. Althusser, "Ideology and Ideological State Apparatuses," 154.
27. Terry Eagleton, *Ideology: An Introduction* (New York: Verso, 1991), 28.
28. Johnson, "The Incentive Fallacy," 625.
29. Eagleton, following his mentor Raymond Williams, has argued that the structure of dramatic realism, even when its contents are seen as radical or progressive as in the case of Ibsen's major plays, reinforces the very social structures it seeks to challenge by presenting a monolithic, complete, inalterable world. "The discourse of the play may be urging change, criticism, rebellion; but the dramatic forms—itemize the furniture and aim for an exact 'verisimilitude'—inevitably enforce upon us a sense of the unalterable solidity of this social world, all the way down to the colour [sic] of the maid's stockings." My present arguments extend this claim; it is not only the conventions of the genre but also the very means of production in creative practice that continually reappropriate progressive, radical, or challenging content to the purpose of reproducing the dominant mode of production. Terry Eagleton, *Literary Theory: An Introduction*, second edition (Minneapolis: University of Minnesota Press, 1996), 162.
30. Roland Barthes, "The Death of the Author," in *Image-Music-Text*, trans. Stephen Heath (New York: Hill and Wang, 1977), 142–48; and Michel Foucault, "What Is an Author?" trans. Josué Harari, in *Aesthetics, Methods, and Epistemology*, ed. James Faubion (New York: The New Press, 1998), 205–22. Barthes's essay first appeared in 1967, Foucault's as a lecture in 1969. David Saunders provides an excellent analysis of Barthes's and Foucault's arguments dealing specifically with their relationship to practical, legal realities. See David Saunders, *Authorship and Copyright* (New York: Routledge, 1992), especially 226–32. I should note that while I do not agree with many of Saunders's conclusions, I find his identification of the problems raised by the contact between postmodern theory and legal practice to be especially clear and insightful.
31. At this point I would be remiss not to point to another seminal essay on the idea of the author, "The Intentional Fallacy" by W. K. Wimsatt and Monroe C. Beardsley in W. K.

Wimsatt, *The Verbal Icon* (Lexington: University Press of Kentucky, 1982), 3–20. Wimsatt and Beardsley argue that the intentions of the author have nothing to do with the meaning of a poem. I do not engage directly with this essay for two reasons. First, though it remains a touchstone, even as something of a relic, in literary discourse, it never gained the same traction in theater studies. Second, and more importantly, its focus is squarely on the critic's engagement with the text as opposed to the general cultural circulation and discourse that Foucault and Barthes focus on and that is more germane to this study.

32. Lawrence Lessig, *Free Culture: The Nature and Future of Creativity* (New York: Penguin, 2004).

33. Siva Vaidhyanathan, *Copyrights and Copywrongs: The Rise of Intellectual Property and How It Threatens Creativity* (New York: NYU Press, 2001), 4.

34. Kembrew McLeod, *Owning Culture: Authorship, Ownership, and Intellectual Property Law* (New York: Peter Lang, 2001).

35. Woodmansee and Jaszi, introduction to *The Construction of Authorship.*

36. Woodmansee, "Recovering Collectivity."

37. Peter Jaszi, "On the Author Effect: Contemporary Copyright and Collective Creativity," in *The Construction of Authorship*, 55.

38. Rose, *Authors and Owners*, 142.

39. Saunders, *Authorship and Copyright*, 227.

40. Ibid., 230.

41. Mark Lemley, "Romantic Authorship and Rhetoric of Property," review of *Shamans, Software, and Spleens: Law and the Construction of the Information Society* by James Boyle, *Texas Law Review* 75 (1997): 873–906.

42. Oren Bracha's project similarly dismisses a narrative of copyright law following the lead of Romantic authorship, but suggests instead a more complex relationship between the two where each borrows rhetorical tools from the other when it is convenient and ignores the other's basic tenets when they become inconvenient.

43. See Peggy Phelan, "The Ontology of Performance: Representation without Reproduction," in *Unmarked: The Politics of Performance* (London: Routledge, 1993), and Peggy Phelan and Marquard Smith, "Performance, Live Culture and Things of the Heart," *Journal of Visual Culture* 2, no. 3 (2003): 294.

44. Philip Auslander, "Legally Live: Law, Performance, Memory," in *Liveness: Performance in a Mediatized Culture* (New York: Routledge, 1999), 150–51.

45. Auslander, "Legally Live," 153.

46. Oliver Gerland, "From Playhouse to P2P Network: The History and Theory of Performance under Copyright Law in the United States," *Theatre Journal* 59 (2007): 94. For much of the nineteenth century, a playwright whose work had been performed but not published owned exclusive performance rights for that work. Once a play was published, however, the play was "dedicated to the public" and any performance of it by someone who owned the text was considered fair use. Congress eventually added a performance right to copyright of dramatic works in order to encourage publication, as many playwrights were not printing their works to prevent unlicensed performances. See Gerland, 79, as well as the cases of *Keene v. Kimball* and *Thompkins v. Halleck.* In England the situation was somewhat different, as performance and printing rights were separate rights as in the United States, but unlike the United States, one did not negate the other. For a good look at the history of this issue in England, see Derek Miller, "Performative Performances: A History and Theory of the 'Copyright Performance,'" *Theatre Journal* 64, no. 2 (2012): 161–78. The point is that Auslander's and Phelan's contention that performance cannot be owned, no matter how theoretically sound, is simply inaccurate, as performance has long been owned, even separately from the works being performed.

47. Anthea Kraut, "'Stealing Steps' and Signature Moves: Embodied Theories of Dance as Intellectual Property," *Theatre Journal* 62 (2010): 173–89.

48. Miller, "Performative Performances," 177.

49. A number of cases dealing with theater helped shape copyright law. In *Daly v. Palmer*, for instance, Augustin Daly sued producers Jarrett and Palmer after the latter produced Dion Boucicault's *After Dark* because Daly claimed that Boucicault's play copied its climactic scene of a train bearing down on the hero tied to the tracks from Daly's *Under the Gaslight.* Daly

won, granting him what was functionally—though not technically—a patent to the plot device of the train, as any other play that wanted to include a similar train scene would need to get his permission first, though this was eventually overturned. See Bracha, "The Ideology of Authorship," 206–7.

Chapter One

1984: The Author as Owner

The year 1984 may not have been the totalitarian nightmare George Orwell imagined, but it did see a certain amount of authoritarian muscle flexing in the world of theater. Over the course of this one year, three playwrights displayed both their hawkish watch over their plays and their readiness to enforce their wills. First, in the summer, Edward Albee closed an all-male production of *Who's Afraid of Virginia Woolf?* in Arlington, Texas. Then Samuel Beckett publicly objected to JoAnne Akalaitis's production of *Endgame* at the American Repertory Theater in Boston. And Arthur Miller became embroiled in a famous conflict with the Wooster Group in New York when he denied them the rights to use the text of *The Crucible* as part of their *LSD: Just the High Points*, a conflict that lasted throughout the year leading to *LSD*'s closing in January of 1985. These cases are hardly rare. Beckett and his estate have either objected to or withdrawn rights from a number of other productions that attempted to reimagine his works on the stage. Albee has also repeatedly shut down productions of his own plays when he has found those productions to deviate from his intentions; more importantly, Albee vocally defends and even celebrates this practice, encouraging other playwrights to follow it. A pattern emerges in the latter half of the twentieth century. A playwright denounces productions of his work, ostensibly on aesthetic grounds. The author, in general, claims that the performance violates his vision or intentions. The producers or performers responsible counter by saying either that the performance represents what they thought to be a faithful interpretation or that their intentionally transformative use of the text does not suggest a lack of respect for either the author or the play. In any case, these arguments play out in terms of competing artistic intentions and questions regarding aesthetic hierarchies in theater. But these arguments also mark another set of assumptions, an undercurrent that not only runs across all these cases but also seems to serve as a kind of common sense, a baseline for argument shared by both playwrights and "deviant" directors. This undercurrent is ideological and reflects the cultural privileging of literary authorship as the model for all cultural production. The concept from literary authorship of the author as *owner* of the work comes into conflict with the developing practices of theater during this period, particularly the movement toward postdramatic theater as a viable model for production. The conflict results not from any sense that ownership of the work is foreign to theater; on the contrary, directors in a postdramatic environment are often deeply invested in the idea that they own their work. The conflict instead results from the assumption that performance must always "serve the text," that the performance is an extension of a preexisting work owned and controlled by the playwright rather than a new work itself. Under this assumption, only playwrights can properly be considered authors and therefore owners. Directors, actors, and designers can only inhabit secondary roles under a system in which ownership and literary authorship are synonymous.

Such a restrictive climate in the age after the death of the author reflects authors' reactionary response to their own obituaries. Authors' shutting down productions of their own works becomes so prevalent in the latter half of the twentieth century due to two historical developments: first, a shift in the U.S. intellectual property discourse toward an ideal of total ownership, and second, the move toward a postdramatic or post-textual theater. I use the phrase "intellectual property discourse" both to include the law itself (legislation and precedent-setting decisions) as well as assumptions about the law. I will argue throughout this book that assumptions about the law often exert greater practical force than the formal apparatuses of the law itself, even when those assumptions go beyond or even contradict the letter and spirit of the law. The movement toward an ideal of total ownership reflects a broadening of neoliberalism's social and cultural influence, an influence that these playwrights help to reinforce through their deployment of its underlying logic despite their often anticapitalist rhetoric.[1] The development of postdramatic theater radically changes the relationships among director, text, playwright, and performance. Each of the playwrights I examine here engages in reactionary behavior to resist the deprivileging of their role and the challenge to total ownership of their work such deprivileging implies. The expansion of the intellectual property regime toward total ownership and the move toward postdramatic theater—even when that move functions as cultural background rather than immediate influence—effectively serve as historical prerequisites for playwright-enforced closures.

Each playwright considered here engages in this reactionary behavior in his own manner. Taken together, their cases suggest the broader scope of the anxiety over the playwright's potentially dwindling power. These cases also expose the ideologies that these playwrights support in trying to maintain the primacy of the text. Each case brings up different aspects of the conflict between constructions of the author-owner and developing theatrical practices. Several instances of Beckett or his estate flexing their aesthetic muscle show how the assumption that the performance is secondary to the text helps reproduce the dominance of literary authorship as the privileged mode of cultural production. The very idea that directors either serve or fail to serve the script supports ideological assumptions about the proper hierarchy between text and performance. I will then turn to Edward Albee's practice of shutting down productions and, more importantly, his defense of the practice. Albee's embracing the ideal of authorship as total ownership has broader ideological implications. Even while Albee decries commercialism and profit motives in the theater as sources of corruption, his deeply ingrained sense of the cultural logic of total ownership helps reproduce neoliberal ideology thereby expanding the notion of commercialism and profit motive as intrinsically good values. Finally, I look at the conflict between Arthur Miller and the Wooster Group as a combination of the threads picked up in the Beckett and Albee cases. The Miller–Wooster Group controversy serves as a site where the aesthetic and ideological issues converge, where both the logic of ownership and the aesthetic ideal of the production's providing a window back to the playwright threaten to short-circuit the possibility of reimagining theatrical practice.

My purpose here is more analytical than corrective. I intend to identify ideological conflicts between the rhetoric and legal practices of playwrights. My point is not that these playwrights should not have these rights, or even that they did anything wrong. My point is to argue that their actions expose ideological assumptions at odds with their rhetoric, and that these assumptions are both influenced by and help reproduce the tripartite cultural construction of authorship that I see functioning and exerting broad influence as the default mode of cultural production in the late twentieth century. I want to highlight the dissonance between these playwrights' practices and their rhetoric and to explore how playwrights flex legal and extralegal muscle to maintain dominant theatrical hierarchies, structures, and modes of production.

THE IDEAL OF TOTAL OWNERSHIP

Playwrights have not always had the right to control who mounted productions of their plays or when and where they were performed. For much of the eighteenth and nineteenth centuries, copyright was conceived strictly in terms of a right to control physical reproduction of texts. The owner of a copyright did not have the right to control or to receive compensation from any uses of the text other than copying. Unprotected uses of the text included everything from translations to performances. Oliver Gerland points out that "until [1856], a copyright owner who had printed and sold copies of a play could not prevent others from staging it. . . . By contrast, plays that had been performed but not printed and sold . . . were fully protected under common law."[2] Performing a play from a published manuscript without the author's permission was considered a perfectly acceptable use of that manuscript. Any owner of a copy of a playscript could claim the right to such use. Copyright law for most of the nineteenth century, then, maintained a deep ontological distinction between the written text and the performed play, a distinction that would become fuzzier as copyright law moved away from a right to print and toward something else. Oren Bracha explains that, for most of the eighteenth and nineteenth centuries, the intellectual property regime in the United States understood copyright as "a limited commercial privilege to engage in a specific economic activity—the printing of a text." Copyright literally functioned as just what its name suggests: a right to copy. After 1856, however, the author of a copyrighted play also controlled the "play-right," the exclusive right to license performances of the play. Even with few changes to the law itself, copyright, over time, "moved much closer to the ideal of ownership as general control over an object of ownership." As Bracha points out, such an ideal of total ownership and absolute control may be untenable as an end but still provides a direction toward which the property regime moves. The ideal of total ownership functions less as a legal reality and more as an extralegal, ideological assumption. Even so, the ideology surrounding copyright has "come to confer on the owner a broad set of powers to dominate numerous aspects and uses of the intangible object of property."[3] Under this ideal, the author-owner of a work owns not only the right to control its reproduction and dissemination in the form in which the author created it but also the right control most transformations or uses of that work. Bracha calls "the work" under this kind of copyright regime "a shape-shifter—an elusive intellectual entity that could assume an infinite number of concrete forms."[4] The work becomes not a discrete entity but instead a category or network containing many different nodes or iterations, all of which fall under the ownership and control of an individual who in turn stands to reap credit and benefit from all uses of and even certain references to the original work. The move to total ownership is the move from an exclusive right to reproduce copies of a text toward an ideal of total control over any and all nodes in a network leading back to the text.

Technically, looking strictly to the letter of the code, U.S. copyright law only grants copyright holders six specific enumerated powers. Section 106 of Title 17 of the U.S. code lays out these rights:

> The owner of copyright under this title has the exclusive rights to do and to authorize any of the following:

1. to reproduce the copyrighted work in copies or phonorecords;
2. to prepare derivative works based upon the copyrighted work;
3. to distribute copies or phonorecords of the copyrighted work by sale or other transfer of ownership, or by rental, lease, or lending;
4. in the case of literary, musical, dramatic, and choreographic works, pantomimes, and motion pictures and other audiovisual works, to perform the copyrighted work publicly;
5. in the case of literary, musical, dramatic, and choreographic works, pantomimes, and pictorial, graphic, or sculptural works, including individual images of a motion picture or other audiovisual work, to display the copyrighted work publicly; and
6. in the case of sound recordings, to perform the copyrighted work publicly by means of a digital audio transmission.

The rights listed above, taken literally, cover a relatively narrow set of powers, mostly the rights to reproduce, create derivative works from, distribute, display, or perform the work under copyright. When Bracha suggests that copyright evolves to confer broad authoritarian power on copyright holders, he does not mean, then, that the letter of the law changed. The law also does not formally acknowledge the idea of the work as a shape-shifter, as a broad domain of control rather than as a discrete entity. These evolutions of copyright occur largely through court decisions and, more importantly, through extralegal assumptions about copyright ingrained in the culture. So while the letter of the law gives copyright holders only these six specific powers, the cultural ideal of copyright confers on copyright holders much greater legal and especially extralegal control over their works, a control often successfully reinforced by fallaciously citing the law, as several cases in this book will show.

That kind of control is inextricable from ownership as a facet of authorship. Ownership is an exclusive right to use. A copyright holder retains exclusive rights to control the specific uses listed above of the cultural objects for which they hold the copyright. Ownership, in the legal sense, provides very limited, specific rights to control use. I may legally own something but exert very little control over it, as many dog owners will tell you. I do, however, retain control over certain rights to use that dog. Such control is, in fact, ownership itself. So ownership in legal terms involves control but does not promise unlimited control over the thing owned. In terms of authorship as the default mode of cultural production, control is both a broader and more essential element of ownership. Arguments that make calls to authorship often treat ownership as a right to total control, control far beyond the scope of the law. As several cases in this chapter will show, ownership as an aspect of authorship often goes even further to include a sense of responsibility on the part of authors to exercise that control. According to the cultural construction of authorship in the late twentieth century, one only owns a work if one can and does exercise total control over it.

One of the major moments in copyright's changing from a protected exclusive right to print to a model of general control and ownership was the introduction of a doctrine of fair use in the late nineteenth century. As Bracha points out, the popular understanding of fair use as a possible emancipatory force against total ownership and control obscures fair use's nature as an expansion of ownership and control.

> Ironically, the fair use doctrine is commonly celebrated today as one of the major safeguards against overexpansion of copyright protection. At the time it was introduced . . . , however, it was a vehicle for a radical enlargement of the scope of copyright. . . . Formerly, infringement was limited to near-verbatim reproduction and all other subsequent uses were considered legitimate. In the new fair use environment, all subsequent uses became presumptively infringing unless found to be fair use.[5]

Bracha points out that almost all nonprinting use was fair use before the introduction of a doctrine that specifically designated which transformative uses were protected. Fair use today covers such uses as parody or citation (with limitations). The law exclusively grants playwrights any rights to use not explicitly protected by fair use; the ideal of total ownership under this property regime helps lead to the conflation of multiple works under an overarching concept of "the work."

Bracha also points out that the questions of ontological distinction between original works on one hand and subsequent works that either adapt, translate, interpret, or otherwise make use of the original work on the other hand intimately entangle with questions of market value.

> One important intellectual influence in this field was again the modern concept of value and the view of the market as the sole institution for allocation of social reward. The abstract, metaphysical debates about the nature of intellectual works were woven with concepts of and assumptions about market value. The two sets of arguments—those dealing with the nature of the intangible object of property and those focusing on market value—were almost always locked together. The one informed and constituted the other. . . . The metaphysical question of the borders of an intangible work was both precipitated and answered by the claim that the author had to collect all the market profits of his work.[6]

The move toward market value as the key prerequisite for copyright protection represents another of the major steps toward the current property regime and the ideal of total ownership. In the 1867 case of *Martinetti v. Maguire*, the court refused to uphold the plaintiff's copyright to the play *The Black Crook* partly on the grounds that the play was, in their view, mere spectacle in addition to being amoral.[7] Since the Constitution justifies governing intellectual property as a means of promoting "the progress of science or the *useful* arts," the court argued, a work that lacked merit and moral substance had no right to be protected. In a sense, copyright law served or had the potential to serve as a means of promoting certain moral and ethical viewpoints. Gerland explains that

> The US Supreme Court's decision in the 1903 case of *Bleistein v. Donaldson Lithographing Co.* (which recognized illustrations used to advertise a circus as worthy of copyright protection) reversed that stance, holding that a work valuable enough to copy is valuable enough to protect (188 US 239).[8]

The court's move to protecting works based on monetary value rather than on its definition of cultural merit reflects a shift in ideas about the work as well as the ideologies that those notions of the work helped to reproduce and reinforce. If the work's protection is based on its monetary rather than cultural value, then the work is primarily a commodity whose market exchange relationships always frame its position in cultural, political, aesthetic, or social discourses. The work's discursive possibilities, even when that work's content is revolutionary, radical, or counternormative, become defined by the mode of production in which the work is produced and circulates. Another key component of the property regime from whence these playwrights draw the ideal of total ownership, then, is that ownership and the need to protect it is ultimately based on monetary and not cultural value, or perhaps more deeply that monetary and cultural value are inextricable.

Mark Rose points to this link between cultural or aesthetic and market value as the essential condition of authorship in the twentieth century. He argues that "the distinguishing characteristic of the modern author . . . is proprietorship; the author is conceived as the originator and therefore the owner of a special kind of commodity, the work."[9] In other words, ownership defines authorship, specifically ownership of the kind of shape-shifting work that Bracha describes. Rose links the conflation of authorship and ownership with the rise of the work as commodity and as a broad aesthetic category rather than a discrete entity. Rose's contention that the primary defining characteristic of contemporary authorship is proprietorship again reflects the broader move toward the ideal of total ownership of artistic labor. In a property regime in which ownership constitutes the most essential element of authorship, aesthetic value cannot be separated from market value, and aesthetic philosophies, theories, and arguments cannot be considered apart from their relationship to market forces. All aesthetic arguments in the era of the author-owner are necessarily ideological arguments grounded in their relationship to capitalism, and the rhetorical content of such arguments often runs counter to the practices of the same social actors making those arguments.

POSTDRAMATIC THEATER

The development of postdramatic theater is an important part of the background of the increase in playwrights' shutting down productions of their own works. The historical overlap between the two is more than just coincidence. Postdramatic theater reflects changing attitudes about authorship and authority, and playwrights react against those same changing attitudes even if not to postdramatic theater itself. Prior to the 1960s, legal conflicts over the rights to perform plays arose, but very few if any cases involved a playwright withdrawing performance rights due to aesthetic differences with the production. So what changed? Hans-Thies Lehmann has argued that the movement away from the text as guiding principle for a theatrical production is the most defining characteristic of emergent theatrical practices in the late twentieth century.[10] Lehmann has thus coined the term "postdramatic theater" to describe that theater in which the text or "drama" serves as one raw material among many rather than as the central guiding principle. Lehmann contrasts postdramatic theater with dramatic theater that is "subordinated to the primacy of the text."[11] He defines postdramatic theater, therefore, not necessarily by historical moment or style but by relationship between text and performance. Postdramatic theater is not theater without texts, but instead theater where the text is not the guiding principle, where the performance is not an extension of the text. The postdramatic theater is a director's or actor's rather than a playwright's theater. Many postdramatic theater practitioners draw on the works of Antonin Artaud to justify their decentralizing texts in the production process. Artaud's major contribution to the movement away from a text-based theater comes in the essay "No More Masterpieces," in which he calls for a rejection of literary classics in the theater, specifically opposing text and performance as distinct and irreconcilable entities.[12] Artaud proposes "to return through the theater to an idea of the physical knowledge of images," a theater that speaks to the public in its own immediate and visceral language rather than in the language of classic texts.[13] Avra Sidiropoulou, in her history of theatrical auteurism, points out that "Artaud conscientiously dismantled the role of the director as mere *explicator* of the dramatic text."[14] But this development does not simply reflect a shift in a battle for power between playwrights and directors. It represents what Lehmann calls the autonomization of theater, a sort of realization of Artaud's call for a theater that speaks in a physical and theatrical rather than literary language. Lehmann argues that

> the autonomization of theatre is not the result of the self-importance of (post)modern directors craving recognition, as which it is often dismissed. The emergence of a director's theatre was, rather, potentially established in the aesthetic dialectics of dramatic theatre itself, which in its development as a "form of presentation" increasingly discovered the means and devices that are inherent to it even without regard to the text.[15]

Similarly, Sidiropoulou argues that the rise of naturalism in the theater in the late nineteenth century created the need for a guiding artistic figure to coordinate the increasing complexity of staging demanded by scenic realism. This text-based movement, then, ironically laid the groundwork for antitextual, directorial auteurism.[16] And Gabrielle Cody argues that auteurism in fact lies at the roots of Western theatrical practice and that its current status as revolutionary only results from a deviation from recent trends.[17] By helping to create the role of the director with a controlling vision, these arguments run, the texts of naturalism laid the grounds for undoing theater's textual basis. The teleology and determinism inherent in such arguments aside, they usefully undercut the idea of postdramatic theater as deviant or playing in bad faith and show that the primacy of the text is historically, culturally, and ideologically bound and not an inevitable or irrevocable development.

Given this radical movement away from the construction of text as central authority, it is perhaps unsurprising that several playwrights have had a reactionary response. These responses especially make sense with regard to the often aggressive nature of other theater artists' rejecting the text. As David Savran puts it, "During the 1970s and 1980s the most important experimental theatre [was] deconstructive in strategy, performing a more or less trenchant critique of theatre and culture from within."[18] Theater practitioners did not so much calmly walk away from text-based theater as lay it out on the table and publicly dissect it. The turn to postdramatic theater in a sense created its own resistance by self-consciously and violently rejecting the long-standing norm of authorial primacy and control. Gerald Rabkin argues that during this period "the function of the playwright was spread among members of the ensemble or subsumed by the director-auteur. Or—as in the early work of Grotowski and Schechner—a classic originary text became the unprivileged ground from which a radical performance text was created."[19] Postdramatic theater not only dilutes the playwright's control but also his credit. But it is important to look beyond the bruised egos and aesthetic power struggles to examine the ideological stakes, the ways in which these playwrights reproduce neoliberal ideologies even as theatrical performance is being reinvented around them.

REPEAT BECKETT

The name Samuel Beckett evokes at least two different responses in scholars and practitioners of theater. The first: reverence. Beckett performed the rare feat of entering theater's pantheon before his death, becoming a dominating presence, emblematic of a hugely influential theatrical movement that reimagined what theater could be and do. He did so, the story runs, by stripping away everything most important about and dear to theater and playing in the ruins of that which remained. The second: fear. Beckett's work must be done, but it must be done correctly. This fear is founded in pragmatic concerns. A Beckett play comes with instant recognition but also heavy limitations backed by a very real tradition of enforcement. Taking creative license becomes a potential financial risk. A closed production loses not only the money already paid for royalties and promotion but also sometimes weeks of lost revenue, a loss that can be devastating for the many theater companies who survive by the skin of their teeth from year to year. Beckett himself notoriously shut down or disowned a number of productions of his own work during his lifetime. This practice continues through his legal representatives, the Beckett estate. Beckett's plays come with a dictum from the playwright himself. Follow the instructions, do the work as it is written. These are my plays. I own them.

But what does it mean to say that Beckett owns these plays? A major goal of this chapter is to interrogate the verb "to own" in a theatrical as well as a broader cultural context in the late twentieth century in the United States. Does it mean he owns the work, the right to use that work, any performances of that work? According to U.S. copyright law as outlined above, Beckett retains exclusive control over a number of rights associated with a particular work, such as *Endgame*, including the right to make and distribute copies, the right to publicly perform and display the work, and the rights for many transformative uses. I will argue that the ideal of total ownership leads to a much broader understanding of his control over the work, an understanding that goes beyond the legal definition of ownership. Such an understanding not only informs Beckett's actions but also, because of its ideological entrenchment as common sense, allows Beckett and his estate to exert even greater practical powers over his works than the law explicitly grants. In this section, I will first trace several instances of Beckett or the Beckett estate shutting down allegedly divergent productions of his work. Then I will unpack the assumptions underlying all of these incidents and conclude by tracing those assumptions through the arguments of both directors and critics. I will argue that the Beckett estate's assumptions about the universality of the hierarchy between text and performance are both theoretically untenable and ideologically reactionary. I will also argue that much of the criticism surrounding these issues, even criticism sympathetic to "deviant" productions of

Beckett's work, does just as much as Beckett's actions to reproduce the ideological assumptions underlying Beckett's total control of the work.

Beckett's fight with JoAnne Akalaitis and American Repertory Theater over their 1984 production of *Endgame*, outlined in the introduction, is the most well-known instance of a Beckett play being shut down in the name of protecting intellectual property. Beckett's control over productions of his works extends beyond the United States, and looking at cases outside the country helps show how the law might play out differently and provide a contrast that helps highlight the assumptions at play. In 2006, L'Agenzia Teatrale D'Arborio in Pontadera, Tuscany, mounted a production of *Waiting for Godot* with two women in the roles of Vladimir and Estragon.[20] Unsurprisingly, and with plenty of precedent, Beckett's estate stepped in and sought an injunction against the production, claiming that the roles were written for two men and that casting women in the roles invalidated the theater company's contract to perform the play. In their complaint, the Beckett estate cited a similar case in Paris from 1992 in which a judge decided that casting women in the roles was a "violation of Beckett's moral rights."[21] The theater fought back, claiming that while the actors were indeed female, the characters were still being played as men, and therefore no violation of the text had occurred. The company had even invited Edward Beckett, Samuel Beckett's nephew and executor of the Beckett estate, to come see rehearsals to judge for himself whether or not the play was a perversion of Beckett's vision, making every effort to ensure that they did not misrepresent Beckett. In this case, the theater company won and successfully completed its run with its two female actors in the male lead roles. The judge presiding over the matter ruled that precluding women from these roles amounted to sexual discrimination and was therefore illegal. Neither the theater company nor the Beckett estate nor even the judge ever questioned the Beckett estate's claims that there exists a correct way of staging the play based on the text, their claim that the text, if adhered to, creates the same staging in all contexts.

Legally, this case came down to an issue of civil rights.[22] But the theater company's original defense relates to the issues of control explored in this chapter. The Beckett estate claimed that the roles had to be played by men to count as men. But the theater company argued that given the conventions under which the production would operate—conventions which would be established by their own instantiation in production—the female actors on stage would count as men within the play. Ultimately, a judge sided with the theater company insofar as their civil rights protecting them from discrimination based on gender were stronger than any concerns that they might be violating the demands of the text. Other cases received less sympathy. Another all-female *Godot* to draw the ire of the Beckett estate was a production by the Manchester, England– bas ed group Grimey Up North intended for the 1998 Edinburgh Fringe Festival. The group argued that their production was not meant as parody but rather was meant to show that the plight of Didi and Gogo was truly universal and not gender-specific. The Beckett estate was not moved by the argument and forced the production to close, leaving Grimey Up North with a loss of the 1,500 pounds they had already spent on publicity.[23] In a statement to *The Independent*, Peter Murphy, the Beckett estate's representative in the matter, was unapologetic.

> Mr. Beckett's writing is extremely specific. You can't get anything more precise. Obviously in this instance it is clear that he didn't give permission for changing the gender of the characters. It is a question of keeping faith with how Mr. Beckett wanted it. One of the characters even has a prostate problem and keeps on having to pee. That doesn't happen to women. One isn't going to allow it to be turned into the problems of the menopause.[24]

Murphy's comments here point explicitly toward a theme running throughout several of these incidents: the issue of gender. His argument not only reproduces ideologies regarding ownership and control but also reproduces gender hierarchies. Although Murphy argues that the gender swapping here only represents a problem because of its alleged anatomical deviance from the script, his focus on the male anatomy and privileging of its structures and its problems along with his implied diminishing of female biological issues clearly suggests a hierarchy. It is also no coincidence that so many of the offending productions deal with gender issues. While Beckett and his estate claim to be defending the text, they also, intentionally or not, defend strict gender distinctions and hierarchies. Most importantly, these cases show that the ideal of total ownership is more than just an American phenomenon and can obtain in any capitalist society with strong assumptions about protecting authorship.

The spirit of the play figures prominently in all these cases. In fact, it comes to stand in for the play itself. In each case, the Beckett estate defined the spirit visually. In *Godot*, the estate believed that the most important factor in preserving the integrity of the work was that the audience see men on stage. It was not enough for them to accept the characters as men within the conventions established by the play. The image of two specifically male tramps played by male actors was more important. And in the Akalaitis *Endgame*, Beckett rendered the spirit of the play inextricable from the image of a spare room with two windows and a door. The Beckett estate believes it has a responsibility to control every embodied performance and more specifically the image it creates.[25] This understanding aligns with the ideal of total ownership and with understanding the production and the script as extensions of a single work, the shape-shifting, amorphous concept encompassing all nodes in a network with the text as origin. They must protect this image from corruption and ensure the network expands only with great care. In a sense, then, the estate sees all performances of Beckett as aspects of the same entity:

a singular image that manifests at different places and at different times or sometimes simultaneously, the correct staging of the text. In order for such a uniquely correct staging of the text—in terms of the resultant physical performance—to be possible, some reliable means must exist through which embodied action can be fixed in language and subsequently retranslated back into the same action, a system, in other words, of scoring movement. Beckett and his estate claim that descriptive language serves as a sufficient means for rendering consistently and readily discoverable the correct way of performing the works. Writing, therefore, essentially becomes an act of ownership and control, and literature becomes further entrenched in its position of power and cultural privilege.

This idea of writing as power and privilege informs and sometimes gets reproduced by theatrical scholarship and criticism. Even Avra Sidiropoulou, whose book otherwise largely serves as a history and defense of directorial auteurism, takes Beckett's side regarding his conflict with Akalaitis, arguing that Akalaitis failed to see that Beckett's text had already taken care of all the directing decisions. In fact, Sidiropoulou's entire chapter on Beckett basically suggests that his texts serve as both text and director, that Beckett is both author and auteur even while the rest of her book defends the practice of rejecting textual control. But Sidiropoulou's inconsistent argument is not alone in criticism reproducing the ideological assumptions underlying Beckett's ideal of the single, correct staging. Much of the discourse, even when claiming to side with directors, proceeds as though the playwright's primacy is a given, a natural fact, the way things are. Many of those who engage in these deviant productions, such as Akalaitis, or advocate them, such as S. E. Gontarski, tend to argue in a way that assumes a hierarchical relationship between playwright, text, and performance rather than suggesting a fundamentally different relationship, such as one in which playwright, text, and performance function as equally important elements in a matrix. Even arguments for iconoclasm or revisionism can reproduce the assumption that the various roles involved in a production must be arranged hierarchically when these arguments focus on rearranging the hierarchy rather than exploring new modes of organizing and categorizing relationships.

Some American critics, particularly those writing in the immediate aftermath of the Akalaitis conflict, defend Beckett's actions and therefore participate in reproducing the neoliberal ideologies underlying those actions. Jonathan Kalb in particular saw Akalaitis's production as a violation of righteous production practices and suggests that her staging deserved the response it got from Beckett. Kalb's arguments participate in reproducing the same ideological assumptions about authorship and ownership that Beckett and his estate reproduce. I direct so much focus to Kalb because his work offers a clear historical snapshot of how these assumptions functioned within the ideological apparatus of American criticism and scholarship in the immediate aftermath of the closures, so I will take time to carefully examine and unpack the assumptions animating his argument. Kalb frames his arguments around a question of the spirit of the play. He argues that "*Endgame* . . . is not about life after nuclear holocaust, which neither Beckett nor anyone else could possibly depict; it is about *our* lives, which are lived under the threat of disaster, nuclear and otherwise."[26] Kalb's argument here suggests an insistence that any one production should be about what the play text is about. The text subsumes the performance's identity because of the former's conventional identity association with the all-encompassing concept of "the work." Kalb does point toward a possibility for considering the production and the text as distinct entities, particularly from the point of view of an audience member unfamiliar with the text: "to the average audience member ignorant of Beckett, objections to this set and music must have seemed very odd; for both elements are powerful as pure theatrics."[27] Kalb assumes that the purpose of the performance should be to teach an audience about Beckett. He says from the outset that, regarding Akalaitis, he is "less interested in her legal and ethical right to do what she did than in the consequences of her aesthetic choices for spectators' perceptions of the play."[28] As I have been arguing, though, this aesthetic argument cannot be separated from the ethical and legal ones. More importantly, this statement assumes as self-evident that it is both the purpose of the play and the responsibility of the director to transmit the aesthetic content of the playwright's intention to the audiences. At the very least, he assumes that all audiences will assume that anything on stage comes from the playwright and, therefore, that directors should try to reflect the playwright's intentions so as not to give audiences a misperception of the playwright. Kalb concedes that "as a visual composition, this stage picture is breathtaking, but theatricality is not the main issue; we must ask whether the design serves the play."[29] The problem here as elsewhere is the conflation involved in using the term "the play." The design may not serve the text, although that is a debatable point, but even Kalb admits that it does serve the production. By asking whether the design serves "the play," Kalb treats these two questions as the same in order to invalidate a choice that works in performance but does not, in his view, conform to the text. That Kalb can see the value in a production he argues is aberrant further suggests that performance's subservience to the text is historically bound and ideologically significant and not, as Kalb and others would have it, a universal value.

Kalb discusses how some directors have managed to violate strict stage directions while still preserving the spirit of the play.[30] He argues that the existence of directors who can stay faithful to Beckett while still evincing scenic creativity suggests that "the problem is not so much directorial freedom as directorial mediocrity, a cast of mind unwilling or unable to recognize that a writer could have anything to teach us about concrete stage action."[31] Kalb allows for freedom only insofar as it promotes faithful executions of the author's works, creating something of a tautological loop validating only productions that serve the playwright's intentions: you can do whatever you want with this text, as long as you do what the text says. And the relative quality of productions is irrelevant to the validity of theater practices that diverge from texts for two reasons. First, many productions that self-consciously deviate from or reimagine a text may seem of inferior quality to many critics because such productions embrace aesthetic values outside those of a traditional, mainstream, text-based theater. Second, even a uniformity of lousiness among such productions would not in itself mean that theater rejecting the sacredness of the text should be feared or banned. Of course, Kalb's assumptions about the primacy of the text run deep, as does his indebtedness to literary constructions of the monolithic author. Kalb makes many appeals to history, suggesting that directors who deviate from or devalue the centrality of texts to a theatrical production in turn "effectively devalue [theater] history by ignoring the accomplishments of others that form their historical context."[32] The "others" here are, naturally for Kalb, authors. The accomplishments of other theater artists do not, in this model, constitute a legitimate aspect of the history of theater. The history of theater, according to the Kalb of 1989, is the history of dramatic literature and the things done to it for better or worse. Interpretation, transformation, or any sort of use other than the one intended by Beckett constitutes "anti-intellectual prejudice and historical naiveté," completely dismissing the possibility of self-aware or conscientious rejection of authorial intention as a valid theatrical paradigm.[33] Again, Kalb's arguments defending authorial control over performance evince the deeply held sense at that moment not only of the text's place at the top of an aesthetic hierarchy of the theater but also of the inherent rightness of such a hierarchy.

On the other end of the spectrum, even those Beckett scholars bemoaning the monolithic control of the Beckett estate have often declined to question the assumption that there exists a single, correct way of transposing the text to the stage. In "Reinventing Beckett," S. E. Gontarski takes a very different stance from Kalb by arguing that the Beckett estate's practice of shutting down Beckett productions runs directly counter to Beckett's spirit, which Gontarski sees as quintessentially revisionary.[34] He points out how both critics and Beckett's estate have undervalued Beckett's own brilliance in revision and reinvention by "delimit[ing] a dynamic process of becoming (or creation) at an arbitrary point—publication."[35] Gontarski then goes on to vent his frustration with the Beckett estate and to suggest ways in which directors might cleverly circumvent the estate's myopic vision without running into legal trouble. In other words, he suggests playing the game to the edges of the rules. On one view, then, Gontarski offers a potential counterargument to Kalb, championing revisionist interpretations and performances. Ultimately, though, Gontarski never challenges the notion that there exists a correct staging of each text against whose grain nontraditional productions of Beckett might intentionally run. Gontarski helps reproduce the ideological assumptions about ownership and control not by overtly defending Beckett's and the Beckett estate's right to control productions as Kalb does, but by creating a framework for authorizing revisionary or nontraditional takes on Beckett that still posits Beckett, the author, as the controller and owner of meaning. Gontarski advocates playing within the system and testing its boundaries without violating them. Beckett and his estate remain in control, the extent of their power and the domain of its influence never actually called into question. His model suggests testing the rules to see how far they will bend but poses no questions as to the way those rules are made or how they function. While Gontarski's argument may on the surface seem radically different from Kalb's, they rest on the same assumptions, namely that the purpose of performing a play is to teach an audience about the author's intentions. Even when Gontarski most wholeheartedly endorses reinventing Beckett, his endorsement rests on the argument that revision best serves the spirit of Beckett. In other words, he calls on directors to reinvent Beckett because, on some deep spiritual or philosophical level, that's what Beckett would have wanted. This argument shows how deeply the ideals of authorial ownership, control, and primacy take root because Gontarski suggests that even iconoclasm, desirable as it may be in the case of Beckett's plays, has to be authorized by the writer.

All of these arguments agree if not on the existence of a "correct" staging then at least on the idea that a performance is necessarily an extension of a text, that the text and the performance are different facets of the same thing rather than ontologically distinct works. Even the relatively progressive or transformative productions still operate under a dramatic rather than a post-dramatic production model in which the performance emanates, in some way, from the text. I would like to suggest a different model for understanding the relationship between texts and performance, one not based on an assumption about the primacy of the text. The arguments above focus on questions concerning how far the director's right to interpret the script extends. When should a director's interpretation of a script acquiesce to a writer's known intention? Does a global faithfulness to interpretation in a production override a local commitment to obey every minute detail of stage directions? But each of these questions already privileges authorship by assuming that a performance or production of a play is, by nature, an extension of the text, another aspect of the same work that the text instantiates. I turn to the concept of types and tokens as an alternative to the interpretation model that offers a means of examining the relationship between text and performance without presuming that the latter is secondary to or derivative of the former. As long as performances are understood to be extensions of texts then any performance not based on a text not only gets dismissed as a failure or bad interpretation but more deeply represents a violation of good theatrical practice and a rejection of the natural hierarchy of the theater. David Z. Saltz argues that interpretation is neither a necessary nor a sufficient way of understanding the relationship between text and performance. Instead, Saltz, drawing on the philosophy of Charles Sanders Peirce and Richard Wollheim, suggests that the relationship between a play text and a performance should be a relationship between a Type and a Token. In *Art and Its Objects*, Wollheim roughly divides art forms into those in which the distinction between types and tokens applies and those in which it does not. Art forms in which the distinction does not apply consist of individual objects as their products and focus of study. Painting and sculpture are examples of such art forms, where the particular object counts as the work of art. For Wollheim, a painting or sculpture only counts as the work of art insofar as cultural conventions say it does.[36] Art forms in which the type/token distinction does apply, on the other hand, are those forms such as literature or music in which a particular instantiation of the work is not the work itself, again according to convention. The work itself is the type, and particular instantiations of the type are tokens. For example, the arrangement of words that makes up *The Great Gatsby* is a type; my copy of the book is a token of that type and is not the work itself. Saltz argues that theatrical performances are tokens of types of types. The first type is the text, the second the production, and the token is the particular performance within a run of that production. Saltz points out that "a dramatic performance *is* the execution of a play. The performance is not something that comes after the actors have said all their lines and followed all the stage directions; it is the very act of saying those lines and following those stage directions."[37] This formulation renders interpretation unnecessary in theater, but also does not demand a monolithic "correct way" of performing a play. Saltz acknowledges that "a materialist critic might worry that to deny the interpretive nature of performance implies a faith that the text can speak to and through the performer directly, transparently, and ahistorically." Instead, Saltz argues, the type/token model "in no way implies that there is a 'pure,' ideologically neutral way of performing a play" and that all productions of a play are equally divergent and therefore equally valid executions of that script.[38] In other words, Saltz argues that viewing performances as executions rather than interpretations of a text validates a wide range of performance choices without demanding any particular interpretative framework or conventions. Saltz's arguments also suggest room for postdramatic theater. A postdramatic production might be a type, any particular performance of which would be a token or instantiation of that type. That such a token may make use of, say, the text of *Hamlet* no more makes it a token of the *Hamlet*-type than *Hamlet*'s use of "The Murder of Gonzago" makes *Hamlet* a token of the Gonzago-type or than Rodin's use of bronze makes the thinker a token of the bronze-type. In other words, the use of the text does not necessarily make a production or a performance a token of that text's type. Viewing productions as types and performances as tokens or even as self-contained art objects using texts as raw material potentially provides an ontological framework in which performances do not necessarily proceed from texts. Beckett, as an author-owner, makes a claim to a version of theatrical production in which everyone is trying to work their way back to the author's intention. Roland Barthes points out that "the Author, when believed in, is always conceived of as the past of his own book: book and author stand automatically on a single line divided into a *before* and an *after*."[39] In the dominant hierarchical view of theater, we could add production to the end of this timeline, so that it comes naturally after author and script, and the line can be easily traced back from production to author. The type/token relationship offers the means to disrupt both this backward tracing and its attendant ideological assumptions about ownership and control. The most important benefit of the type/token model for the present study is that it opens up the possibility for understanding performance not as an extension of the text but as a distinct work with only a categorical relationship to the text. Furthermore, severing the causal ties between text and performance helps open up the possibilities for models of theatrical production other than type and token as well, including models such as the one employed in the Wooster Group's *LSD* in which the text serves not as the type or original work but as a raw material.

While convention dictates that a performance executing a particular script counts as a token of that script's type, determining whether or not a particular performance counts as an execution of a particular script depends on a separate set of conventions that are more contentious and fluid. Beckett says only those performances that follow the script to the letter count as executions. For Beckett, the question is simple: either the performance follows the directions or it does not. But finding a consistent test for whether or not a performance executes a script is trickier than it may seem. One possible test asks whether all the words of dialogue are spoken as written. But this test leaves no way to determine fidelity in cases of plays without dialogue such as Beckett's *Act Without Words*. So one could add the requirement that the performance follow all stage directions. But this test, too, runs into problems. Something like an all-female *Godot* could make the claim that it was following the directions to the letter because the script never explicitly states that the characters are men. An all-female *Godot* could even claim that the characters in the production *were* men, even though they were played by women. As long as they counted as men in the production, such an argument might run, whether the person playing them were male or female would be irrelevant. Though courts have not yet accepted such an argument—again, the L'Agenzia Teatrale D'Arborio case was settled on an issue of civil rights overriding author's rights, not on an acceptance that the author's rights were not violated—they very easily could, but doing so would mean challenging the extralegal assumption that authors have the right to exercise control over not only the uses of the text explicitly numerated in copyright law but also over all nodes in the expansive network of the work. Whether a play executes a script is subject to argument and must be determined on a case-by-case basis by looking to current conventions of language and representation to see if what is onstage can count as an execution of the script. An audience or a director might recognize a performance as a token of a certain play-type, as an event that executes the script, even if the author of that play-type disagrees. As Saltz puts it, "a performance is a token of a particular play for a given community if, and only if, that community sees the performance as fulfilling the constitutive requirements of the play."[40] That these conventions are malleable and subjective in no way validates the claims such as those made by the Beckett estate to a kind of exclusive ability to determine whether or not a performance executes a text.

The contract between a playwright and a producing entity often gives the playwright or her representative the final say in whether a play has faithfully executed a text. This arrangement leaves a producer who intended to faithfully execute a text but accidentally ran afoul of a playwright very little recourse. Playwrights' contracts often include language to the effect that the play shall be presented exactly as written, but, as the above examples demonstrate, determining the felicity of that execution is not so clear-cut. Disputes in these cases default to the assumption that the playwright is right, leaving very little if any room for directors to argue that they did, in fact, execute the script as written. Of course, such controls are within playwrights' rights, and by agreeing to these contracts, theater companies accept that playwrights have the final say over whether or not the production executes the text. Playwrights shutting down productions of their own works is, then, not a legal issue in the sense that the legal questions are more or less settled, and changes to those issues would require wholesale changes to the system of production. The point here is to point out the underlying ideologies that system of production embraces and reproduces. Because standard contracts imbue playwrights with so much discretionary power and leave so little room for mediation in cases where directors honestly and sincerely believed they were following the script but failed to execute it faithfully in the playwright's eyes, the current production system defaults heavily to the interpretation model and to authorship and its attendant values of ownership and control over the text and all its extensions.

Understanding how the type/token model can reframe the production process is not a matter of immediate, practical, legal efficacy, then, but is instead a matter of seeing other possibilities for modes of production to undercut the dominant mode's claims to universality and neutrality as common sense. Under the type/token model, Akalaitis's *Endgame* does not have to be read as an interpretation of Beckett's *Endgame* at all, faithful or against the grain. Rather, Akalaitis's *Endgame* just is an execution of Beckett's script. In other words, a performance of Akalaitis's production is a token of the *Endgame*-type rather than an interpretation of *Endgame*.[41] The distinction is important because where an interpretation-based understanding of performance suggests a causal link between text and performance, the type/token relationship creates a purely conventional link between text and performance. Convention suggests that performances that execute the "instructions" of a particular script are performance-tokens of that text-type. Akalaitis's *Endgame* is only a token of the *Endgame*-type because a set of conventions exists that sorts performance-tokens primarily according to the particular text they execute. As Saltz points out, "types in general, and plays in particular, are what some philosophers call 'sortal concepts.' Tokens are things, actions or events. Types are categories that we use to identify things, actions, or events."[42] The relationship between text and performance becomes less deterministic/teleological and more categorical/conventional. The conflict between Beckett and Akalaitis is not actually about her freedom to deviate from or add to the script. Instead, it is about what counts as an execution of the script. Akalaitis herself insists that she was following the script, reverently even. In an interview with Kalb, she says that, while working on the ART *Endgame*, "every pause was . . . almost sacred."[43] She simply saw the setting as one of the director's necessary choices even while following the script. Beckett, however, insists that the language of the script ensures an eminently iterable performance, a one-to-one relationship between text and stage-image where choices are unnecessary. Only a very specific sequence of images and actions counts as a faithful execution of the script. Akalaitis argues that a number of different stage-images, including hers, count as executions of the script with equal fidelity, pointing out that "there have been plenty of productions of *Endgame* which interpreted the design widely."[44] Beckett and Akalaitis, then, differ not over a particular production design but over the proper roles of directors and designers.

At stake, then, in the conflict between Beckett and Akalaitis are the conventions under which a performance counts as an execution of a script, not the conventions guiding the underlying assumption that any performance *using* a text-type must be a token *of* that type. But neither considers the possibility of relationships between text and performance other than execution. Consideration of such relationships would recognize the contingent and arbitrary nature of the relationship between text and performance. When Akalaitis or anyone else defends a production diverging from the norm of the *Endgame*-type by arguing that her production still represents a faithful execution of the script, she cements the underlying logic that performances always represent extensions of the script. Reproducing this underlying logic thereby reinforces the ideological underpinnings of Beckett's practice of shutting down productions of his own work. My point here is that Akalaitis, Gontarski, Kalb, Sidiropoulou, and even L'Agenzia Teatrale D'Arborio, despite their wide array of differing arguments, all further cement the Beckett estate's iron grip over productions by trying to argue in terms of fidelity to the text. By arguing that they actually were serving the text or the spirit of Beckett, these performers and critics maintain the theatrical hierarchy in which the text must be served and the playwright is both primary artist and author-owner of both text and performance. Such rhetoric supports a continued acceptance of the dichotomy of roles the Beckett estate offers in relation to Beckett and his works: fawning acolyte or iconoclastic rebel. This dichotomy, in turn, exacerbates one of the major effects of the interpretation model of performance: reproducing structures of ownership and control derived from literary modes of authorship under capitalism.

So what does it matter if Beckett, his estate, his defenders, and his detractors help reproduce capitalist relations of production? Such reproduction matters at least in part because of its dissonance with Beckett's anticommercial rhetoric. The American premiere of *Waiting for Godot* provides a clear example of Beckett's ostensible anticommercialism. The first American production of *Godot* at the Coconut Grove Playhouse in Miami in January of 1956 was famously a failure, with half of the audience leaving in disgust. In a letter to Alan Schneider, director of the production and, eventually, Beckett's hand-picked preferred American director,[45] Beckett suggests that its commercial failure represented an artistic triumph in that it resisted easy commodification.[46] Beckett dismissed the success of previous European productions as "the result of a misunderstanding" and suggests that the commercial failure of Schneider's production is the result of Schneider's having "succeeded better than any one [sic] else in stating [the play's] true nature." Beckett further speculates that Schneider avoided the "half-measures and frills . . . that 90% of theatre-goers want" to his commercial peril but to the artistic benefit of the play. Throughout this letter, then, Beckett diametrically opposes commercial success and artistic integrity. For Beckett, commercial failure only proves artistic prowess because it shows an unwillingness to pander to audiences and suggests an achievement of artistic complexity and richness beyond mere entertainment. But Beckett's practices of exercising total authorial ownership and control reproduce the very underlying structures of capitalism, suggesting that Beckett's anticommercialism is purely rhetorical. Stephen John Dilks argues that even this ostensible anticommercialism was itself commercially motivated, that Beckett's proclamations of pride at failing to achieve market success were in themselves marketing tools. In other words, according to Dilks, Beckett's repeated claims to have failed in the market were ultimately the secret to his success in the market.[47] Dilks suggests that Beckett's glorification of the Miami production's failure served as a means to promote the New York production by appealing to cultural elitism, foregrounding the difficulty of the play and offering New York audiences an opportunity to prove their intellectual superiority to the provincial citizens of Miami. And, as Dilks points out, "selling Beckett as a failure worked," as the New York production went on to great critical and financial success.[48] In spite of claims to disdain commercial success as a violation of the purity of the art and artist, Beckett's insistence on authorial control and ownership along with his use of anticommercial rhetoric as a marketing tool help to reproduce the very underpinnings of commodification, commercialism, and, in the context of the late twentieth century, neoliberalism's valorization of the individual will and competition over all other ethical and social systems. The problem with this contradiction is not hypocrisy. The stakes are much higher than that. The problem is that these ideological assumptions run so deep that even those who would reject or resist the systems such assumptions support often make use of and therefore reproduce those systems.

LEASING ALBEE

Edward Albee has, by his own admission, shut down many productions of his own work over his career.[49] But one case in particular exemplifies Albee's belief that the playwright should function as a particular kind of author-owner whose realm of ownership and control extends to the decisions made by directors and actors in every production of his plays, no matter how small. Albee closed a production of *Who's Afraid of Virginia Woolf?* in Arlington, Texas, in 1984, a production so small that it almost certainly would have escaped wider notice had Albee not decided to make an example of it. Dov Fahrer, a local director and head of an actor's studio in Arlington, approached the play with the idea that both heterosexual couples were actually deeply disguised homosexual relationships, an interpretation of which Albee is aware and which he has since publicly denounced.[50] Fahrer, having no access to Albee's opinions about that interpretation of the play, acquired an all-male cast and began rehearsing. The play garnered the ire of three Arlington City Council members, and they attempted to shut down the productions on the grounds that it promoted such immorality as homosexuality. Ironically, this reactionary attempt to censor the production on the grounds that homosexuality is immoral drew Albee to take sides with the city council after the conflict between the council and Fahrer had garnered some national press. The group pushed on as long as it could, even violating the city council's ban, but after only three performances seen by a total of fewer than three hundred people, Albee's agent Esther Sherman served the theater with a cease and desist order. In a statement to the Associated Press, Sherman said that "the arrogance of this group is truly offensive. They have no respect for the author's work." She also quoted Albee as saying to her that the play should only be performed "with all characters as the gender in which they were written. . . . This is not a gay play, and that's all there is to it." Albee also responded to the production by saying that while directors should be allowed a certain amount of creativity, they do not have "permission to distort."[51] Albee's strong sense that any production of a play necessarily reflects the playwright's intentions rendered the size of the audience or potential for national exposure irrelevant. Because the production, in his view, always represents the playwright, the director's choices represent arrogance. Albee's position in this case and others espouses a deep belief in the ideal of total ownership.

Albee's authoritarianism regarding productions of his plays rests on his assumption that all productions attempt or should attempt, with varying degrees of success, to reproduce an ideal production upon which the playwright bases his writing. During an interview with Ted Chapin as part of American Theatre Wing's career guide series, Albee says that he took up directing his own plays because "it occurred to me that nobody has the access to exactly what I saw, what I heard when I was writing the play that I do."[52] Again, Albee assumes that the purpose of a performance is to provide access to the text and that audiences will assume everything represented on stage reflects the intention of the playwright, that audiences have no concept of directorial choice. He even suggests that directing his own plays functions as a kind of favor to the audience because he can offer the closest vision of what "the author want[s] the play to look and sound like."[53] Even better than the author-owner, according to Albee, is the author-director, who protects his work by taking control of the directing process and eliminating any chance of divergent executions of his script. Rakesh Solomon's book on Albee's directing practices, containing a prefatory endorsement by Albee himself, is pointedly titled *Albee in Performance*.[54] Given that the book covers only those productions directed by Albee, yet calls itself, broadly, *Albee in Performance*, Solomon's title suggests that Albee is only truly performed when Albee directs the production. Solomon explicitly argues that Albee falls in a long line of great writer-directors in the theater including Shaw, Beckett, and Brecht who protect the integrity of their work by taking control of the direction themselves, of making use of their "exclusive access" to the ideal form of the play. In fact, Solomon suggests that playwrights who refuse to direct their own work may be abdicating their responsibility to see their concept all the way through to its execution.[55]

Elsewhere, Albee has taken even further this argument that the director's goal should be to reproduce the playwright's mental image of the play during composition. Albee even argues that open-mindedness on the part of a playwright regarding directorial freedom represents an act of bad faith and threatens to undermine the integrity not only of his own work but of the theater in general.

> If an author gives up his authority to a director in script changes, to actors, to producers, to backers, that's in dereliction to his own responsibility to himself. I would imagine that directors can make it a director's theater only if they do (1) the work of dead playwrights, or (2) the work of playwrights who are so weak or such bad writers that they can't keep it their own theatre.[56]

This argument explicitly invalidates the rise of auteur directors, devised pieces, ensembles, and any other kind of postdramatic theater, not to mention dramatic theater that attempts to any extent to be playful with the text. By laying out the conditions for directors to "make it a director's theater," Albee presumes that the theater is, by its nature, a playwright's theater. He also equates an inability or just disinclination to control performances with bad writing. During the American Theatre Wing interview, Chapin supports Albee's assertion that directors exist to recreate playwrights' imaginations on stage. After acknowledging that the play comes from Albee's subconscious, he attacks productions such as Fahrer's that take a script in directions other than the stated intention of the playwright. Chapin argues that "for a director to say, 'Oh, well, your subconscious was saying something other than what you thought it was saying,' is a little presumptuous."[57] Albee very well could have misinterpreted his subconscious, but, more importantly, Chapin's argument assumes that the point of producing a play is to work backward to its author's subconscious and that every director approaching a play attempts such psychological mining. A divergent production might not be a failed execution; it might not be an execution at all. It might be doing self-conscious violence to the text. Or a director might not care about the text or author's intent at all and instead be using the text simply as a raw material. Or a director might, following Wimsatt and Beardsley, believe that an author's intention is fundamentally unknowable. The point is that Albee's and Chapin's insistence on the extension model as the only tenable relationship between text and performance reproduces the author-owner's privileged place as the ideal model for a cultural producer.

Albee often equates leaving to directors choices about execution with weakness or bad writing. In another interview, Albee again relates his notion of the ideal performance but also explicitly states his critique of the autonomy of the director, reinforcing his vision of a theatrical hierarchy with the literary text on top.

> Ideally a playwright can get his play from a page onto the stage and back to the audience, rather like playing tennis against a backboard. But this very seldom happens, because you have to deal with human beings. You have to deal with actors and the director. No performance of a play that is halfway decent is ever

> as good as the performance the author saw when he wrote it. You must accept this as fact. . . . But the most disturbing thing is the encouragement that has been given to directors and actors—mostly directors, I suspect—in the United States in the past fifteen years, to consider themselves coauthors of a work. The corruption . . . has gone so far that many playwrights compose their plays on the assumption that the director and the actor will do their work through them. The ideal is that . . . the author's intention is so precise that any sentence that comes in the middle of a play can be spoken only in one way and understood only in one way.[58]

A number of points here call for unpacking. First, Albee implies that productions necessarily represent *degradations* of plays. Because "no performance of a play that is halfway decent is ever as good as the performance the author saw when he wrote it," according to Albee, performances of "good" plays are necessarily flawed by virtue of being performances. Albee even offers a corollary, suggesting that poorly written plays have better performances because they leave more up to the director and actors, who, because of this challenge and freedom, will produce better work than if they were trying and failing to reproduce the work of a "good" writer.[59] Or, stated more succinctly, "a bad play could be improved by production, a first-rate play can only be proved, not improved, by production."[60] This argument relies on an assumption that the production is secondary to the script. Second, Albee decries directors' claims to be coauthors of *a work*. He embraces the notion of the work as a shape-shifter, the entirety of nodes in a network originating from a single, authored text. Albee tells his playwriting students: "you take the credit and you take the blame" for every performance of their plays.[61] Albee, then, sees control over productions as not only the playwright's right but also responsibility, a responsibility based in his assumptions about the natural relationship of productions to texts. That he sees these relationships as "the right way" is evinced by his sense that the rise of postdramatic theater represents a corruption of good practices. Writers such as Charles Mee who intentionally leave production choices up to directors, in Albee's view, betray their own kind by giving in to bad practices and denying not only their right but their responsibility to control productions. In other words, Albee's sense of total ownership runs so deep that any playwright who thinks otherwise is, by definition, a bad or weak writer.

Albee further evinces his sense of total ownership as well as his embrace of an expansive concept of "the work" in his understanding of playwrights' legal rights to ownership. In order to explain how playwrights' ability to control productions is protected, Albee uses market relationships to describe the difference between writing for the stage and writing for films. As opposed to screenwriters who sell their work along with the rights to change or use it in any way, playwrights, in allowing theaters to produce their works, "are leasing the production rights. We retain absolute ownership of the play."[62] If by ownership of the play Albee means control of those rights specifically granted by copyright such as rights to reproduction, distribution, and public exhibition, then he is right. Playwrights retain those rights to lease again as opposed to screenwriters who generally sell those rights. The right to use the text in a theatrical performance returns to Albee, and he may lease it again, always retaining "absolute ownership of the play." But slippage occurs here. Albee leases the production rights, the *rights to use* the play in performance, not a discrete thing called "the play." When Albee leases his play, he does not send out a prepackaged production as many mega-musicals do with their touring companies. The point is that when Albee says he retains complete ownership of the play, it seems to mean to him that he owns not only, say, the right to produce tokens of the *Woolf*-type but also all tokens of that type. Technically speaking, copyright law grants Albee the right to control where, when, and by whom the script is used in production. The particulars governing how that right to use may or may not be executed depends on the particular contract between Albee and the theater company in question. If I lease a car, the law grants the owner the ability to lease the right to use that car for a period of time. The law does not specify the conditions of that lease; the particular contract says what I can and cannot do with the car. Albee's idea that the law endorses his particular uses of his control is again an example of the assumed relationship between Romantic ideology and the law and how that assumed relationship exerts force in excess of the law itself. In other words, while Albee appeals to copyright law as an endorsement of his total control, much of the extent of his control actually comes from contract norms in theater rather than the U.S. code concerning the law. Those norms are in many ways self-regulating within the theater industry, meaning it is more the theater industry than the law that reproduces authorship as the default mode of cultural production.[63]

In terms of ownership, this default to authorship leads to an expansive notion that playwrights own and control all productions of their plays. Albee suggests that an ideal form of the play exists, the recreation of which should be the goal of any company producing it. But choices are always necessary in theater when instantiating tokens of types. Choices are also necessary in printing a book, choices about font, design, even kind of paper. But, by convention, these choices do not affect the identity of "the thing" in literature. *Gatsby* is still the same *Gatsby* whether printed in Helvetica or Garamond. The font might affect one's reading *experience*, but one would still be reading *Gatsby*. Choices in theater greatly impact "the thing" of the performance, however. Again, individual performances of plays are tokens of types of types, so two productions making different choices with a text are fundamentally different things even though they are also, in another sense, the same play. Furthermore, playwrights' ability to lease performance rights, let alone control individual productions, is a relatively recent development of the movement toward an ideal of total ownership. It is in this climate that Albee's and Beckett's assumptions about broad control over works make sense, then. The structures of ownership and assumptions about intellectual property law reproduced by theatrical practice suggest a web of connections from the text all leading back to and therefore owned by the author.

Albee's views of the relationships between the text and the work and his attempts to control the work go a long way toward reproducing the ideologies underpinning the very sort of commercialism he often claims to find so appalling. Albee has referred to Broadway producers as "criminals" and has suggested that profit motives encourage producers and dramaturgs to make plays more "safe" for audiences, corrupting the integrity of the writers and the purity of their vision and craft in the process.[64] Albee has also said that "the further you get away from the commercial theatre on Broadway, . . . the more life plays have. Most of what's done in commercial theatre is dead before it starts. And what isn't, two thirds of that is killed by the time it opens."[65] But Albee's practices of shutting down productions of his work and his insistence on maintaining playwrights' total ownership and control over all productions does at least as much work toward reproducing the underlying ideological structures of capitalism as any Broadway producer or dramaturg could ever hope to do. Albee functions as part of an ideological cultural apparatus—the mainstream theater—that supports commercialism's practices even while rhetorically decrying its underlying philosophies. When Albee appeals to the law to support an ideal of total ownership of the entire network of connections emanating from his text, he reproduces the underlying assumptions about ownership that inform our current intellectual property discourse, the discourse that both supports and is supported by the "criminals" on Broadway whose commercialism, according to Albee, corrupts writers and forestalls the emergence of great new American plays.[66] Althusser argues that many ideological state apparatuses interpellate subjects as free so that they will freely submit to being subjects. I propose that, here, popular conceptions of the law and general ideologies of authorship interpellate writers such as Albee as owners so that they will accept and support an underlying concept of ownership serving capitalist interests even when it goes against their aesthetic and philosophical convictions.

In the particular context of the late twentieth century, then, exercising strong control over productions inevitably reproduces neoliberal ideology. Harvey points out that this apparent contradiction between revolutionary aesthetics on one hand and an ideology that serves the smallest, wealthiest portion of the population on the other is actually a feature of neoliberalism itself and one of the keys to its widespread acceptance.

> Neoliberalization required both politically and economically the construction of a neoliberal market-based populist culture of differentiated consumerism

> and individual libertarianism. As such it proved more than a little compatible with that cultural impulse called 'postmodernism' which had long been lurking in the wings but could now emerge full-blown as both a cultural and an intellectual dominant. This was the challenge that corporations and class elites set out to finesse in the 1980s.[67]

As postmodernism gained ground as a kind of common sense among artists and intellectuals, it may have seemed to offer some degree of emancipation from the author because of the individual author's disappearance into the discourse. However, the very notion of discursivity, with its never-ending series of exchanges of signifiers, resembles nothing so much as the neoliberal notion of the market as a model for all social and cultural institutions. The death of the author is not a disappearance of the author or even of the role of the author but a transformation of the role of the author from a creative artist to an individuated identity or "brand" tied to ownership rights over particular original goods within a marketplace. Harvey points out that "capital is not a thing but a process in which money is perpetually sent in search of more money."[68] Another effect of authorship and the neoliberal assumptions it inscribes on creative practices is that, by transforming creative works into capital, the work loses its identity to the totality of the system of exchange in a way that is remarkably similar to postmodern and poststructuralist theories of the ways discursivity endlessly defers the identity and meaning of the work and the artist. To follow Harvey's phrasing, the work is not a thing but a process in which signifiers are perpetually sent off in search of more signifiers, all of which come back under the control and ownership of the author-function or author-brand. Authorship's main function under such a system is to serve as a means of indexing works to owners to ensure their control over and exclusive right to profit from those works.

But how can Albee endorse so strongly through his actions the capitalist relations of ownership that make possible the very commercialism he sees killing the theater? Albee and Beckett both treat the ideal of total ownership as common sense, as the way things should be. Also, like Beckett, Albee ostensibly bemoans the theater's tendency to pander toward "literate middle-browism" and to reject any iconoclasm.[69] Cultural hegemony helps explain how both of these authors, each anticommercial in his own way, can not only internalize but vigorously defend one of the major underpinnings of capitalist commercialism. As Gramsci argues, cultural hegemony is the means by which a dominant class maintains support from a suppressed class by successfully ingraining the moral and intellectual beliefs of the dominant class as beneficent or at least neutral "common sense" for all classes.[70] Harvey points out that neoliberalism constructed much of its consent, as he terms it, not through coercion or forced regulation, at least not at first, but through a variety of cultural and institutional channels.[71] I argue that theater, and particularly the increasingly widely accepted "common sense" of the playwright as author with ultimate authority, functions as one of these channels by which the ideas of neoliberalism become widely accepted and held even by those who might resist their outcomes. The cultural logic of ownership, therefore, is flexible enough to endear itself to anticapitalist thinkers without actually losing any of its practical force.

Albee's stated distaste for the "criminals" of Broadway and their practice of degrading plays by making them safe for audiences also conflicts with his practice of shutting down productions, especially considering the types of productions he tends to shut down. The Fahrer *Woolf*, for example, incurred Albee's wrath in part because he felt it made the play "a gay play," or a play primarily about issues of homosexuality. Albee has also shut down or refused permission to numerous productions of *Who's Afraid of Virginia Woolf?* due to attempted casting of mixed-race couples, a black George and a white Martha, for example.[72] Albee has shut down such productions, he claims, because he finds it unacceptable "to play around with an author's text to make it address an issue the author didn't intend to address."[73] Albee's complaint here assumes that having a mixed-race couple on stage necessarily makes the play *about* race. Aside from the reductiveness of this argument and its low estimation of audiences, it again expresses a resistance to a perceived thematic and argumentative change to the script. Albee's rhetoric in defending his shutting down these productions, then, always hinges on his not wanting the productions to address or exhort issues other than the ones he intended to address in writing the play because he sees all performances as extensions of the text and therefore of himself. While these claims purportedly rest on the rights of the playwright, in each case Albee's actions work toward maintaining both heteronormativity and racial uniformity on stage. In other words, they make the productions "safer" commercially by appealing to hegemonic ideals about dominant or normative heterosexual, single-race relationships. Albee's insistence on what I am calling "safe" casting also contradicts Solomon's characterization of Albee's casting practices. Solomon argues that just as Albee "eschews detailed character description" in his texts, he goes into casting with no preconceptions about the physical characteristics or personality traits he desires in actors.[74] Instead, Solomon argues, Albee cares much more deeply about performers' skill and intelligence. Clearly, this ideal of open-minded casting does not play out in the cases mentioned above. The contradiction arises from and reproduces the privileging and naturalization of hegemonic norms. Albee has no idea what his actors should look or act like, in these cases, except that they should be white and straight, even in cases where he does not specify the characters' race or sexuality anywhere in the text of the play. The framing of this privileging as a matter of obvious and natural fact instead of an ideologically loaded choice further exemplifies the extent to which Albee, despite his anticommercial, anti-mainstream rhetoric, reproduces the assumptions that support the hegemon.

Finally, Albee's assumption that the performance and the text function as extensions of a single work protected under the ideal of total ownership adds a new dimension to the interpretation question and the type/token relationship. Two of Albee's ideas figure prominently here: the performance as window to the text and the playwright, and the performance as an always flawed reproduction of the ideal production envisioned by the playwright during composition. As Saltz points out, this model of reproducing the ideal production encounters deep theoretical problems, including but not limited to the fact that no matter how closely a reproduction comes to the ideal or even the original production, it is still at best a "copy or imitation."[75] The author's idealized performance is not the type of which a performance is a token. Any production of *Who's Afraid of Virginia Woolf?* might be an imitation of Albee's idealized version, the version he "saw" when writing the play and the version to which he has privileged access, but even the most faithful imitation would still not be an instantiation of that, which is why the idea of leasing "the play" rather than the rights to use the play cannot hold. The relationship between the text and the performance is not one of ontological and aesthetic identity, but is instead an ideologically loaded categorization based on arbitrary and contingent conventions. Types are sortal concepts, and the criteria for grouping or sorting tokens into type-classes are purely conventional. The reason we can say a performance of Fahrer's all-male *Woolf* and a performance of the original Broadway production of *Woolf* are both performances of Edward Albee's *Who's Afraid of Virginia Woolf?* is not that both are tokens of the same type, but instead that both are tokens of production-types executing the same text-type and that we tend to group production-types according to the text-type they execute. The play-type is a sortal concept used to identify that set of productions that execute a particular play text. The production-type is a sortal concept used to identify that set of performances historically linked to a particular rehearsal process. These definitions are historically contingent upon changing conventions. Saltz points out that "to say that a type 'exists' is just to say that the concept *functions* in our discourse and thought; and to say a token 'exists' is just to say that it *instantiates* a type."[76] So the type of *Who's Afraid of Virginia Woolf?* exists because it functions as a way for us to categorize a set of productions and performances, even if those performances are radically different. And the performance tokens of Fahrer's or the Broadway production are only tokens of *Woolf* insofar as they are understood to instantiate the *Woolf*-type. The process of determining to which type a particular performance-token belongs depends upon historical conventions and has high ideological stakes. Placing performances executing the text of *Woolf* within the category of *Woolf*-performances relies on an assumption that executing a work equates to extending that work at least insofar as any market value gained from that use should benefit the author of the original work. This convention of categorization further evinces the cultural privileging of texts as source for and authorizer of performances.

USING MILLER

But what about a piece that uses a play text but in no way posits itself as a token of that play's type? In this section, I will look at an example of a production that uses a play text, but claims not to be a production of that play. More specifically, I will explore how such a claim functions under both a regime of idealized total ownership and a dominant conventional understanding of performances as secondary to and derivative of texts. The Wooster Group's famous conflict with Arthur Miller over the former's use of *The Crucible* provides just such a case. As part of their *LSD: Just the High Points*, the Wooster Group planned to present a highly stylized take on Miller's *The Crucible*. Miller resisted such use and ultimately forced the group to shut down the production, even though by the end of their rehearsal process the show used Miller's script barely if at all. Miller even objected to and was able to prohibit the Wooster Group's increasingly oblique references to his text, prohibitions that in many cases exceeded the letter of the law. A number of issues arise from this case. Miller's inability or unwillingness to separate any use of his text on stage, even as a quotation or reference, from an instantiation or token of the *Crucible*-type reveals the ever-broadening scope of the ideal of total ownership. Miller's reactionary actions also provide a clear example of interpellation, in which a social actor—Miller, in this case—becomes co-opted to support and reproduce the very structures and systems he would resist. Thomas P. Adler argues that "Miller's action [provides] a fascinating case study in the ongoing debate over who 'owns' or maintains interpretive authority over the written text when it becomes a performance text—the author or the director."[77] Adler points to the salient issues, but I would like to direct his lines of inquiry along a slightly different vector. Adler's statement of the issues suggests an unproblematic identity between ownership and maintaining interpretive authority over the written text. I would like to continue to trouble this identity, separating out the limited set of rights granted by legal constructs of ownership on one hand and the ideal of total ownership as a broader set of real powers—including maintaining interpretive authority—on the other. Adler also suggests that the problem in the Miller–Wooster Group confrontation occurred when the written text became a performance text. Adler's comment, while trying to put performance on equal footing with writing by calling a performance a text, actually recreates the very cultural hierarchy that privileges writing because he implies that for performance to be equally valid it must be raised to the level of a text.[78] And aside from Adler's reproducing the cultural hierarchy privileging texts, this statement underestimates the complexity of the relationship between the text of *The Crucible* and the production of *LSD: Just the High Points*.

Miller's battle with the Wooster Group was long and complex. The Wooster Group first started working with *The Crucible* in November 1982 and contacted Dramatists Play Service to inquire about the performance rights, which DPS said were unavailable at that time in New York. In January of the following year, Elizabeth LeCompte, director of the Wooster Group, reached out to Miller's agent, Luis Sanjuro, who said he would have to see what they were working on. In September 1983, after seeing a rehearsal, Sanjuro suggested the group invite Miller, who did not see the show until October. A week after seeing the show, Miller instructed his agency to deny the Wooster Group permission to use excerpts from *The Crucible* for three reasons: he considered their production a parody of his work, he thought audiences might confuse the show for a production of his work, and he worried that, because of the latter reason, the Wooster Group's show might draw audiences away from a commercial revival of *The Crucible*. The Wooster Group continued to rehearse and rework the piece over the course of the next year, severely cutting their work on *The Crucible* to one twenty-five minute segment of four in *LSD: Just the High Points*. The group began performing the piece in September 1984, prompting Miller's attorneys to issue a cease and desist order in early November, two years after the group had first started working with the text of *The Crucible*. At this point, the Wooster Group replaced *The Crucible* with a new, original text called *The Hearing* by Michael Kirby. *The Hearing* moved the basic plot and scenarios of *The Crucible* to 1950s suburbia with new characters and dialogue. Any time one of the performers in *The Hearing* "accidentally" said a line from *The Crucible* or referred to another character by the name of their corresponding character in *The Crucible*, a buzzer would sound, making Miller's control a part of the performance.[79] Miller continued to threaten to sue, even though the text in use was no longer *The Crucible*. The new version of *LSD* closed on January 8, 1985, halfway through its intended run, largely because the group could not afford to fight Miller if he had actually taken the case to court.[80] The closing cost the theater an estimated $10,000 from lost revenues: 5 percent of their annual budget.[81]

Miller called the Wooster Group's use of *The Crucible* "a blatant parody."[82] Not only was this not the group's intention, but, ironically, if the Wooster Group had insisted it was a parody they might have been able to claim fair use. Miller later admitted to Don Shewey of the *Village Voice* that the idea that he was trying to protect his economic interests by preventing a production that might preclude the success of a Broadway revival was a "smokescreen" and that he was actually trying to keep the play from being presented in a way he felt was not in line with his intentions.[83] Under either justification, this move reinforces structures of ownership because of its assumptions about control of all nodes in the network of "the work." More importantly, both justifications assume that any performance using *The Crucible* is *The Crucible*, that to include his text in a token is to instantiate the *Crucible*-type. Now it is not only executions of an author's text that come under the author's ownership but seemingly any use or even reference. Convention governs the categorization or sorting of performance tokens into types. The dominant convention in the twentieth century was to say that a performance was a token of whatever play-type (script) it executed. This sorting convention privileges an author-centric, text-based model of dramatic theater. But the Wooster Group's *LSD* is not an instantiation or token of the *Crucible*-type. It uses parts of the *Crucible*-type, words of dialogue from the script of Arthur Miller's *The Crucible*, but because it couches those words within the context of a performance that openly and critically engages *The Crucible* it does not instantiate the *Crucible*-type, is not a token of it. In effect, the performance puts quotation marks around the *Crucible*-type whereas something like the Akalaitis *Endgame* still executes a script albeit in a manner other than the manner preferred by the script's author. As LeCompte puts it, "I used Miller's play like an icon, like a piece of culture. It's almost like using a piece of the American Flag in a mosaic. People remember when they saw the play, what they thought about it. It sets off all sort of reverberations."[84] For LeCompte, not only is *LSD* not a production of *The Crucible*, it does not even really use the *Crucible*-type so much as it references that type's cultural "reverberations" or associations. Miller's unwillingness or inability to separate out the concepts of use and instantiation shows how deeply the concept of the work as a shape-shifter, an entity that can change forms while still maintaining its essential identity, remains entrenched. Miller's conflation of use and instantiation provides a way of maintaining not only exclusive rights to financial benefit but also aesthetic control, even limiting other artists' ability to comment upon or allude to his work if he disapproves of their commentary.

The Hearing, the Wooster Group's original, 1950s-set response to the script, might have been completely protected under the law had it been presented as part of *LSD* or even as an original play, depending on the extent to which it could be seen to parody, to respond to, or to draw inspiration from *The Crucible* rather than to adapt it. Again, none of the enumerated exclusive rights of copyright holders prevent references to or responses to other texts, only derivative works. And perhaps *The Hearing* would have been protected under the law, but the Wooster Group lacked the funds to really fight in court, even though the law might have been on their side.[85] Miller, therefore, only had to threaten legal action, even legal action beyond the scope of the law, to limit what the Wooster Group could do even with regard to the themes of his work and their cultural associations. As Bracha points out, ideas about the law and its relationship to authorship often exert force in such cases in excess of the letter and spirit of the law.[86] For Miller, his total ownership of *The Crucible* even extends to the ideas contained in the script, granting him the right to control others' use of the social critique associated with the play. Woodrow Hood argues that Miller's efforts to limit even references to or protected transformative uses of *The Crucible* purely for its cultural value suggest that Miller views *The Crucible* less as a rarefied work of art to be preserved and more as a commercial "brand" whose identity must be maintained.[87] As David Savran points out, Miller's authoritarian actions run counter to the arguments of the play itself.

> Arthur Miller's threat of legal action has proven the veracity of the Wooster Group's demonstration. It has confirmed the suggestion that the sphere of interpretation is not a pure, aesthetic realm but the world of political power. In this world, Miller's own reading of the play is distinguished from all others not because it is more correct but because it is empowered with the force of law. By insisting on his own interpretation, Miller has, ironically, aligned himself with the very forces that *The Crucible* condemns, those authorities who exercise their power arrogantly and arbitrarily to ensure their own continued political and cultural domination.[88]

Savran draws attention to an important tension between the content of Miller's collectivist, antiauthoritarian argument and his participation in reproducing neoliberal ideology, which resists any and all kinds of collectivity, through his actions. Although Savran points to the conflict between Miller's and the Wooster Group's interpretations, it is not so much Miller's reading or interpretation that's privileged but his right to control use of and even references to the text. Unlike the other cases discussed so far in this chapter where postdramatic theater served as a kind of background noise, a mounting threat to the established order, this is a case of a postdramatic theater project being invalidated and suppressed by a theater industry deeply entrenched in the dramatic mode. Miller's power is in one sense based on the "force of law," but more specifically it is based on the extralegal ideological force of the law, the cultural ideas about the law, enforced not by the courts or by statutes but by inequalities between social players in terms of means to litigate.[89] This tension between Miller's political philosophy and his authoritarian, capitalist actions again has to do with the ideological state apparatus of intellectual property interpellating him as an owner to the point that, even against his espoused political beliefs, he engages in actions that support the neoliberal ideologies underlying the structures of ownership that prop him up both financially and artistically. While Miller's work critiques authoritarianism and profit-motive-as-ethic his professional practices depend upon and in turn bolster those very ideas.

1984

I opened this chapter by pointing out that three of these major closings occurred in 1984 and playfully suggesting a link between such closings and an Orwellian Big Brother system. Some may object to this association, arguing that just because theatrical conventions shift and new practices emerge, playwrights are not under any obligation to "get with the program," to roll over and accept a model of theatrical production that deprivileges the text and therefore greatly diminishes the significance and power of authorial intent. But my point is not that these playwrights are nefarious Big Brother types. The point, instead, is to expose the dissonance between their anticommercial rhetoric and the ideologies they support in defending authorship. In other words, the playwrights are not Big Brother; they just reproduce the dominance of the hegemon for which Big Brother serves as a symbol. In each of these cases, authorship serves as the default mode of cultural production, meaning that assumptions about authorship serve as the standard against which other modes of cultural production are judged. The playwrights in question, the critics discussing them, and even the laws to which they appeal place authorship in this default, dominant position. The point of my argument is, again, not to call hypocrisy on anyone. Pointing out hypocrisy is a much lower-stakes argument than showing that progressive rhetorics are ineffectual when employed in conservative apparatuses. My argument is a question not of hypocrisy but of expediency. If this argument were about hypocrisy, it would need to prove that the authors' anticapitalist rhetoric reflected their actual politics more than their actions. Even if the authors discussed in this chapter are being disingenuous in their anticapitalist rhetoric or if their actions reveal their politics more earnestly than their rhetoric, that does not diminish the point that their practices and not their rhetoric carry the greater political force. Because, while they may argue for anticapitalist ideologies, sincerely or not, their practices reaffirm and reproduce capitalist structures of production. Sincerity, irony, and therefore hypocrisy are somewhat moot points when the point is the dissonance itself between rhetoric and practice and that the practice is what matters in terms of maintaining status quo or resisting it. To conclude this chapter, I will look at a series of debates over how playwrights, the law, emergent practices, and philosophical and theoretical trends should respond to one another. Rather than situate myself among the "shoulds," I will explore how authorship's position as the default mode of cultural production runs through these discourses as a sort of guarantor of neoliberal ideology's dominance. The debates about whether playwrights—or directors, for that matter—should or should not accept shifting hierarchies obscures an important ideological question: what consequences and implications come from holding on to dominant structures and practices regardless of the content produced therein?

Several critics responding to the emergence of postdramatic theater and playwrights' shutting down or objecting to productions in the immediate aftermath of the 1984 closings try to strike a balance between celebrating new models of production and maintaining the playwright's authority. Gerald Rabkin, writing in 1985, argues that an overly hasty cheering of the director's emancipation from the playwright risks devaluing the work of playwrights to the point that playwrights will no longer want to write plays.[90] Rabkin argues that "those of us sympathetic to the destabilizing of the author's patriarchal authority over his *text* must also recognize the importance of protecting the author's personal right to his work."[91] In the same year, Mel Gussow, responding to the controversy surrounding the ART production of *Endgame*, suggests that while "Miss Akalaitis should be allowed her share of directorial license," Beckett also "has every right to protect the letter as well as the spirit of his words."[92] Rabkin and Gussow both suggest a balancing act, then, an appreciation for a director's theater tempered by a respect for the playwright's vision or intention. But ultimately such arguments replicate an aesthetic hierarchy with the text on top because they depend on the interpretation model of production. In other words, even when arguing that directors should be given a certain degree of interpretive freedom, they maintain the assumption that a director's function is secondary to the text.

These assumptions about the cultural logic of ownership run so deep that they allow Rabkin to advance a completely unreliable picture of the relationship among authors, texts, the market, and the law. Rabkin sees the law and capitalist systems failing to protect authors or respect their authority, their aesthetic control of their works. In fact, the opposite is true. Responding directly to the idea that the law or production practices should adjust to an aesthetic discourse in which authors have been declared dead, Rabkin argues that "Barthes's insistence upon the disseminative power of the text does not logically abrogate the author's ownership rights over his work."[93] Rabkin's assertion here is right but does not illuminate much, other than the rather obvious fact that the law is not beholden to aesthetic theory or philosophy. He also argues that "historically the author's rights which emerge with capitalist individualism have always been rendered precarious by the marketplace."[94] Author's rights are not made precarious by the market, as Rabkin claims, but rather are bolstered by it, and in turn the logic of protecting those rights bolsters the market. Even the very cases he discusses, such as the Akalaitis *Endgame* case, show that authors exercise enormous powers. Those powers grow specifically out of the market, not as protection against it. The constitutional justification for copyright law is to encourage the progress of the arts, and copyright law since the late nineteenth century has assumed that encouraging the progress of the arts means protecting financial incentives to create. Beckett can shut down productions of his work not in order to protect himself from the market but in order to operate within it. Without market value, the thing Rabkin claims endangers playwrights, Beckett would not have the rights and powers he does. As with my discussion of Kalb earlier, this analysis is meant to unpack a snapshot of critical assumptions at the time rather than respond to an argument. What Rabkin's arguments show about criticism at the time, then, is a desire to celebrate new modes of production tempered by the deeply ingrained, almost intractable cultural logic of capitalism.

The cultural logic of ownership and an assumption about authorship's position as default mode of cultural production underscore all of Rabkin's arguments, and Rabkin's arguments all help reproduce the ideal of total ownership by presenting its supposed absence as a cause of peril or creative persecution. Instead, its actual presence supports vested interests its presence actually represents. His claims reproduce authorship's position as the default mode of cultural production by suggesting that other modes of production and theoretical models that decentralize the text represent threats to authorship. Without getting into the argument of whether greater control of texts by authors is somehow morally or aesthetically desirable in all cases and contexts, the point is that in the context of the latter half of the twentieth century, the control of authors was great, quite the opposite of Rabkin's image of the victimization playwrights supposedly faced at the hands of auteur directors and the very market whose assumptions protects their rights. The emerging postdramatic moment operated under a different logic about the central authority of the author, a logic in many ways running counter to dominant neoliberal ideologies. These authors' exercising something approaching total control ultimately reproduces the market-relation-as-ethic-and-aesthetic they each decry in their own ways, and the critics who rely on authorship as the default mode of cultural production in turn bolster neoliberal ideology's position as "common sense."

These conflicts between authorial ideology and artistic practice extend beyond the world of the theater. In fact, they relate to a broader conversation about the relationship between changing philosophies and creative practices on one hand and—some argue—a relatively stagnant legal system and set of cultural institutions on the other. These conversations play out mainly in scholarship on literature, so I will take some time to lay out that discourse and its relationship to authorship as the default mode of cultural production before exploring how theater uniquely complicates it. Rose, who suggests that ownership is the fundamental condition of modern authorship, is not alone in examining the relationship between changing aesthetic practices and theories and the institutional functions under whose jurisdiction they operate. Martha Woodmansee and Peter Jaszi have both argued that policy and industry practices could and should change to reflect changes in aesthetic philosophy and artistic practice. In fact, the volume they edited sets out, in part, to provoke such changes. Woodmansee claims that because the law has not, according to her, responded to "the 'critique of authorship' initiated by Foucault," it does not reflect the practicalities and needs of contemporary creative artists. Therefore, she sees a "pressing need to reestablish communication" between artists, cultural critics, and legislative and judicial bodies.[95] Jaszi takes an even stronger stance, suggesting that current copyright law "[forces] all writing into the Procrustean doctrinal model shaped by the individualistic, Romantic concept of 'authorship.'"[96] Jaszi and Woodmansee suggest that the default to authorship harmfully restricts writing practices.

David Saunders offers an opposing view, strongly resisting the idea that just because practices and philosophical trends change the law should follow.[97] While Saunders is right to suggest that the law has no obligation to adjust to aesthetic or philosophical trends, the force of his arguments threatens to obscure how the law's manner of operation reproduces capitalist relations of production and resists or reappropriates the development and proliferation of anticapitalist performance practices. Saunders's response is crucial to understanding this process of reproduction because it too supports neoliberal ideology by invalidating art's and philosophy's ability to challenge or comment on it from a position outside the market. Throughout his book, Saunders argues that the law is not beholden to art or philosophy, and that arguments such as Woodmansee's or Jaszi's fail to recognize that the law is the law and art is art. Responding to Rose's critique of the authorship-ownership conflation, for example, Saunders argues that

> Poststructuralism is claiming here to speak with the epochal voice of universal history. It is as if a linguistically rectified theory of authorship—it is now 'language' not the author that makes sense—could debunk the law of copyright as an arbitrary short-circuiting of the infinite possibility of language. But legal procedures and judgements do not have as their purpose the enunciation of endless meanings.[98]

While I agree with Saunders that copyright law has no inherent obligation to be beholden to critical and aesthetic theory, his seeming dismissal of such theories' jurisdiction for commenting upon the law's aesthetic or extralegal implications does not follow. Elsewhere, he points to a commentary about artistic appropriation from a copyright lawyer, saying that "as a copyright lawyer[,] the writer recognizes that if there is a legal problem there can only be a legal answer."[99] And in terms of legal efficacy, that may be true. But aesthetics and theory may certainly have an answer to a legal problem, even though that answer does not have legal force. Such an answer may, however, have real, efficacious extralegal force. Saunders ignores the extralegal implications of the law or at least the validity of commenting on them. Theorists and artists are certainly within their rights to critique the law if not to demand it to change. But then again, the law's purported purpose is to protect artists, having its constitutional basis in the government's right to promote creative and intellectual activity, so why should artists and critics not comment upon the law qua law albeit from the perspective of aesthetics or philosophy?

Saunders's resistance to such commentary supports authorship's place as the default mode of cultural production. Saunders repeatedly decries arguments such as Rose's, Jaszi's, and Woodmansee's, arguments he claims exert "pressure to subordinate positive law to the direction of aesthetics."[100] But Saunders seems to want to subordinate aesthetics to the direction of positive law. For Saunders, the author-owner construct is not just the default relationship between cultural producer and cultural product; it is the only justifiable relationship because it reflects his understanding of the law. Saunders's arguments that legal questions about aesthetics can only have legal and not aesthetic answers ultimately implies that the state should control the arts' structures of production and that the arts' modes of production must in turn support dominant models of exchange. Saunders's position, insisting on the law's speaking exclusively for and to itself, then, constitutes a reproduction of neoliberal ideologies because it actively steps in to reclaim the author/owner/individual from the peril of disappearing into the collectivity of the discourse and insists that no matter how strong the consensus regarding the author's death, her authority cannot be stripped away unless the law decides independently of its own will to do so.

Rose addresses the question of why the law does not reflect aesthetic and philosophical developments in a way that by no means suggests that the law be "subordinated" to aesthetics.

> Why, then, don't we abandon copyright as an archaic and cumbersome system of cultural regulation? Why don't we launch into the brave new world that Michel Foucault imagines at the end of 'What Is an Author?' where the authorial function disappears and texts develop and circulate, as Foucault puts it, 'in the anonymity of a murmur'. [sic] The institution of copyright is of course deeply rooted in our economic system, and much of our economy does in turn depend on intellectual property. But, no less important, copyright is deeply rooted in our conception of ourselves as individuals with at least a modest grade of singularity, some degree of personality. And it is associated with our sense of privacy and our conviction, at least in theory, that it is essential to limit the power of the state. We are not ready, I think, to give up the sense of who we are.[101]

Far from demanding that the law reflect artistic practices or aesthetic philosophy as Saunders claims he does, Rose offers a nuanced take on the relationships among society, culture, and the law. He suggests that as much as writers may resist the institutions and ideologies from whence copyright comes, they also find validation in copyright's interpellating authors as owners. For Miller, Beckett, and Albee, authorship's place as the default mode of cultural production reflects the capitalist hierarchies and commercialism they reject as well as the position of exclusive credit and control they defend. The author-owner construct is both a symbol of the enemy and an encapsulation of their identities. The role this construct creates for these writers allows them the freedom to speak against capitalist structures and neoliberal ideologies while simultaneously rendering them complicit in reproducing those same structures and ideologies. This contradictory identity with the author-owner construct is common to artists in many art forms throughout the twentieth century, but theater further complicates this relationship because of the multiplicity of creators involved in any theatrical work.

Even those theater artists whose practice seems most antithetical to authorship's place as the default mode of cultural production can adopt authorial roles and operate under the cultural logic of capitalism. Charles Mee, who has built his reputation and career around rejecting an authorial position, even more strongly reproduces capitalist assumptions by becoming something of an antiauthorial author, commodifying the very resistance to commodification. Mee asks that anyone

> feel free to take the plays from this website and use them freely as a resource for your own work: that is to say, don't just make some cuts or rewrite a few passages or re-arrange them or put in a few texts that you like better, but pillage the plays . . . and build your own, entirely new, piece—and then, please, put your own name to the work that results.[102]

Mee expresses his anxiety over maintaining a space for authorship even as he claims to reject it. I read Mee's positioning as an attempt to maintain the author's place in the postdramatic theater. I'll nominally give up some of my control, he implies, as long as I still get to be the author. W. B. Worthen has also pointed out that while it suggests malleability and an open-source ethos, "this proviso also seems to articulate an anxiety and nostalgia for the identity and propriety of the printed work."[103] Mee's career, then, exemplifies authorship's abilities to maintain its structures by appropriating its own resistance. Despite his ostensible openness and self-proclaimed denial of originality, Mee ultimately reproduces institutional and critical assumptions about authorship. In an introduction to an interview she conducted for *TDR*, Mee's daughter, Erin Mee, talks about her experiences directing her father's plays and offers the standard narrative of Mee as an antiauthorial author.[104] Erin Mee explicitly distances her father from the kind of control other author-owners have exercised, saying that Mee "wouldn't try to close down *Endgame* because JoAnne Akalaitis hasn't followed his stage directions word for word" or "ask the Wooster Group to 'cease and desist' from staging parts of *The Crucible* in ways he didn't originally envision."[105] She also points out that she gets to play a more active role when directing her father's plays than when directing other plays. "I'm not just *allowed* to bring my ideas to the production; I'm *expected* to do so . . . I get to be who I am: a creative artist, not an interpretive artist."[106] Instead of writing plays to be served, she suggests that Mee "writes blueprints for events. For spectacles. For festivals."[107] But here, she calls his plays "blueprints," suggesting a grand design to be followed. And in all of her comments about the special relationship between director and text in a Mee play, the text still serves as a point of origin, even if the paths running from that origin diverge. The play still comes first and the director second, not only historically but also creatively. She implies that Mee plays transform the director's role from interpretive to additive but not generative. Mee—and here I mean not Charles Mee the person but the "brand" of Charles Mee—nominally sacrifices control over the performance event to ensure that event continues to proceed from a text, thereby maintaining text-centric structures and production practices. Mee provides the opportunity for directors to be more than "just interpretive artists" while maintaining the text's position at the origin point of a production process. By creating texts more amenable to postdramatic production practices, Mee helps to maintain the dominance of the author-owner construct even in an emerging, antiauthorial mode of production.

The relationship among the law, neoliberal ideology, and constructs of authorship and ownership takes on personal in addition to political dimensions. Rose points out that during a key period of copyright law's development in the late nineteenth century, the idea emerged that "a work of literature belonged to an individual because it was, finally, an embodiment of that individual."[108] Beckett echoes this idea during a conversation during which an interviewer asks him about

> directors preferring to work with dead authors. 'But I'm not dead yet,' [Beckett] said. 'Not quite. I'm a dying author, certainly.' [He] then asked him why it was less important to respect an author's text after he's dead, and [Beckett] answered, 'Well, just because then you can't hurt his feelings.'[109]

In the theater, though, a number of different artists apply their energy and personality to a work, so the model of a work emanating from or functioning as "an embodiment of" an individual author necessarily diminishes the work of other practitioners. Beckett's feelings are hurt because of his assumption that authorship sits both at the top of a theatrical hierarchy and at the origin point of a line ending in performance. According to these arguments, the figurative death of the author can only obtain in theater on the condition of the literal death of the specific author in question. But even that does not hold. The Beckett estate continues to enforce the will of Beckett. And, as I argue in the next chapter, Jonathan Larson's literal death did not impede his individualistic authorial intention from exerting legal and financial force in the authorship dispute surrounding *Rent*. The cultural logic of total ownership and the idea of the author-owner are so ingrained that even literally dead authors continue to exert control over their texts and thereby reproduce an author-centric mode of production.

The practice of playwrights shutting down productions of their own plays continues, alive and well, to the moment of this writing. One recent case involved David Mamet shutting down Alchemist Theatre's production of *Oleanna* in Milwaukee, Wisconsin, after just one performance on June 19, 2014. *Oleanna* centers on Carol, a college student accusing her professor, John, of harassment and rape. The issue here, as in several of the Beckett and Albee cases, was gender-blind casting. In Alchemist's production, the role of Carol was played by Ben Parman. According to a statement made by Erica Case and Aaron Kopec, the producers of the show, they did not change the character Carol's gender even though they cast a man to play her. They explicitly claim that they "did not change the character of Carol but allowed the reality of gender and relationship fluidity to add to the impact of the story."[110] This idea seems to have played well to the audience, as Mike Fischer's review, published in the same issue of the *Milwaukee Journal Sentinel* as the story about the closure, consistently refers to Carol with feminine pronouns and acknowledges the gender identification issues.[111] This situation is somewhat unusual because Alchemist Theatre kept the casting a secret until opening night. The cease-and-desist only went out after reviews appeared online revealing that Carol was played by a male actor. In all of these cases, however, the playwrights acted as though copyright law entitled them to control casting decisions along race and gender lines. However, U.S. copyright law itself grants only ownership over the right to perform the work publicly, not the right to control every aspect of such performances. That greater right to control performances comes from the temporary licenses playwrights grant producing entities whereby they essentially lease the performance right that copyright law grants them with added stipulations. Increasingly, however, cultural assumptions erroneously ascribe such powers to copyright law itself, as seen throughout this chapter. Thus one only has to reference copyright law to wield great practically enforceable power even if such power is in excess of the law itself. Theaters seldom if ever fight back in such cases by making the claim that they have faithfully executed their contracts; a lack of such resistance to cease and desist orders stems at least in part from a widespread belief that as soon as an author claims "copyright," the game is over even when a theater might have a valid, legal defense worth pursuing.

Because of the gender identification issue, this is not just a conflict between the rights of the playwright and the rights of the director or actors but is also, in a very real way, about the legal status of sex and gender. Mamet rejects the performance out of hand because of a male actor playing a female character, dismissing the notion that a male body can count as a woman. That the theater closed the production rather than fight back suggests a lack of parity among parties in terms of ability to litigate rather than an actual rightness on Mamet's part or wrongness on Alchemist Theatre's part, especially considering that cross-gendered casting is as old as theater itself. Fischer's review of Alchemist Theatre's single performance even argued that Mamet's script provides support for a transgendered reading, noting that "Carol refers to herself at one point as 'of doubtful sexuality' and as having overcome sexual 'prejudices' and 'humiliations.'"[112] Moreover, copyright, as practiced here, gives Mamet the right to decide unilaterally that someone identifying as female does not actually count as female even in the context of a performance of a play. A lawyer might argue that Alchemist Theatre's production did not violate the stage directions, that the character of Carol was a woman just as in the script but happened to be played by a man and argue that shutting down the production amounts to discrimination. Who can say how much traction such an argument might find, but my hunch is not much. The U.S. legal system has shown again and again its strong preference to uphold the ideal of total ownership even beyond what its own strictures dictate. In fact, given the current political and judicial environment, I suspect that Mamet could successfully shut down a production in which an actor who identified as trans-woman played Carol. My point is that Mamet shutting down productions of his own work constitutes an act of reproducing an author-centric mode of production as well as cis- and heteronormative assumptions about gender and sexuality.

All of this is intended to point out the ideological stakes in these superficially aesthetic and legal conflicts and to examine the hegemonic roles adopted by playwrights at certain points in the history of this period. The writers examined in detail here all participate in reproducing dominant ideology, an ideology they resist rhetorically, by assuming total control over an extensive work that includes the text and all performances executing that text. What causes Albee and Beckett and Miller to conflate type and token, however, is not an ontological issue but an ideological one. In other words, they see "the work" not so much as an entity but as an ideal of total control over all nodes in network because of the deeply ingrained cultural logic of total ownership. They make appeals to the law that assume an endorsement of ownership and control far greater than the law itself actually provides for. In the late twentieth century, the ideology of authorship is, in practical terms, more powerful than the law itself in regulating performance practices and always does so toward the end of reproducing capitalist models of production. Authorship's position as the default mode of cultural production helps reproduce dominant ideologies and also limits the very creative freedom copyright law is meant to support and encourage. As the next chapter will show, even those artists most attuned to the ideological stakes of performance practices and most committed to resisting neoliberal ideologies occasionally default to authorship's assumptions and thereby reproduce the very thing they set out to challenge.

NOTES

1. Many of my arguments in this chapter hearken back to Frederic Jameson's central thesis, that while many have seen the rise of the postmodern as populist and egalitarian in its dissolution of the high art–mass culture divide, postmodernism actually heralds the culmination of capitalist ideology because all cultural logic takes on its assumptions about commodities, capital, competition, and exchange. Frederic Jameson, *Postmodernism, Or, The Cultural Logic of Late Capitalism* (Durham, NC: Duke University Press, 1991).
2. Oliver Gerland, "From Playhouse to P2P Network: The History and Theory of Performance under Copyright Law in the United States," *Theatre Journal* 59 (2007): 79.
3. Oren Bracha, "The Ideology of Authorship Revisited: Authors, Markets, and Liberal Values in Early American Copyright," *Yale Law Journal* 118, no. 2 (2008): 231.
4. Ibid., 228.
5. Ibid., 229.
6. Ibid., 241.
7. Ibid., 206–7.
8. Gerland, "From Playhouse to P2P Network," 77, n. 7.
9. Mark Rose, *Authors and Owners: The Invention of Copyright* (Cambridge, MA: Harvard University Press, 1993), 1.
10. Hans-Thies Lehmann, *Postdramatic Theatre*, trans. Karen Jurs-Munby (New York: Routledge, 2006).
11. Ibid., 21.
12. Antonin Artaud, *The Theater and Its Double*, trans. Mary Caroline Richards (New York: Grove Press, 1958).
13. Ibid., 74–75, 79.
14. Avra Sidiropoulou, *Authoring Performance: The Director in Contemporary Theatre* (New York: Palgrave, 2011), 14.
15. Lehmann, *Postdramatic Theatre*, 50.
16. Sidiropoulou, *Authoring Performance*, 14–15.
17. Rebecca Schneider and Gabrielle Cody, eds., *Re:direction: A Theoretical and Practical Guide* (New York: Routledge, 2002), 125.
18. David Savran, *The Wooster Group, 1975-1985: Breaking the Rules* (Ann Arbor: UMI Research Press, 1986), 221.
19. Gerald Rabkin, "Is There a Text on This Stage? Theatre/Authorship/Interpretation," *Performing Arts Journal* 9, no. 2/3 (1985): 143.
20. Barbara McMahon, "Beckett Estate Fails to Stop Women Waiting for Godot," *The Guardian*, February 3, 2006, available at http://www.guardian.co.uk/world/2006/feb/04/arts.italy (accessed December 5, 2011).
21. Ibid.
22. Of course, legal systems vary significantly from country to country, and terms such as "civil rights" and "moral rights" have very different meanings in the United States than they do elsewhere. My point in looking at these incidents and the arguments surrounding them is not so much to explore the legal issues themselves as to look at the assumptions such arguments reveal about cultural production.
23. Sarah-Kate Templeton, "Beckett Estate Rules Out Female Version of Godot," *The Scotsman*, July 27, 1998; and Raymond Duncan, "Waiting for No Woman," *The Herald*, July 27, 1998.
24. Peter Murphy, quoted in Louise Jury, "Death and the Artist," *The Independent*, August 2, 1998.
25. Apparently, the Beckett estate finds no production too small to control. Whereas the Warner and Akalaitis productions were relatively prominent and large-scale, the Grimey Up

North and L'Agenzia Teatrale D'Arborio productions were relatively small. The Beckett estate also shut down another, even smaller production of *Godot* headed to Edinburgh and put together by high school students in London because they set and performed the play in a bathroom. Harry Michell, the seventeen-year-old who directed the production, was out roughly $1,400 on the publicity he had spent on the show. The students were resourceful, however, and instead wrote and performed a new play called *Still Waiting for Godot* about two theater critics who show up to the bathroom to review a production of *Waiting for Godot* unaware that it has been canceled. See James Bradshaw, "Plumbing a Beckett Play, Finding It Flush with Obstacles," *Globe and Mail*, August 29, 2009; and Mike Wade, "Plumbing the Depths? Actors Take to the Toilet," *London Times*, August 15, 2009.

26. Jonathan Kalb, *Beckett in Performance* (Cambridge: Cambridge University Press, 1989), 81.

27. Ibid., 80.

28. Ibid., 72.

29. Ibid., 81.

30. Ibid., 153.

31. Ibid.

32. Ibid.

33. Ibid., 154.

34. S. E. Gontarski, "Reinventing Beckett," *Modern Drama* 49, no. 4 (2006): 428–51. See also S. E. Gontarski, "Editing Beckett," *Twentieth Century Literature* 41, no. 2 (1995): 190–207. Gontarski makes a similar argument here about Beckett's essentially revisionary spirit by looking at Beckett's own process of editing and suggesting continuing editorial revisions.

35. Gontarski, "Reinventing Beckett," 430.

36. Richard Wollheim, *Art and Its Objects*, second edition with six supplementary essays (Cambridge: Cambridge University Press, 1980), 74–84.

37. David Z. Saltz, "What Theatrical Performance Is (Not): The Interpretation Fallacy," *Journal of Aesthetics and Art Criticism* 59, no. 3 (2001): 303.

38. Saltz, "The Interpretation Fallacy," 306. It is worth noting that Saltz departs from Wollheim on this point. Wollheim very much sees performance as a form of interpretation. The point is that the type/token model in itself does not necessarily remove interpretation from the text/performance relationship.

39. Roland Barthes, "The Death of the Author," in *Image-Music-Text*, trans. Stephen Heath (New York: Hill and Wang, 1977), 142–48.

40. David Z. Saltz, "When Is the Play the Thing?—Analytic Aesthetics and Dramatic Theory," *Theatre Research International* 20, no. 3 (2002): 271.

41. Actually, Saltz would call a performance of the Akalaitis production a token of a type of a type. The first type is the *Endgame*-type, of which the Akalaitis production is a token. But the production is also a type of which the individual performances are tokens both of the production-type and the *Endgame*-type.

42. Ibid., 269.

43. JoAnne Akalaitis, quoted in Kalb, *Beckett in Performance*, 166.

44. Ibid.

45. Barney Rosset has suggested that the failure of the Miami *Godot* in fact led to Schneider's status as preferred director because Rosset and Beckett felt such a sense of loyalty and appreciation to Schneider's having taken the heat for the production's failure. See *Waiting for Beckett*, directed by John L. Reilly (1994; New York: Global Village, 1994), VHS.

46. Maurice Harmon, ed., *No Author Better Served: The Correspondence of Samuel Beckett and Alan Schneider* (Cambridge, MA: Harvard University Press, 1998), 8–9.

47. Stephen John Dilks, "Portraits of Beckett as a Famous Writer," *Journal of Modern Literature* 29, no. 4 (2006): 161–88. See also Stephen John Dilks, *Samuel Beckett in the Literary Marketplace* (Syracuse, NY: Syracuse University Press, 2011).

48. Dilks, "Portraits of Beckett," 168.

49. The exact number of such closures as well as their dates and locations are elusive. Despite consistent accounts from both Albee himself and others that he has shut down "a

number" of all-male productions of *Who's Afraid of Virginia Woolf?* the only case mentioned with any specificity is the one directed by Dov Fahrer described in this paragraph. For this reason, I focus in this section more on Albee's comments about the practice of shutting down productions throughout his career than on particular incidents. For some examples of such general comments, see David Richards, "Edward Albee and the Road Not Taken," *New York Times,* June 16, 1991; Hap Erstein, "Directing, Sexuality—and Indecent Exposure," *Washington Times*, February 28, 1992; Phillip McCarthy, "The Man Who Cried Woolf," *The Age*, August 18, 2007. This list is representative and not at all exhaustive.

50. "Career Guide: The Playwright," American Theatre Wing website, http://americantheatrewing.org/careerguides/detail/the_playwright (accessed April 11, 2013).

51. "Albee Seeking to Close an All-Male *Woolf*," *New York Times*, August 3, 1984.

52. "Career Guide: The Playwright."

53. Edward Albee, quoted in Matthew C. Roudane, "A Playwright Speaks: An Interview with Edward Albee," in *Critical Essays on Edward Albee*, ed. Philip C. Kolin and J. Madison Davis (Boston: G.K. Hall and Co., 1986), 198–99.

54. Rakesh H. Solomon, *Albee in Performance* (Bloomington: University of Indiana Press, 2010).

55. Ibid., 1–2.

56. Edward Albee, *Stretching My Mind* (New York: Carroll and Graf, 2005), 32.

57. "Career Guide: The Playwright."

58. Edward Albee, quoted in Digby Diehl, "Edward Albee Interviewed," in *Conversations with Edward Albee*, Philip C. Kolin, ed. (Jackson: University of Mississippi Press, 1988), 33.

59. Ibid.

60. Edward Albee, quoted in Peter Adam, "Edward Albee: A Playwright Versus the Theatre," in *Conversations with Edward Albee*, ed. Kolin, 137.

61. "Career Guide: The Playwright."

62. Ibid.

63. These contract norms are codified, just not in U.S. code. The Dramatists Guild offers a "bill of rights" for dramatists in addition to form contracts for members to use. This bill of rights lays out the guild's assumptions of the basic rights of dramatists, including the rights of playwrights to have their play presented exactly as written as well as the explicit right to attend all rehearsals and performances, together endorsing playwrights' control over productions. http://www.dramatistsguild.com/billofrights/.

64. Ibid. See also Stephen Bottoms, "Borrowed Time: An Interview with Edward Albee," in *The Cambridge Companion to Edward Albee*, ed. Stephen Bottoms (Cambridge: Cambridge University Press, 2005), 231–50, especially 236.

65. Albee, quoted in Adrienne Clarkson, "The Private World of Edward Albee," in *Conversations with Edward Albee*, ed. Kolin, 81. See also Bruce J. Mann, "Interview with Edward Albee," in *Edward Albee: A Casebook*, ed. Bruce J. Mann (New York: Routledge, 2003), 129–45, especially 142–43; and Bottoms, "Borrowed Time," 238.

66. "Career Guide: The Playwright."

67. Harvey, *A Brief History of Neoliberalism*, 42.

68. David Harvey, *The Enigma of Capital and the Crises of Capitalism* (New York: Oxford University Press, 2010), 40.

69. Albee, quoted in David Richards, "Edward Albee and the Road Not Taken," *New York Times*, June 16, 1991.

70. Antonio Gramsci, *Selections from Cultural Writings*, ed. David Forgacs and Geoffrey Nowell-Smith, trans. William Boelhower (Cambridge, MA: Harvard University Press, 1985), 420–21.

71. Harvey, *A Brief History of Neoliberalism*, 39–40.

72. Phillip McCarthy, "The Man Who Cried Woolf," *The Age,* August 18, 2007, 19.

73. Quoted in McCarthy, "The Man Who Cried Woolf."

74. Solomon, *Albee in Performance*, 14.

75. Saltz, "The Interpretation Fallacy," 305.

76. Saltz, "When Is the Play the Thing?" 269.

77. Thomas P. Adler, "Conscience and Community in *An Enemy of the People* and *The Crucible*," in *The Cambridge Companion to Arthur Miller*, second edition, ed. Christopher Bigsby (Cambridge: Cambridge University Press, 2010), 89.

78. See Saltz, "When Is the Play the Thing?" 271. Saltz points out that the use of the phrase "performance text" has been a strategy for validating performance as a self-sufficient form and not as derivative or secondary to written works. However, the term "performance text" maintains textual supremacy through a rhetoric of elevation and assimilation. This strategy of "validating" performance by "raising" it to the level of the text also, I think, suggests a kind of critical anxiety over engaging with or analyzing anything not easily divided into discrete works, an anxiety caused by the need ingrained in the cultural logic of capitalism to understand all cultural production in terms of commodities and exchange.

79. Savran, *Breaking the Rules*, 191–93.

80. Nan Robertson, "Dispute over 'L.S.D.' Appears Ended," *New York Times*, January 10, 1985.

81. Samuel G. Freedman, "Play Closed After 'Crucible' Dispute," November 28, 1984.

82. Arthur Miller, quoted in Robert Massa, "Arthur Miller Clings to *The Crucible*," *Village Voice*, December 10, 1983.

83. Savran, *Breaking the Rules*, 193.

84. Quoted in Samuel G. Freedman, "Who's to Say Whether a Playwright Is Wronged?" *New York Times*, December 23, 1984.

85. Woodrow Hood, "Please, Steal My Art: Does Intellectual Property Law Hinder Creativity? Or, Can We Stop Talking about Intellectual Property Law and Talk about Creative Practice Rights?" *Wake Forest Journal of Business and Intellectual Property Law* 12 (2012): 418.

86. Bracha, "Ideology and Authorship," 190.

87. Ibid.

88. Savran, *Breaking the Rules*, 219.

89. According to a 2013 study by the American Intellectual Property Law Association, the average cost of litigation for a copyright infringement case that goes to trial ranges from $373K to $2.1M depending on the amount of money sought in damages and the assessed value of the copyrighted works in question. While playwrights with backing from publishing companies might be able to afford to take such cases to court, they operate in the knowledge that theater companies who often operate at the edge of their budgets from year to year likely have little means to pursue a case even if they have a solid legal defense. The result is that theater companies are far more likely to shut down a production than to fight for one even when they could win. Enforcement of intellectual property rights, in practical terms, is sometimes based more on economic disparity and assumptions about the incontrovertible rights of authors than on actual intellectual property law.

90. Rabkin, "Is There a Text on This Stage?" 142–59.

91. Ibid., 155. Emphasis original.

92. Mel Gussow, "Critic's Notebook; Enter Fearless Director, Pursued by Playwright," *New York Times*, January 3, 1985.

93. Rabkin, "Is There a Text on This Stage?" 154.

94. Ibid.

95. Martha Woodmansee, "On the Author Effect: Recovering Collectivity," in *The Construction of Authorship: Textual Appropriation in Law and Literature*, ed. Woodmansee and Peter Jaszi (Durham, NC: Duke University Press, 1994), 28.

96. Peter Jaszi, "On the Author Effect: Contemporary Copyright and Collective Creativity," in *The Construction of Authorship: Textual Appropriation in Law and Literature*, ed. Woodmansee and Jaszi, 55.

97. David Saunders, *Authorship and Copyright* (London: Routledge, 1992).

98. Ibid., 223.

99. Ibid., 230.

100. Saunders, *Authorship and Copyright*, 227.

101. Rose, *Authors and Owners*, 142.

102. Charles Mee, The (Re)making Project website, last accessed November 6, 2013, http://www.charlesmee.org/about.shtml.

103. W. B. Worthen, *Print and the Poetics of Modern Drama* (Cambridge: Cambridge University Press, 2005), 98.
104. Erin B. Mee, "Shattered and Fucked Up and Full of Wreckage: The Words and Works of Charles L. Mee," *TDR* 46 (2002): 83–104.
105. Ibid., 85.
106. Ibid., 85.
107. Ibid., 83. Her use of the words "spectacle" and "festival" as evidence of nondramatic models of production will pop up again in my discussion of Jean-Claude van Itallie's assertion that labeling *The Serpent* "a ceremony" was little more than a nominal nod to a stylistic movement within an otherwise traditional, drama-centric production apparatus.
108. Ibid., 114.
109. Kalb, *Beckett in Performance*, 78–79.
110. Chris Foran, "Mamet Letter Forces Alchemist to Cancel *Oleanna* after One Performance," *Milwaukee Journal Sentinel*, June 20, 2014. Mamet has not, as yet, publicly commented on the closure.
111. Mike Fischer, "Alchemist Theatre Delivers Intense Take on David Mamet's *Oleanna*," *Milwaukee Journal Sentinel*, June 20, 2014.
112. Fischer, "*Oleanna* review."

Chapter Two

"A Necessary Myth": The Author as Individual

Next to an unassuming doorway at the cramped-looking 632 St. Peter's Street in New Orleans's French Quarter hangs a plaque denoting the space as the site where Tennessee Williams composed *A Streetcar Named Desire*. This plaque plays into a larger trend of centering a play's history on the playwright as an individual author. It implies the central importance to *Streetcar* of Williams's lonely work in a small space. Williams's individualism, protected by his isolation at the stage of composition, serves as a guarantor for quality and an origin for any charting of the play's history or legacy. The image of the individual genius toiling away in a cramped room validates the play by playing into Romantic literary tropes valuing the individual genius of a writer. But the story of cultural production does not end with the lonely writer in theater.[1] The necessity of collaboration among various artists in creating a fully realized theatrical piece undercuts the tenability of narratives treating a play as the extension of a unique, individual genius. Even in models of production in which the playwright functions as the primary artist, her work forms only one part of the final product of a performance. Martha Woodmansee points out that there was a time when even literary models of cultural production viewed writers as one artist among many contributing to the final product of the book, a view that was slowly overturned as the central defining metaphor for authorship evolved from tradesman-like craft to divine inspiration.[2] Woodmansee's study suggests that relationships between writer and finished product other than the twentieth-century model of authorship are not only theoretically possible but have obtained in the past. Individual authorship is neither a necessary precondition for nor an inevitable development of playwriting practice. Because of the collaboration necessary in mounting nearly any play, lonely individualism is also not a construct particularly well suited to theatrical production. But perhaps my claim that individualism does not fit well with the collaborative nature of theater conflates two modes of cultural production, separated by both convention and chronology in the development of a performance: the authorship of the play could proceed in the literary model with the individual author and the collaboration could happen after the fact among directors, actors, and designers. As I argued with regard to Albee, Beckett, and Miller in the previous chapter, the separation between playwrights' practice and the work of other theater artists does not always remain so clean. But, more importantly, the problems of applying the individual author construction to theater become exacerbated in the period from the 1960s to the present by the growing role of collaboration at the stage of initial development and composition. This period saw the rise of collaborative ensemble theater, the continuation of collaboration in musicals, the expansion of the role of dramaturgs, and the proliferation of developmental workshops, all signs of collaboration's increasing importance in the practice of generating or composing texts for the theater. The ideal of the author as a unique individual conflicts with the reality of collaboration in this period not only during the rehearsal process but also during the conceptualization and composition stages.

In what follows, I will look at the production histories and legacies of the Open Theatre's *The Serpent* and the Broadway musical *Rent* to show some of the consequences of the ideological conflict between an individualistic authorship model and collaborative theatrical practice. These conflicts often create turmoil in terms of theater's internal ethics while also leading to material, often financial consequences resulting from imposing the literary individual genius model of authorship onto the culture of collaboration in theater. The first half of this chapter focuses on *The Serpent*, often hailed as one of the great examples of the collaborative practice that was the hallmark of 1960s revolutionary theater companies. Many narratives of theater in this period characterize the prevalence of collaboration within these theater companies as a means of putting into practice rhetorics and political philosophies running counter to dominant ideology. The production history and legacy of *The Serpent*, in spite of its position in theater history books as a prime example of '60s collaborative theater, shows how a dominant ideology can reappropriate even a revolutionary practice. What began as a process of reinventing what theatrical performance could be ended as an emphatic reactionary assertion of literary authorship as the default mode of cultural production because of its affinity with neoliberal ideology's praise for the individual. The second half of the chapter follows a case with a different trajectory, a trajectory of the literary model of authorship inscribing individuality onto a creative practice with a long tradition of collaboration. The importance of collaboration throughout the history of American musical theater contrasts sharply with the distrust of collaboration and default to individual authorship displayed in the controversy surrounding the authorship of *Rent*. The repeated attempts by Jonathan Larson and his estate to quash any narratives of collaboration in accounts of *Rent*'s developmental history as well as the courts' privileging individualism suggests that the radical movements of the 1960s not only failed to unseat literary authorship and the capitalist mode of production it supports but in fact led to a reactionary reassertion of those forces' dominance.

THE "MYTH" OF COLLABORATION IN *THE SERPENT*

In their introduction to *Restaging the Sixties: Radical Theaters and Their Legacies*—arguably the definitive text for teaching the radical theater movement of the 1960s—editors James Harding and Cindy Rosenthal argue that "the radical theaters of the 1960s coalesced around responses to issues of authority and community, both as these issues related to their position vis-à-vis society at large and vis-à-vis theatrical practice in particular."[3] Harding and Rosenthal also use the terms "theater" and "collective" almost interchangeably, as all of the theaters they consider in their book, including the Living Theatre, the Open Theatre, and the Performance Group, organized themselves as collectives to varying degrees. The avant-garde theaters of the 1960s, they suggest, shared two key features: collectivism and a mission to respond directly to issues of authority and community. According to Harding and Rosenthal, these collective, antiauthoritarian groups provided "a direct challenge to the normative cultural values of bourgeois society, a challenge that overlapped with a tendency among all group theaters to question the traditional structures of mainstream theater and the authority of the literary dramatic text."[4] They explored "countercultural aspirations" of blurring the distinction between rehearsal and performance, a pursuit "directly tied to the goal of reorganizing the means of production."[5] By focusing more on process than product, these collectives found a way to resist commodification while still sharing their work with an audience. They did away with hierarchies and authoritarian structures in their own organizations, hoping to model within the change they hoped to see without.

> Substantial effort was made to allow creation to emerge from a largely non-hierarchical distribution of labor among collective members. Making theater was in this respect as much an experiment in the practice of radical democracy as it was an exploration of the possibilities of theater as such. Challenging not only boundaries of theater, collective creation was thus intended to model the sociopolitical ideals espoused by the collectives themselves.[6]

These groups, then, were collective, idealistic, antiauthoritarian, and anticapitalist. As such, they threatened an established order.

Theater traditionalists recognized the potential threat collaboration presented to established artistic hierarchies almost immediately. In his introduction to *The Best Short Plays of 1969*, editor Stanley Richards dismisses the work of those collective groups contemporary with his volume.

> The playwright, unquestionably, forever will be the focal and motivating force in the theater regardless of other evolutions, transmutations or regional relocations. Yet, I can just hear refuting murmurs in the wings about several widely-publicized production groups that have eschewed, almost obliterated, the dramatist in favor of concentration upon weird body movements, grunts, groans, punctuating burps, self-conscious improvisations and shivering shapeless backsides. I am sure Shakespeare's bones must rattle whenever these self-indulgent advertisements in egotism and purgation are billed and sold—at considerable admission prices!—to the public as "significant drama."[7]

Of course, as both a playwright and editor of an ongoing series of play collections, Richards had financial stakes in maintaining a text-based theater, but his comments neatly encapsulate the mistrust of collaboration's aesthetic validity as well as the sense that dramatic theater's place in the mainstream is the result of its serving a universal hierarchy rather than a function of its reproducing that hierarchy. Richards's distrust of collectivity presages neoliberalism's insistence that "all forms of social solidarity [be] dissolved in favour [sic] of individualism, private property, personal responsibility, and family values."[8] The distrust of collectivity has high political and social stakes for both '60s ensemble theaters and the traditional, mainstream theater establishment. The radical theaters Harding and Rosenthal describe threaten text-based theater's self-image as the rightfully intrinsic norm for theatrical production. The collaborative, collectivist practices of these theaters and conservative responses, such as Richards's, to these practices suggest that collaboration and the removal of the individual author stood poised to activate anticapitalist ideologies in an immediate and practical way.

But Harding and Rosenthal's account only tells part of the story. In fact, one of the most celebrated examples of this type of theater not only deviates from these collectivist ideals, but does so in a way that deeply reaffirms and reproduces neoliberal ideology by rejecting, denying, and ultimately commodifying the ostensible collectivity of the group who created it. The Open Theatre's *The Serpent*, directed by Joseph Chaikin and collaboratively developed from 1967 to 1968, began life as a perfect example of 1960s radical collective theater but became a perfect example of the very author-centric, commodified theater against which groups such as the Open Theatre defined their ideology and their purpose. Many accounts of the radical theaters of the '60s, however, not only include *The Serpent* but cite it as a prime exemplar of collectivist theater's artistic success.[9] The transformation of *The Serpent* from postdramatic experiment to dramatic text exposes the pressure the ideal of individualistic authorship exerts on even radically collectivist theater and the ways in which the ideology of authorship regulates creative practice.

The Open Theatre came into being at a moment of radically reimagining the possibilities of the American theater. Joseph Chaikin had first come into the world of experimental theater through his work with the Living Theatre. Dissatisfied with the Living Theatre's increasingly narrow focus on a "dramaturgy of political confrontation," Chaikin created a new workshop composed of actors and writers interested in using theatrical practices to explore important ideas even if those explorations did not yield commercially viable performances as a result.[10] In place of a commercial production model, Chaikin's company initially operated as a collectively funded, not-for-profit theater where everyone involved in its projects contributed to the group's coffers to ensure their creative independence from market forces.[11] To ensure they would never need to sell out, in other words, company members bought in. Chaikin also received an NEA grant for $5,000 that he used to bring in outside teachers such as Kristin Linklater and yoga master Swami Satchidananda.[12] The Open Theatre, then, relied on collaboration in their business practices as well as their creative practices. They made the actor not only the dominant artist but also an equal shareholder. In this way, the Open Theatre, at least initially, fulfilled the promise of avant-garde theaters of the 1960s in the United States. Rather than simply creating works with an anticapitalist message, they structured their production apparatus along noncapitalist lines. Their mode of production was every bit as revolutionary as the content of their work.

Their idealistic vision only lasted so long, and the Open Theatre did eventually have a commercial success that challenged their commitment to such goals. This success came with a production of Jean-Claude van Ittalie's play *America Hurrah.*[13] It caused shockwaves in the group that reconfigured its philosophy, structure, and composition because, as Gene A. Plunka notes, "suddenly, the ensemble, previously dedicated to non-commercial laboratory experimentation, was now interested in the fruits of commercialism."[14] Chaikin felt that many of his actors had become too enamored of their own commercial success and indie-darling fame, so he assembled a mostly new group of eighteen actors for a workshop in which they would explore the Bible through physical improvisations and other acting exercises.[15] Though Chaikin was more interested in exploring the life of Christ, the workshop quickly narrowed its focus to the story of Genesis. Even this narrowing of focus suggests the egalitarian, collaborative spirit of the ensemble as Chaikin let go his original vision in deference to the group's collective interests.

The group maintained this collaborative, exploratory spirit from the workshop's inception in early October of 1967 through the end of November that same year. At that point, van Itallie started coming to the workshops with the understanding that he would shape and solidify the group's explorations into a cohesive and iterable form. Robert Passoli describes van Itallie's proposed role in the process as one of a collaborator working among many others, a collaborator whose work, by definition, had to leave room for the actors' continued input and influence.

> Eventually van Itallie took over the writing. His task vis-a-vis the workshop was to satisfy two demands advanced by Chaikin. First, that the additional material must be concerned with exile, alienation, and man's aloneness—the principal themes of the workshop's version of the story of Adam. Secondly that the workshop dynamic of exploration and discovery should somehow be built into the eventual piece. That is, something had to be left open for the actors to investigate in *performance*.[16]

As described above, *The Serpent* represents a radical shift away from earlier dominant trends in American theater. Most notably, the text is secondary in this ideal version of *The Serpent*, both chronologically and in the aesthetic hierarchy of the performance. The Open Theatre's work fits into the model of postdramatic theater especially as it is defined in opposition to dramatic theater that is "subordinated to the primacy of the text."[17] Postdramatic theater creates new hierarchies of performance and rejects the construct of authorial intention as infallible word of god. As idealized by Chaikin and the performers, *The Serpent* was a piece whose text grew out of the performances rather than the other way around. The words in *The Serpent* functioned in service of the actors and their actions rather than as the gospel truth, a set of instructions to be followed devoutly, or a mystery to be pondered and unraveled in performance. Once again, the group's mode of production and organization of labor were set to reflect their politics. As a work of postdramatic theater, *The Serpent* represents a reinvention of the theater in which the drama—if it even exists—and its author no longer call the shots. Unless you ask that author.

In a 1970 documentary on *The Serpent*, van Itallie discusses his role in the creation of the piece.[18] Van Itallie's reflections on the project consistently suggest a less complete rejection of the drama-based model of theater than other accounts of *The Serpent*'s production history and legacy. I will quote van Itallie at length because his take on his own role within the process bears close scrutiny.

> It was conceived of as a piece in which the actors would be priests in a sense. That there would be a feeling of oneness. In the sense that the congregation feels that the priest is questioning the same sorts of things that they're questioning. I didn't come to *The Serpent* until it was two months in progress and my job then was how to put some of the impulses that the actors had had and that Joe had had concerning Genesis into a shape that would be meaningful to an audience and into words because most of their original explorations were wordless. It's an exploration of a feeling or it's a looking for a direction. The

> lines get rather blurred in terms of who's doing what. The actors suggest words or reject words. They have ideas about how something should look. Joe does the directing, and each word that's in *The Serpent* is written by me except for the begats which I stole from the bible. Then the question becomes how do you keep this excellent thing which the actors have created and keep it fresh and also give it enough of a shape that it'll be recognizable and that'll make the point that you want it to make where you place it. One thing to do then of course is to give it words. Not necessarily to put words in a person's mouth but to give for instance the words in a narration or in a chorus or different words to different actors. The word is one element, I think the most important element, in terms of shaping an impulse. It's always the top of the iceberg. It's always what clicks everything else into place.[19]

Van Itallie offers several conflicting ideas not just about his own position in this local process but also about the general role and function of the author and the text in theater. Van Itallie begins by placing the actors in the dominant creative position, calling them priests and acknowledging their primary creative role in shaping the piece. He then describes his role as that of shaping raw impulses and putting words to movement. Almost immediately after, though, he points out that all of the words are his. Van Itallie then gives credit to the actors for the quality of their imaginative work but immediately stresses that without his contribution the work is incomplete, cannot communicate, does not count. He then vacillates through the rest of his response between ceding and claiming sole authority over the piece. His claim to not putting words in anyone's mouth seems like a denial of power and exclusive agency, but his immediate positioning of himself as narrator restores his status as author. Perhaps the most telling phrase comes near the end when he says that "the word is one element, the most important element." The comma there represents the instantaneous switch from a postdramatic framing of collaborative creation to a traditional, dramatic conception of the author as individual genius or primary artist. He positions the word—and by extension, the author—as a point of origin, a source, a guiding principle in a supposedly collaborative process. As time has passed, van Itallie has presented an increasingly cynical view of collaboration while ever more vehemently defending the primary function of the author and language's privileged role in theatrical production. In a retrospective of the Open Theatre published thirteen years after the documentary containing the interview quoted above, van Itallie decries the "myth that everyone was equal, that the pieces were created by everybody. It may have been a necessary myth, to facilitate the actors' commitment to the material. Yet it was a myth."[20]

Van Itallie dismisses the "myth" of collaboration as nothing more than a tool to mollify egotistical actors who fail to understand their subordinate position in the theatrical hierarchy. This dismissal clearly demonstrates the dissonance between innovative or even revolutionary theories of theatrical creativity on one hand and deeply entrenched ideologies governing constructions of and assumptions about authorship on the other. While the theatrical practice of the Open Theatre rejects the very idea of an author in favor of an egalitarian, communal model of production, van Itallie's claim to primacy reinstates old hierarchies. This is not to say that Chaikin's and the actors' conceptions of the group represent an intrinsically superior, teleologically utopian progression against which van Itallie's self-image as author operates. Instead, I wish to expose and explore the cultural forces at play in the conflict between van Itallie and the rest of the Open Theatre as well as the stakes of this discord. In what follows, I will point out several sites of conflict between ideals of collaboration and assumptions about the intrinsic or natural status of individual authorship. These discordant moments raise two important and related questions. First, what makes the assumption of the author as individual so hard to shake? Second, what consequences result from this assumption's intractability? The answers to these questions lie in the interactions between sometimes conflicting, sometimes complementary cultural forces influencing production of both dramatic texts and theatrical performances.

The history of *The Serpent*'s creation clashes with van Itallie's argument for the play as a product of his own individual creativity. Anxiety over the issues of attribution and ownership first infected the group during a tense boat ride to Rome where *The Serpent* was to premiere, kicking off a European tour. The piece still lacked a finalized form when the group set sail on April 25, 1968.[21] Van Itallie, Chaikin, and Roberta Sklar put the titles of the different segments on note cards and van Itallie went off on his own with the cards to determine the final order.[22] Like Tennessee Williams in a cramped apartment in New Orleans, van Itallie retreated to the isolation of his small stateroom on the boat carrying them across the Atlantic so that his individual genius could operate without outside interference. The actors quickly came to perceive this simple act of shuffling cards as an act of profound violence and betrayal. The actors generally felt that they had previously all had equal share in the project and that van Itallie's making unquestionably final decisions on his own robbed them of their contribution. His decisions, they felt, essentially amounted to his ripping their work out of their hands and reshaping it in his image, especially since much of what was cut came from the actors while van Itallie's contributions, such as the medical scenes drawn from his personal experiences dealing with his mother's illness, remained in the final product.[23] The ensemble was so upset that "several members set up secret meetings to discuss the alterations" during which they commiserated about having their work effectively erased.[24] Feelings of ill will and unease persisted throughout the tour, and the collaborative spirit more or less vanished.

> By June, after a month of touring, the demoralization was staggering. The actors moved around Europe like tourists, hanging out in groups of four and

> five, seeing the sights, and coming together only when necessary—for travel, rehearsal, and performance.[25]

The group's mood and spirit of collaboration had both plummeted since the early workshops that, according to Chaikin, "couldn't have been better" because "everyone was deferential to everyone else, and [they] maintained a strict, though unspoken, rule of friendliness among one another."[26]

These personal conflicts reflect a deeper ideological conflict resulting from a complex network of competing ideological assumptions: van Itallie's, the group's, and broader cultural ideologies. Terry Eagleton's systematic categorization of such types of ideology provides useful terms for untangling this web of cultural forces at play in the creation of a work of art.[27] I turn to Eagleton's system in order to examine the relationships among the conflicting ideologies of the various parties involved in creating *The Serpent*. Eagleton stresses that these categories do not define universal conditions or relate to any specific ideologies; rather, they are a means of separating out types of ideological forces. The content of each category, then, may vary radically among different times and places. Their utility lies not in revealing anything about dominant ideologies in general, but in facilitating separation of ideological forces across different levels of production. Eagleton first defines the General Mode of Production and the Literary Mode of Production. The General Mode of Production is basically the dominant mode of economic production in a given context whereas the Literary Mode of Production refers more specifically to models of literary writing and authorship, of which there may be several at any given time. Eagleton emphasizes the nondeterministic nature of his modeling, explaining that he uses "the term 'general' not because economic production is ever anything other than historically specific, but to distinguish economic production from the Literary Mode of Production."[28] The General Ideology of the given moment, produced by the General Mode of Production, is the dominant set of assumptions about production, a set of ostensibly "common sense" assumptions serving hegemonic interests.[29] Finally, Authorial Ideology and Aesthetic Ideology function not so much as distinctive ideologies in relation to the General Ideology but rather as roles available within the General Ideology for the author or aesthetic theory. In other words, these categories delineate "[modes] of insertion of authorial and aesthetic formations into the hegemonic ideology as a whole."[30] Eagleton also includes text as one of his sites of alternate ideologies, but I divert from his definition because the idea of text becomes much more complicated with regard to theatrical performance, so using Eagleton's category of text (always literary for his purposes) would not serve the present investigation. In fact, Eagleton himself understands the complexity of the situation.

> Drama, strictly speaking, belongs to a distinct mode of production from literature, characterised [sic] by its own relatively autonomous forces and relations. Dramatic *texts* may belong to the Literary Mode of Production, depending upon the historical character of the theatrical mode of production; but the assimilation of drama to literature is an ideologically significant appropriation.[31]

Eagleton's last comment here about the "assimilation of drama to literature" being an "ideologically significant appropriation" sheds some light on the conflicts between van Itallie and the Open Theatre. After all, much of the conflict between the two rests on van Itallie's insistence on the inevitability and necessity of literature's appropriating drama while the Open Theatre was founded upon resisting just such appropriations.[32]

The company's internal distress serves as a microcosm of conflicting ideologies and an example of the difficulty of activating a truly resistant or revolutionary Aesthetic Ideology within an existing General Ideology. Van Itallie's Authorial Ideology as an insertion into the General Ideology posits himself as the traditional white male individual genius author. He nominally allows the company its resistant, collectivist Aesthetic Ideology only insofar as it keeps them happy and only for as long as he needs to maintain the illusion of collaboration. He asserts the rightness and dominance of his vision of the Authorial Ideology while the entire company sits literally trapped on a boat in the middle of the ocean. They cannot walk out. They cannot back out of the tour. They are effectively held hostage while van Itallie claims his role as first and final word regarding the construction of the piece, his role as the singular author. His actions on the boat reflect his broader Authorial Ideology. His denial of the possibility of a truly collaborative authorial or aesthetic position within the General Ideology—his claim that collaboration is merely a necessary myth and not a viable mode of production—performs a common function of the Authorial Ideology with regard to the relationship between the Literary Mode of Production and the General Mode of Production within late twentieth-century American capitalism. As Eagleton explains, "in developed capitalist social formations, then, the most significant relation of [the Literary Mode of Production] to [the General Mode of Production] is that of the [Literary Mode of Production]'s function in the reproduction and expansion of the [General Mode of Production]."[33] By replicating a dominant mode of literary production, that of the single, often white male author, van Itallie participates in the General Mode of Production and its reproduction of its own means of production, the General Ideology, in this case neoliberalism. But why is individualism with regard to authors such an important part of the General Ideology? The answer has to do with authorship's role in reproducing capitalist cultural hegemony. Cultural hegemony designates the means by which a dominant class maintains support from a suppressed class by successfully ingraining the moral and intellectual beliefs of the dominant class as "common sense" for all classes.[34] In this case, the idea of the author as the individual genius constitutes a subset of the ideal of individualism, of the neoliberal ideal that individual self-interest serves progress better than collective considerations. Through forces of cultural hegemony, that individualism has become a "common sense" assumption, to the point that van Itallie can reject the ensemble's collectivist Aesthetic Ideology as a fantasy. The conflict between van Itallie and the rest of the Open Theatre becomes more than just personal bickering among artists with big egos and fragile self-esteem; it becomes a site for reproducing assumptions intrinsic to capitalist ideology through the violent repression of collectivist ideologies. But the stakes of the conflict do not stop with either personal hurt feelings or microcosmic victories for neoliberal ideology. The conflict also has both immediate and far-reaching practical ramifications for those involved.

Van Itallie's anxiety over controlling the play extended beyond the original process of its creation. On his own, and without input or approval from the actors, van Itallie reworked *The Serpent* and published it, after which it circulated as would any other play text, with companies paying for the rights to perform it.[35] Van Itallie attended some early performances by groups other than the Open Theatre, finding at least one of them "abysmal."[36] In fact, he hated the production so much that he wrote an angry letter to the director and provides excerpts from that letter as a preface to the play, a kind of warning about how and how not to perform "his" work. Throughout this letter, van Itallie repeatedly exposes his reliance on assumptions of single, individualist-genius authorship despite the collaborative realities of the process of creating *The Serpent*. His anger toward the production arises mainly from the fact that the actors seem to have improvised words during the performance.

> There are certain precise and taxing techniques necessary to acting a play like *The Serpent*. . . . [I]nventing words a la Second City of ten years ago has nothing to do with these techniques at all, and only distracts and detracts from the piece. What of "improvisation" you say. Aren't ensemble companies supposed to improvise? The word "improvisation" is an overused one and means a lot of different things to different people. What it does *not* mean for a play like *The Serpent* is verbal improvisation in performance.[37]

Van Itallie frames the object of his displeasure as more than just a violation of the integrity of his own work. Rather, the actors' deviating from the script represents a transgression of territorial lines that van Itallie would like to maintain. His dismissive reference to Second City suggests he views improvisation as a passing fad causing actors to forget their place.[38] When the actors try to play playwright, he argues, both the performers and the text suffer. "Actors are not," van Itallie says, "poets, at least not while they're on their feet in front of an audience."[39] Improvisation—specifically nonverbal improvisation by van Itallie's preference—belongs only in the "beginning of rehearsals by the ensemble" and should consist of "exercises toward the material, and an opening of the actors to it, a personalization—but performance itself must be tight, i.e. the logic of the play, its thrust, has to be clear."[40]

Not only does this argument again assert the subservience of the actors to the words and structure the playwright provides, but it also downplays the importance of improvisation as a generative creative practice and therefore bolsters van Itallie's claim to sole ownership of the text of *The Serpent*. If improvisation only functions properly as a warm-up or preliminary rehearsal exercises for actors, as a way of "opening of the actors" to the material, then the actors' improvisations in Chaikin's Bible workshops cannot be considered part of the writing process. Van Itallie has even occasionally claimed that he wrote more or less independently of the actors' work, denying the actors access to anything other than a secondary, subservient role in the production process.

> When I wrote, I never worked directly from the verbal improvisations of the actors. It is enough for actors to do what they are doing and not have to write on their feet too. I wrote from the emotional totality of the sounds and movements of the actors. It would be closer to the truth to say that the improvisations inspired the playwriting.[41]

In other words, van Itallie's view of improvisation supports his holding on to traditional, drama-centric theatrical hierarchies but also his erasing the contributions of his collaborators in the creation of *The Serpent*. Van Itallie's viewpoint here also aligns with Stanley Richards's dismissing collective theater groups as a momentary distraction from the proper history of dramatic theater. Richards echoes van Itallie's claims that collaborative exercises mostly function to keep egotistical, overreaching actors happy until a text is delivered, arguing that "the grunts, groans, etc. may be emanating sparks, but the true torch, the *only* torch, is ignited by the dramatist."[42] Comments such as this implicitly link the revolutionary, exploratory spirit of the avant-garde theater of the '60s with a dangerous upsetting of hierarchical structures and of individualistic authorship's place as the default mode of cultural production. Richards links the freeing of the body and the dissolution of traditional narrative structures with the unseating of traditionally dominant white male figures. Van Itallie's actions suggest a return to authorship that rejects not only collaborative generative practices but also egalitarian organizations of labor. The final line of van Itallie's letter leaves no question about his understanding of authorship and ownership regarding *The Serpent*: "for a company coming to the text in order to perform it, even *as* a ceremony, it is a play in the very usual sense that if you vary the text you do so at your own peril . . . and mine apparently."[43] Van Itallie's assumption that all productions of *The*

Serpent reflect directly on himself further highlights his sense of sole authorship and ownership. Despite his claim that *The Serpent* "attempts to break some kind of barriers in theatrical form," he ultimately retreats to traditional assumptions about the primacy of the text and therefore the ultimate authority of the playwright.[44] The text is the blueprint, and only an architect should be allowed to create or alter it.

Van Itallie suggests that labeling *The Serpent* "a ceremony" only serves as a nominal nod to experimentation and innovation.[45] He reduces the anticapitalist, revolutionary ideologies of radical '60s theater to a marketing catchword. Despite its unusual structure and lyrical use of language, van Itallie insists that *The Serpent* is a traditional play with a single author: himself. In this way, collaboration becomes a kind of branding; the very thing that was meant to be the means to resist capitalism and commodification becomes a tool for selling the play as a commodity in a capitalist model of exchange. One of capitalism's great strengths in terms of its intractability comes from this kind of reappropriating rhetorics of resistance as brands and slogans for commodities.[46] As Harvey points out, such flexibility in adapting and embracing its own resistance is one of neoliberalism's keys to success in terms of ingraining itself as the dominant ideology; the proponents and beneficiaries of neoliberalism found ways to appeal to the spirit of individual freedom present in the many countercultural movements of the 1960s while jettisoning or downplaying their calls for collectivism.[47] In fact, even movements that ran ideologically opposed to neoliberalism could be co-opted by reframing the movements themselves in terms of market logic, characterizing the freedom to express oneself as a process of exercising choice as consumers not only of "particular products but also with respect to lifestyles, modes of expression, and a wide range of cultural practices."[48] Van Itallie's discussions of the word "ceremony" as a stylistic label of his play—a commodity to be reproduced, sold, licensed—is a kind of avant-garde theatrical Hot Topic, selling antiestablishment-tinged goods through traditional establishment structures of exchange that support capitalism's continued dominance as "common sense" as well as authorship's role as the default mode of cultural production. Like Beckett using the commercial failure of the Miami *Godot* as a means to sell the New York production by marketing the play's unmarketability, van Itallie uses the Open Theatre's anticapitalist rhetoric as a branding tool to appeal to a subset of consumers within a capitalist marketplace who want to obtain a certain kind of cultural capital and antiestablishment veneer but who have no real interest in alternative organizations of labor or ideologies.

Van Itallie's claim to total ownership and the resulting assumption that all productions of the work reflect upon (and therefore, in a sense, serve) him provides another example of his Authorial Ideology helping the Literary Mode of Production to reproduce dominant ideological assumptions. In addition to arguments about aesthetic integrity and the hierarchy of creative roles in theatrical production, van Itallie appeals to copyright to make claims about the intrinsic rightness of individual authorship. The law does not *cause* van Itallie to privilege individualism; instead, the law provides a means for ensuring the reproduction of assumptions about the nature of authorship, including the assumption that individualism is its natural state. When van Itallie retreats to individualistic, single-author assumptions of artistic production, he participates in recreating competition-based models of creativity and in reinforcing the apparent inevitability of hierarchies of artistic merit among theater practitioners. Again, the reasons for his doing so rest on the benefits various cultural and social forces, such as copyright law, offer. The idea of intellectual property, in this case, interpellates artists as owners so that they will submit to a structure of ownership not necessarily aligned with their politics or philosophy.[49] In this light, I read van Itallie's resistance to transformative or revolutionary Aesthetic Ideologies as a result of his desire to protect the author's role as unique creator and therefore owner of cultural products. He supports the ideologies that support capitalist modes of production because these ideologies interpellate him into a locally dominant subject position. To acknowledge the ensemble's contributions as equal or even substantial would not only mean sacrificing his ability to claim sole ownership for artistic merit but would also represent a broader-scale rejection of the very possibility of his identity as an author as he understands it to function.

The most important textual site of conflict over the authorship of *The Serpent*, then, in terms of both cause and consequence, seems the most innocuous: © Copyright, 1969, by Jean-Claude van Itallie.[50] The potential difficulty in recognizing this line as a site of conflict arises primarily from its effective erasure of other voices. In other words, even as it fulfills his claims to individual authorship it denies that anyone else, such as the actors who at the very least helped develop the published text, might have ever claimed otherwise. And, to be fair, the ensemble members never challenged this copyright claim. The point is not about what the law actually did or even what it might have done in this case. Those questions are relatively simply answered. Van Itallie successfully claimed a copyright that his potential co-authors never challenged for their potential share. The important implication for the present study is the way in which this copyright claim writes a narrative of creative practice. This simple line in the title page of the printed version of *The Serpent* writes its own history of a single-author, independent creation, and unquestionable individual ownership. Even under simpler circumstances, though, such a claim might face challenges. In his critique of John Searle's response to "Signature Event Context," Derrida finds a number of conflicting assumptions operating in Searle's acknowledgments and copyright statement. Derrida suggests that Searle fails to recognize the argumentative nature of these textual sites.

> If John R. Searle owes a debt to D. Searle concerning this discussion, then the "true" copyright ought to belong (as is indeed suggested along the frame of this *tableau vivant*) to a Searle who is divided, multiplied, conjugated, shared. What a complicated signature! And one that becomes even more complex when the debt includes my old friend, H. Dreyfus, with whom I myself have worked, discussed, exchanged ideas, so that if it is indeed through him that the Searles have "read" me, "understood" me, and "replied" to me, then I, too, can claim a stake in this Copyright Trust. And it is true that I have occasionally had the feeling—to which I shall return—of having almost "*dictated*" this reply. "I" therefore feel obliged to claim my share to the copyright of the *Reply*.
>
> But who, me

Derrida does not actually suggest changes to copyright policy here. Instead, he points to copyright as a site for claims about authorship that privileges both ownership-centric models of authorship and individualism as a prerequisite for authorship. Van Itallie's claim, then, proves even more problematic. The metaphorical shareholders in the copyright trust of *The Serpent* could also arguably function as literal shareholders. And their role in creating the piece extends far beyond consultation or suggestion.[51] By most accounts, including van Itallie's early reflections on the process, the ensemble played an integral and formative role in creating the piece from its earliest foundations. Derrida critiques Searle's simultaneous claim to an individual, unique subjectivity and acknowledgment that his thinking exists as part of a complex series of relationships and influences that even includes Derrida. Van Itallie not only denies the traces of his functioning within such a network but more boldly takes credit for the labor of others, labor he has earlier acknowledged and even deferred to. In short, the copyright claim performs three key extralegal functions. First, it erases the work of the ensemble. Second, it cements van Itallie's assumptions about the inevitable ascension of the individual as opposed to the corporate or collective author. Finally, by appearing so inconspicuously at the beginning of the text, on a page ostensibly devoted to bureaucratic minutiae, it treats those assumptions as natural, as common sense, thereby completing the process of framing the play within van Itallie's Authorial Ideology of unique creativity and total control.[52]

Cultural assumptions about copyright law facilitate van Itallie's ability to claim individual ownership and create a narrative of independent creation. Several legal scholars have pointed to what they see as a deep contradiction between the alleged purposes of copyright law on one hand and the ideologies it supports and reproduces on the other. Siva Vaidhyanathan argues that copyright laws do not simply offer benevolent protection to artists but also "expose and depend on American ethical assumptions and cultural habits."[53] Vaidhyanathan goes on to argue that while intellectual property laws originally protected artists and ensured due acknowledgment and compensation for creative work, they have now gone too far toward protecting publishers and producers at the expense of an open creative exchange. Lawrence Lessig makes a similar argument in *Free Culture*, arguing that the unbalanced power of those who think they stand to lose money through fair use and public domain has corrupted the once noble purpose of intellectual property.[54] However, both Lessig and Vaidhyanathan believe in the existence or at least possibility of a nobler version of copyright law and assume that it lies rooted in the need for protecting artists' rights to benefit from their own creations. Lessig firmly states his belief "that 'piracy' is wrong, and that the law, properly tuned, should punish 'piracy.'"[55] But this rhetoric takes for granted that creative works must function as a species of property capable of being stolen. This nostalgic view of a time when intellectual property law served as a kind of ideologically neutral guardian angel for artists risks eliding copyright's already self-effacing role in reproducing both cultural hegemony and the very notion of intellections as property.

Oren Bracha, on the other hand, complicates both those narratives that overstate the continued influence of Romantic constructions of authorship in intellectual property law and those that suggest that intellectual property law has betrayed its own underlying ideals.

> Copyright law has many features that are diametrically opposed to the fundamental tenets of original authorship, but at the same time it is saturated with concepts that are directly traceable to these tenets. Modern copyright's rules of ownership often favor corporations and other commercial entities at the expense of actual creators of works, but at the same time copyright is justified on the basis of authors' rights, and many of copyright's rules—sometimes the very rules that deprive authors of ownership—are constructed in terms taken from the vocabulary of authorship.[56]

Copyright proves rhetorically malleable; appeals to it can employ anticapitalist vocabulary to reinforce capitalist interests. The very idea of the copyright symbol suggests a threat to one's work and a need for protection, but the idea of "protection" presumes a very particular way of understanding the identity and valuation of a work. Furthermore, the copyright symbol itself, the symbol of protection, can in fact become a means of robbing others of the rights associated with the products of their labor. Van Itallie's copyright claim uses the language and symbols of artistic protection to deny due credit and compensation to other artists.

Van Itallie's role in supporting dominant ideologies and repressing collectivist, revolutionary ideologies complicates narratives positing *The Serpent* as a paragon of radical theater. Harding and Rosenthal point to the ideological relationship between theatrical practice and the general mode of production. They argue that collaborative groups such as the Open Theatre "stood in marked contrast to the reified strictures of commercial theater and had radical implications for the organization of labor more generally."[57] The production history of *The Serpent* does indeed suggest a relationship between theatrical practice and the general organization of labor, but rather than representing the model for emancipation from capitalist structures as Harding and Rosenthal suggest many 1960s theaters represent, *The Serpent* shows just how hard resisting those "reified strictures" can be. *The Serpent*'s "implications for the organization of labor" are far from radical; it implies that dominant ideologies and the general mode of production can overwrite or reappropriate even radical resistance. Even narratives that expose the occasional failure of radical theater to resist dominant ideologies sometimes overlook radical theater's role in reproducing those ideologies. David Savran implies that such failures suggest a corruption of radical theater from an outside force, attributing the decline of the avant-garde in part to "the increasing exploitation of nonprofit theaters for their artists and product by commercial producers intent on replenishing their stores of cultural and symbolic capital."[58] *The Serpent*'s trajectory from an experimental piece privileging performance over text to a printed text with rights for rent written by a single author suggests that the influence of commercialism on the avant-garde may be less unilateral. No outsider transformed the process from collectivist to individualistic and capitalist; the change originated not only within the group but with one of its most iconic figures of revolt and innovation. The avant-garde, at least in the case of *The Serpent*, had built into itself the means to transform into its own rhetorical opposite, the idea against which it ostensibly defined itself: the commercial, which measures success in terms of competition among individuals.

The stakes extend beyond a philosophical debate about the reproduction of means of production. More broadly, imposing literary assumptions about authorship onto theater threatens to invalidate theater's own internal culture, history, and even ability to construct and maintain its own conventions. This treatment of theater as derivative of or dependent upon literature risks more than just reputation or ego; it threatens to undermine collaborative theatrical practice. The assumption that literary authorship represents the highest, ideal, or correct version of cultural production lies at the heart of the tension over *The Serpent*. Van Itallie retreats from theatrical to literary conventions over time. His early work in the process embraced collaboration and displayed an understanding of his role as that of one craftsmen among many. As time moved on, he became more and more insistent upon asserting himself as The Author of the piece. Even the way van Itallie spoke about the process changed over time. In interviews immediately following the process, van Itallie refers to the words of the piece as one element among many. Just a few years later, he asserts that the idea of collaboration was always a myth in the process used by Chaikin and himself to let the actors think they were contributing so they would not distract from his individual, literary, authorial labor.

Van Itallie's authorial ideology, then, participates in an established pattern of authors' reinforcing ideological assumptions that may not only be aesthetically restrictive and regressive but also, in other cases, may have more immediate, material consequences. To see how such consequences might play out as a result of privileging an individual-genius model of authorship, I turn to the controversy over the authorship of *Rent*.

THE THREAT OF COLLABORATION

Musicals in general create problems for individual-genius models of authorship. Often featuring collaboration among two or three writers spread across the disciplines of lyricist, composer, and book writer, musicals embrace collaboration and acknowledge cocreation far more often than nonmusicals. In an interview on the American Theatre Wing's website, musical book writer Peter Stone says that a book writer, a lyricist, and a composer together constitute an author and that alone each is only "one third of an author."[59] Shared credit forms an integral part of the history of musicals; many of the great, canonical musical writers come in pairs: Rodgers and Hammerstein, Kander and Ebb, Lerner and Loewe, to name a few.[60] Even in cases where common attributions fail to foreground collaboration, sole accreditation in popular parlance does not completely erase contributions either in terms of recognition of collaborators' work or in terms of material benefits such as royalty payments for those collaborators. For example, if I ask a theater student who wrote *A Little Night Music*, *Sunday in the Park with George*, *Sweeney Todd*, and *Into the Woods*, that student would likely tell me those were all Stephen Sondheim shows, of course, but Sondheim wrote the book on none of the above. However, any script or promotional materials for these shows list their respective book writers, and those writers still benefit from the labor they contributed to those projects. The norm of collaboration and cocreation extends beyond the initial creation of musicals, too. Producers staging revivals often commission rewrites and reworkings of individual songs or even of broader structure either by the original author(s) if still living or by a new writer, adding yet another collaborator to the trust. Examples of such reinventions include David Henry Hwang's recent reworking of *Flower Drum Song* and Arthur Laurents's recent production of *West Side Story* with new Spanish-language lyrics and dialogue translated from the original script by Lin-Manuel Miranda. In both of these cases, the later writers functioned as contractors, workers-for-hire in a model similar to that used among screenwriters in Hollywood. Acknowledgment of additional work does not in either situation undo or change early attributions of authorship. Bruce Kirle argues that the norm of revision lies at the heart of the American musical.

> Musicals wed text, performance, and reception to create meaning within specified historical contexts. Works-in-process, they are open and fluid, subject to a great deal of variation, even subversion, in the way they are performed. As such, in their original productions or over time, they often assume lives of their own that can be quite independent from the original intentions of their authors.[61]

Musicals' existence in such a state of essential incompleteness renders individual authorship in the literary mode a concept ever more alienated from the historical conventions of the genre.

Yet despite the continuation and even expansion of collaboration at the heart of the musical, literary assumptions about the individuality of the author begin to take deeper root throughout the late twentieth century with serious, material consequences, particularly with regard to the controversy surrounding the authorship of *Rent.*[62] Lynn Thomson, a dramaturg hired to help Jonathan Larson in the final stages of *Rent*'s development, sued Larson's estate for cowriting credit and attendant financial compensation. The causes and implications of this case turn on ideological forces reinforcing the centrality of individualism in constructions of the author. The question of authorial intention and identity has an added emotional component in the case of *Rent*, given Larson's tragic death due to Marfan syndrome just before the play opened. Questioning Larson's individuality and singular genius as the sole source of conception and composition for *Rent* becomes even more difficult, then, because it runs the risk of also questioning the narrative of a young, impoverished artist becoming the posthumous hero of a movement by making the definitive generational statement about the AIDS epidemic. In other words, Larson's individuality serves as the foundation for constructing not only an author but also a symbolic cultural figure behind which a generation and a cause rallied. That same individuality, though, also reproduces neoliberal ideology by reaffirming assumptions that valorize the individual and sow suspicion of collectivity and collaboration.

The myth of *Rent* as the brainchild of Jonathan Larson bears little resemblance to the actual history of the musical's creation. Faye Buckalew points out that "from the very beginning, the development of . . . *Rent* relied upon collaboration"; the idea to make a modern-day *La Boheme* originated not with Larson but with playwright Billy Aronson, who asked Larson to collaborate as composer in 1989.[63] In fact, when Aronson left the project in 1993, he and Larson both signed a formal agreement that required Larson to acknowledge Aronson's contribution especially with regard to conceiving the project.[64] Not only is *Rent* not the product of Larson's lonely labor in a drafty room, it is not even his idea. After Aronson's departure from the project, Larson got development support from the New York Theatre Workshop. Over the next two years, Larson worked alone, refusing the workshop's continuous offers of aid in the form of outside collaborators.[65] The New

York Theatre Workshop presented an early version of *Rent* written entirely by Larson—with some possible remnants of Aronson's contributions—as a workshop production late in 1994.[66] The general reaction to this performance both from the workshop itself and from other theater professionals in attendance was that the concept was promising but the script itself was lacking.[67] Under these conditions, the New York Theatre Workshop again urged Larson to accept the help of an outside collaborator. Larson may have resisted in part because of his own investment in the promise of the role of author as individual genius. In one of his earlier works, *tick tick Boom!*, Larson's autobiographical narrator expresses his desire to become the defining voice of a generation of musicals by single-handedly creating the "*Hair* of the '90s."[68] Larson felt he could not be the voice of a generation as part of a team. But with the pressure rising and the risk of not having his play produced at all becoming increasingly possible, Larson finally agreed to accept a collaborator.

The New York Theatre Workshop hired Lynn Thomson to help Larson with *Rent*, particularly with regard to narrative structure, in May 1995.[69] Thomson, who taught playwriting classes at NYU, signed a contract promising her $2,000 and a credit as dramaturg but containing no guarantees about copyright or ownership of the final piece.[70] The language of Thomson's contract as well as her initial informal understanding of her role in the process suggested that she would do little if any actual writing and would instead serve more of an editorial or consultant role, "asking questions and coaxing solutions out of Larson," rather than generating any new or original material for the play.[71] Even at this point, Thomson's contributions made her part of the informal, extralegal copyright trust of *Rent* of the kind suggested by Derrida. In other words, even had her contribution remained limited to consultation, her very presence in the process undermines the myth of authorship as a unidirectional force originating from the inspiration and individuality of a unique, unnetworked consciousness. But the extent of Thomson's contributions only further complicates the story of Larson's individual authorship, taking Derridean play about the insecurity of identity into a much more practical realm with immediate, material consequences for those involved. The metaphor of the copyright trust became more prescient for Thomson and Larson as the nature of their working relationship started to evolve.

> [Thomson and Larson] rewrote the script of *Rent*. Working closely together, Thomson and Larson did most of the revisions alone in Larson's apartment. In their working relationship, they shared artistic control over the direction the script was to take. Choices about what was to be included in the script were arrived at through agreement. When artistic disputes arose, Thomson at times deferred to Larson's ideas, and at other times Larson deferred to Thomson's. Despite Thomson's previous expectations, her work with Larson began devel-

> oping into a relationship more akin to that of coauthors than that of dramaturg/playwright.[72]

Williams's solitary room had become the collaborative space of Larson's apartment.[73] Not only had Larson begun to buy into the collaborative process he had so adamantly resisted, but apparently he had even begun to appreciate Thomson's help. Larson reportedly told Thomson that he would never deny her contribution and even credited her below Aronson on some drafts.[74] While Larson's place as primary author never came into question, his claim to sole ownership and reluctance to risk that claim softened in response to the successful collaboration. And the collaboration was successful. The New York Theatre Workshop decided to go forward and produce the version of the script that Larson and Thomson completed in late 1995. That production then moved to Broadway, though Larson would tragically not live to see its Broadway premiere in 1996.

Just how much did Thomson contribute to the final version of *Rent*? According to Thomson's appeal, the two "entirely rewrote or substantially altered" some 1,212 of the script's 2,542 lines.[75] Roughly 48 percent of the final, performed version of *Rent*, then, arose directly from their collaborative work, about 9 percent of which came exclusively from Thomson, numbers that even the Larson estate did not contest at trial.[76] Quantifying the amount of work Thomson put in somewhat misses the point at least with regard to the ideological assumptions at play. Even one line from another party would be enough to undercut the veracity of the literary model of unique individualism and genius as the basis for authorship. But the extent of the collaboration, its constituting the labor on half of the final version of the script, highlights the problems with understanding *Rent* as the brainchild of Larson, as a cultural statement from a unique, representative voice of a generation. Larson's giving into collaboration and loosening his commitment to the idea of author as individual suggests a trajectory toward his accepting a more corporate model of authorship. This individual acceptance of collaboration aside, the stakes of the dissonance between cultural assumptions about authorship and the reality of *Rent*'s creation form the basis for a conflict that continues to challenge constructions of authorship in both philosophical and legal terms.

Because the nature of Thomson's collaboration with Larson had evolved beyond her originally limited role of outside consultant, Thomson believed she was entitled to more credit and compensation than she had been granted under her original contract. After Larson died,

> negotiations began between Thomson and Larson's heirs over what would be a fair division of *Rent* royalties. When on-going negotiations broke down, Thomson sued the estate of Larson for 16 percent of Larson's share of the royalties. This amount reflected Thomson's belief that she was entitled to

> approximately one-half of one-third of the royalties since substantial changes to at least one-third of the script resulted from her collaboration with Larson.[77]

The U.S. District Court for the Southern District of New York heard Thomson's original suit, and Judge Lewis A. Kaplan determined that Thomson was not entitled to joint authorship based on the standard set by the case of *Childress v. Taylor*.[78] Not to be deterred, Thomson then filed an appeal with the U.S. Court of Appeals for the Second Circuit, arguing that Kaplan's decision had not appropriately applied the *Childress* test.[79] The decision of the appeals court quotes Thomson as saying that she had "virtually no disagreement with the District Court's findings with respect to what happened between her and Jon Larson, or with respect to the evidence of Larson's intent."[80] In other words, Thomson and the courts agreed on all the facts; they differed in their understanding of the precedent set by *Childress*. *Childress v. Taylor* had become (and remains) the precedent against which all other joint authorship cases would be judged by expanding the standards for joint authorship set forth in section 101 of the 1976 Copyright Act. These standards of joint authorship bear close scrutiny because of both their impact on the *Thomson* case and their implications about authorship's institutionally privileged role as the default mode of cultural production.

The court in *Childress v. Taylor* came up with a two-pronged test for joint authorship based on the court's reading of the 1976 act. Both prongs have been called into question by legal scholars and even rejected in some subsequent court cases, but the *Childress* test served as the basis for determining joint authorship in *Thomson v. Larson*. The first prong requires all authors to contribute independently copyrightable material, and the second prong requires that all authors intend to function as coauthors of the work in question. Both sets of requirements must be met in order for joint authorship to obtain. A brief history of the facts of the *Childress* case is necessary in order to understand the exigencies, implications, and complications of this two-pronged test. *Childress v. Taylor* dealt with a dispute between playwright Alice Childress and Clarice Taylor, an actor. Taylor had conceived of a play based on the life of comedian Moms Mabley and contacted Childress in 1985 to see if Childress would be interested in writing the piece for Taylor to perform.[81] Childress declined the offer, but when the Greens Play Theatre reached out to Taylor to help develop and produce the show in 1986, Childress got on board with the project.[82] The theater only gave the pair six weeks to write the script before rehearsals would need to begin, so Childress and Taylor divided the labor. Taylor's interest in the project had already led to her compiling a great deal of research on Moms Mabley through interviews and documents, so she shared her research and consulted with Childress, who wrote the actual script.[83] Taylor also shared her ideas about what moments and characters should be included in the script with Childress and continuously looked over drafts of scenes as they were completed.[84] Viewing Taylor's contributions as secretarial or editorial and not authorial, Childress filed for and received sole copyright for the play, including material added throughout the course of the initial run.[85] When Taylor attempted to perform the show again without first securing Childress's permission, Childress sued Taylor for copyright infringement.[86]

Taylor's defense rested on her claim to joint authorship of the work, as she could not very well infringe upon her own copyright.[87] As *Thomson v. Larson* would later, *Childress v. Taylor* ended up in appeals with the Second Circuit, and it was here that the court developed the two-pronged test for joint authorship. Despite her conceptualizing the project and intensive research and editing labor, Taylor clearly failed the first part of the court's test based on the 1976 act because nothing she contributed could have been independently copyrighted.[88] Though this first test exposes a clear privileging of expressive work over conceptualization, research, and editorial work under copyright law, the second part of the joint authorship test, the requirement that all parties involved intend to function as coauthors, has more direct bearing on the investigation at hand as the *Thomson* ruling in both the District and Second Circuit courts hinged on it. The second test is also where the court in *Childress v. Taylor* most dramatically altered the scope of joint authorship standards from the 1976 act. Technically, once the court had established that Taylor's contributions did not meet the criteria for the first part of the test, the question of intent became moot because both criteria must obtain to establish joint authorship. But the court considered the question of intent of both parties and ultimately found that Taylor's claim to joint authorship also failed this test.

The Copyright Act of 1976 requires that two or more authors intend to merge their work into a new whole in order for all to have claim to joint authorship.[89] The *Childress* court expanded on this requirement, saying in its decision that the involved parties must intend to be joint authors in order for joint authorship to apply.[90] The distinction between the intent to merge work required by the 1976 act and the intent to enter into a joint authorship relationship required by *Childress* is subtle but crucial. Whereas the intent to create a joint work only requires that the authors intend for their contributions to form part of a larger whole, the intent to function as joint authors requires all parties to intentionally and willfully enter into a business relationship as joint authors. In the *Childress* case, Childress's rejection of Taylor's suggestion that they work as joint authors proved to the court that Childress did not intend to enter into a joint authorship relationship. That Taylor continued to work on the project after this rejection effectively constituted, to the court, a waiver of any rights to the work as she knew that Childress had no intentions of entering into a joint authorship relationship. Since not all parties intended such a relationship, the court found that Taylor's claim to joint authorship also failed the intention test. The court's decision therefore created a precedent that would be applied in *Thomson v. Larson* of looking past the strictly creative interactions between authors claiming joint authorship to examine the understanding all parties had during the process of creation regarding the business relationship between them. The court's added specificity regarding the intention requirement was meant to address "the fear that editors and research assistants might fall under the statutory definition of a joint author if intent is considered to be the intent to merge rather than the intent to be a joint author."[91] The court's fear arises directly from the facts of the case, as Taylor's contributions largely consisted in the passing on of information already available in the public domain and coming up with ideas.[92] Neither of these contributions constitutes copyrightable work; therefore neither Childress nor Taylor could have reasonably expected that their collaboration constituted a joint authorship agreement. The court's test sought to protect the spirit of the law by protecting owners of copyrighted material from specious claims against their ownership rights of their works; this protection in turn would preserve the constitutional purpose of copyright law to encourage creativity and innovation by protecting creators' interests in their own works. As the application of the test in *Thomson v. Larson* shows, however, the standards created in the *Childress* decision fail to account for cases in which there is reasonable, factual doubt about discrepancies of business expectations between collaborators because Thomson's claim clearly meets both standards for joint authorship of the 1976 act itself in that Thomson and Larson were both aware that her independently copyrightable material was going to be merged with his into a joint work. The expansion of the second prong of the test is also, arguably, redundant, because the work of editors and researchers is already excluded from joint authorship protection because it fails the first test by not being copyrightable. The reasons for the court's decision with regard to intention in some ways fit the facts of the case but also narrowed the scope of necessary intent and raised the burden of proof for intent to such a degree that the standard arguably puts secondary collaborators at a significant disadvantage, a disadvantage that Lynn Thomson experienced firsthand.

In *Thomson v. Larson*, both courts agreed that Thomson's claim to joint authorship satisfied the first requirement for joint authorship: copyrightability. There was no question that Thomson contributed a substantial amount of actual lines to the script, expressive work that, taken out of context, Thomson could have copyrighted on her own. There was also no question that Thomson and Larson both intended to merge their independently copyrightable works into a joint work. In fact, the court's admission that Thomson contributed independently copyrightable work to *Rent* led to a third and final case that was settled out of court in which Thomson asserted her right to prohibit the use of the portions of *Rent* the court acknowledged she had written.[93]

According to the court, Thomson failed the second part of the *Childress* test, mutual intent to enter into a joint authorship relationship, because she failed to establish Larson's intent to enter into such a relationship. Using the *Childress* precedent, "the court looked for indications of Larson's intent in billing, copyright registration, interviews, contracts, and other secondary sources."[94] Thomson's intent never even came into consideration, as the court interpreted *Childress* to mean that all parties had to express mutual intent to enter into a coauthor relationship. Under this interpretation, the lack of such intent on the part of any of the involved parties—Larson—sufficed to reject claims of joint authorship. The court also declined to consider whether Thomson had reasonable expectations regarding Larson's intent to enter into a joint authorship, a curious lacuna especially considering Judge Kaplan's acknowledgment in his closing statement that had Larson lived, he probably would have given Thomson credit and the issue would have been moot.[95] The court, therefore, implicitly recognized not only the probability of Thomson's claims that Larson intended for her to receive some amount of authorial credit and attendant compensation but also the court's own deviation from the perceived spirit of the collaboration in the name of following the *Childress* precedent to the letter and looking to secondary sources to ascertain intent. For Thomson, then, the specific circumstances of the *Childress* case had pushed the law toward such a strong single-author bias in the name of protecting individual creativity that collaborators retain virtually no protection from exploitation outside of the mercy of the primary authors with whom they collaborate.

Several legal scholars have suggested that *Thomson v. Larson* exposes the problems with the *Childress* test precisely because of the test's ill fit to the reality of collaborative writing practices. My contention is that while *Thomson v. Larson* applied the *Childress* test correctly, that test itself reveals an ideologically loaded institutional default to individual authorship. In other words, the *Larson* case shows the law functioning as it is designed to do, by reproducing the means of reproduction of capitalism. In engaging with the legal discourse, then, I am less interested in the matters of law and fact for their own sakes than in the ideological implications of a court decision that set precedent expanding the requirements for joint authorship claims beyond what the code itself requires. Faye Buckalew argues that the *Childress* precedent places far too much weight on the intentions of primary authors.

> When two people have been sufficiently involved in determining the expression of a copyrightable work . . . it should become necessary at least to examine the intent of the person claiming secondary authorship. Such an examination would not only protect lesser known authors from more powerful authors but also allow the court to determine if there was a reasonable misunderstanding that led the secondary author to provide work for which he or she deserves adequate protection and remuneration. Such protection would

> ensure that the purpose of the Copyright Act—to promote the useful arts—would be better furthered.[96]

She suggests that the law leaves secondary authors open to exploitation, as even a secondary author led to a "reasonable misunderstanding" about the nature of the collaboration has no legal recourse. Even at the risk of facilitating exploitation, the court goes out of its way to privilege individual authorship. Steven Kan characterizes Taylor and Thomson as "Good Samaritans" and Larson and Childress as "Opportunists." He argues that the standards of joint authorship set in *Childress v. Taylor* ensure that Opportunists in cases of "Good Samaritan v. Opportunist would always prevail under the adopted mutual intent standard because it is biased in favor of the dominant decision maker over and against the true joint author."[97] The moralistic tone of his choice of words aside, Kan effectively highlights the law's bias toward naming a single party the author of any work. Jane Lee, among others, argues that contract law stands better suited to deal with joint authorship because it places the responsibility of disentangling the complicated questions of relative attribution onto those actually involved in the creative process.[98] However, Lee's stance does little to protect collaborators who lack legal savvy from potential exploitation. Arguments such as Lee's fail to sufficiently account for "the Thomson court's reliance on Childress's porous doctrine—in particular misguided faith in contract to prevent copyright disputes—[that] underscores the need for a clearer joint authorship background rule."[99] Paulette Fox also points out that while contract law could in many cases preempt these disputes, copyright law should not therefore be let off the hook for its responsibility to protect collaborators and their contributions.[100] The court entertained evidence on both sides as to whether Larson intended to enter into a joint authorship relationship, even accepting that Larson made verbal commitments to give Thomson credit, yet still decided Larson did not intend to enter into such a relationship on the basis of program notes and copyright filings from before Thomson's entry into the project. This decision further highlights the court's bias toward single authorship. The court only had evidence of his intent to function as a single author predating his accepting the collaboration with Thomson. There's no way the evidence from that time could have suggested otherwise because Thomson had not yet entered the picture. At best there was no evidence of his intention about entering a joint authorship relationship with Thomson either way, and the court even acknowledged that he had probably changed his mind not to mention the fact that there was no question whatsoever of their mutual intent to join their independently copyrightable works into a joint work. In spite of all of this, the court defaulted to an assumption of single authorship. Of course, this case in some ways presents unusual circumstances, particularly regarding Larson's untimely demise. As nearly all involved parties, including the courts, acknowledge, Larson may very well have made good on his alleged promises and given Thomson credit and due compensation.[101] Had Larson lived, would he have made good on his promises? Would Larson have worked out an equitable agreement after the fact that more accurately reflected Thomson's final role in the creation of *Rent*? Ultimately, these questions are irrelevant to the issue of the law's role in reproducing literary authorship ideologies. Whatever Larson may or may not have done does not change the court's interpretation and use of the standards of joint authorship in *Childress v. Taylor*. In the situation presented to them, even with evidence strongly suggesting a joint authorship relationship, the courts deferred to a strong bias favoring individual authorship.

What implications does the institutional and cultural default to individual authorship over collaboration have for the future of *Rent* and the musical in general? In contrast to Bruce Kirle's assertion that incompleteness and malleability play essential roles in defining the very character of the American musical, the specter of Larson's mythological status as sole, individual creator of *Rent* threatens to stagnate and fix it. Larson's posthumous legal victories depended upon and reinforced ideological assumptions about individual genius and the role of inspiration in creating works. As these assumptions, based on literary modes of production as well as broader cultural assumptions about competition, begin to saturate theatrical culture, theater's own creative practices could become untenable. The "unfinished" musical and the tradition of coming to new iterations of musicals with a spirit of reinvention could become a thing of the past, seen as an outdated practice running counter to the cultural privileging of individualism over collaboration. As for *Rent*, the legal and cultural forces reifying the play as evidence of Larson's status as both individual genius and speaker for a generation render the possibilities for reimagining even parts of the script unlikely at best, impossibly fraught with potential legal complications at worst. Such reimaginings are in no way necessary for the continued success of the musical as a genre, nor would their disappearance represent the passing of some nostalgia-soaked golden age to which musicals should return. The point here is that the source of these changes, the root of collaboration's declining status, is an inscription of dominant values from the culture of one art form to another through the vehicle of the law as an ideological state apparatus. The aesthetic ideology of twentieth-century American literary production, the most egocentric qualities of which have become co-opted by the general ideology of the state in order to render neoliberal ideals about individualism and competition into common sense assumptions about the nature of authorship, has come to dominate the aesthetic ideology of theater despite the ill fit of this ideology to actual theatrical practices. Peter Jaszi characterizes the *Childress* case as an example of "copyright's recursive insistence on forcing all writing into the Procrustean doctrinal model shaped by the individualistic, Romantic concept of 'authorship.'"[102] Jaszi somewhat overstates the law's influence here; the high burden of proof for claims of collaboration set by the *Childress* court suggests a legal default to individualism rather than a trend of forcing all writing to fit a single model. Nevertheless, this default has important practical and ideological consequences. It places a nearly insurmountable burden of proof upon a secondary author and gives a primary author virtually unlimited power to deny claims of secondary contribution. Following the way the *Rent* court applied the test, any primary author would simply have to claim that she never intended to enter into a legal joint authorship in order to maintain total control over, credit for, and compensation from a coauthored work. Because the law reinforces the literary ideology and gives it muscle, new and old theatrical practices stand at risk not only of a kind of aesthetic invalidation but also of legal vulnerability to exploitation, showing that the law, in practice, serves less as a protection for artists and more as a means of assuring the reproduction of the means of production.

SPACE FOR COLLABORATION

The questions of authorship surrounding *Rent* and *The Serpent* point to the roles the ideals of collaboration and individualism play in both production practices and in constructing narratives of theater history. In both cases, the ideal of individualism as part of the general or dominant ideology subverts collaboration's status as a valid artistic practice, but this subversion occurs differently in each case. In *The Serpent*, the attempt at a collaborative process resulted in a product with a single author who not only took over the writing process but attempted to rewrite the production history to completely discount the contributions of other collaborators. Van Itallie attempted to characterize the process as an individual intellect forced to make nominal concessions of credit to a group in order to maintain a happy working environment through flattery, yet the story of *The Serpent* remains a touchstone of the history of collaborative theater practice. Its place as such in theater history narratives erases the ideological conflict between individualism and collaboration. These narratives follow van Itallie's example, paying lip service to the idea of collaboration but ultimately privileging individualistic literary authorship as the default mode of cultural production. The *Rent* case and the controversy surrounding it, on the other hand, foreground the conflict between individualism and collaboration. While Thomson's conflict with Larson and his estate place the ideas of individualism and collaboration under closer scrutiny, it also shows that individualism remains privileged both aesthetically and legally. The contribution of a collaborator, according to many arguments of the case, threatens to devalue the work of an artist, to somehow make it less worthy of praise, admiration, or even attention than a work completed by a single individual. The courts in both *Thomson* and *Childress* effectively treat those claiming to be collaborators as guilty until proven innocent of attempting to extort credit and compensation from the "true" author of a text. Rachel Shteir's retrospective on the impact of the *Thomson* case on dramaturgy suggests that the case's legacy has mostly taken the form of either sympathetic indignation for Thomson or a cautionary tale about dramaturgs' need to protect themselves with contracts.[103] The ideologically loaded default to individualism creates two kinds of problems for collaborative practice in theater. Practical problems, primarily tensions between collaborators, in the historical moment in which the collaboration takes place often result from an unwillingness on the part of one or more parties to let go of the privileged construction of individual genius author. Historiographical problems—a lacuna regarding the reactionary politics at play in an ostensibly revolutionary production or a dichotomous, he said she said debate overshadowing the political and ideological stakes of conflicting claims about collaboration—create the risk of constructing a narrative in which authorship's privileged role among modes of cultural production and artistic practice remains an unexamined assumption. The case of *The Serpent* in some ways shows this subversion more strongly because the dominant narratives in theater history continue to treat a triumph of individualism, authorship, and the dominant ideology as a prime example of successful collaboration and revolutionary practice. Authorship and its attendant ideologies maintain their dominant position by inscribing authorship onto its countermovements and detractors.

Is collaboration a necessary myth for theater history, too? Do we extol the virtues of collaboration while ignoring the huge role individualism plays in our narratives? Not always. Collaborations do not inevitably result in such ill will or regressive, conservative assertions about authorship.[104] As I discussed earlier, collaboration permeates the history of musicals to the point that musicals have more great teams than great individual authors. And even authors whose names carry connotations of individual genius such as Sondheim more often than not give credit and compensation to their collaborators. Thomson's fight for credit and compensation is more exception than rule. The two cases studied here represent a danger, though, of defaulting to a distrust of collaboration and an almost defensive preference for Romantic notions of the author as individual genius over theater's native amiability toward collaborative practice. Dominant modes of cultural production evince an ideological preference for singular authorship, and hegemonic forces such as copyright law, play publishers, and even theater history textbooks reinforce claims to the neutrality and inevitability of such preferences. By using individual authorship as a default, cultural institutions further the proposition of the author's essentially individualistic nature as a self-evident and universal truth. But imbedding that assumption as "common sense" actually requires constant renewal and institutional support. The increasingly tenuous validity of the collaborative practices that the culture of theatrical artists has long embraced suggests that this assumption continues to take greater hold as the theater, even the revolutionary theater, ever more strongly reproduces dominant ideologies through its practices. Legal scholar Douglas M. Nevin argues that "by distributing disproportionate ownership interests among only certain members of a collaborative team, copyright law has forced the theater industry to ignore the collaborative process that defines the art form as one living, breathing whole."[105] Like Jaszi, Nevin oversells the law's ability to dictate theatrical practice, but his point that copyright law favors individual authorship over other modes of cultural production remains salient. Ryan J. Richardson points out that "while the outcome of Thomson fits squarely within a reasonable reading of the law," it also strongly suggests that "copyright law, as currently applied, is inflexible."[106] Again, the law may be doing what it is supposed to do, but "what it is supposed to do" is, often, to reproduce a capitalist mode of production. Richardson agrees with the *Thomson* court's decision but also with those critics who see that decision as a sign that copyright law cannot adapt to the realities of modes of cultural production in the late twentieth century. Richardson further points to the problem with this ill fit between copyright and practice: copyright's "all-or-nothing approach to joint authorship, galvanized by the rigid requirements of Childress, arguably fails to incentivize collaborative writing and permits those with presumed creative control to reap the rewards of others' labor."[107] The law does not mandate the forms that theatrical practice may take, nor does its default to or preference for individualistic literary authorship prohibit collaboration. Copyright law and other cultural institutions can, however, either make collaboration so suspect as to render artists vulnerable as in the case of *Rent* or allow the very idea of collaboration to be co-opted as little more than a marketing tool serving a completely individualistic, capitalist model of production as in the final product of *The Serpent*. A narrative such as the myth of *The Serpent* as an exemplar of '60s collaborative theater practice belies the significant role that authorship, particularly authorship's demand for individualism, plays in theatrical practice.

In the case of *The Serpent*, the imposition of literary modes of authorship onto a creative process drawing from theatrical tools and traditions led to sore feelings, a possible distrust of future collaborations for those involved, and a legacy of individual authorship of a particular work that erases the contributions of a number of artists. In the case of *Rent*, the dominant literary ideology of authorship and its preferential legal status have robbed a cocontributor of not only her credit but her due financial compensation. If *The Serpent* is a case of collaboration gone sour, *Rent* is a case where collaboration was always an idea to be resisted, denied, in favor of individual recognition. In both cases, however, literary models of authorship work to render the collaborative practices native to theater aberrant or illusory, not representative of true artistry. True artistry, or the concept of artistry that best reinforces dominant ideologies governing cultural production, is individualistic and competitive, the rewards of critical renown and commercial success providing incentive to create. This is not to suggest that theater represents some idyllic or utopic space of pure egalitarianism corrupted by market relationships. Certainly theatrical collaborations go more and less smoothly and many cases of uncredited contribution probably never go to court or receive public notice of any kind. The point here is that collaborative creation of theatrical works is a practice native to the culture of theater, understood and widely accepted. But when dominant ideologies of authorship, based in the distinct though related field of literature, pressure theatrical practice to default to assumptions about creativity and hierarchies of artistic value favoring individualism and can back up that default with legal force, theater's ability to define its own concept of artistic legitimacy becomes tenuous.

NOTES

1. Of course, the story does not necessarily end with the writer in literature, either. Editors often have heavy influence in final products, sometimes leading to troubled authorship claims. The case of Raymond Carver and his editor Gordon Lish offers one of the most prominent examples of the scandal caused by an undisclosed collaboration upsetting the myth of the individual genius. The short story collection *What We Talk About When We Talk About Love*, arguably Carver's most well-known work, was heavily edited by Lish. Lish even gave the collection its iconic title, changing it from Carver's original title, *Beginners*. Lish's contributions included not only cutting and fine-tuning but also adding entirely new lines, some of which went on to be counted as some of Carver's most iconic. Some estimates suggest Lish cut as much as 55 percent of Carver's original manuscript. The revelation of this relationship led to wide-ranging discussions about who actually authored the stories, the proper relationship between editors and authors, and whether the history of collaboration robbed the works of some of their artistic merit because they did not emanate from a single, individual genius (i.e., the idea that collaboration is somehow cheating or cheap). See Simon Armitage, "Rough Crossings: The Cutting of Raymond Carver," *New Yorker*, December 25, 2007; David Eric Tomlinson, "Editorial License: Raymond Carver and Gordon Lish," *Zouch Magazine*, October 24, 2011; and Giles Harvey, "The Two Raymond Carvers," *New York Review of Books*, May 27, 2010.

2. Martha Woodmansee, "The Genius and the Copyright: Economic and Legal Conditions of the Emergence of the 'Author,'" *Eighteenth-Century Studies* 17, no. 4 (1984): 425–48. See also Martha Woodmansee, "On the Author Effect: Recovering Collectivity," in *The Construction of Authorship: Textual Appropriation in Law and Literature*, ed. Woodmansee and Peter Jaszi (Durham, NC: Duke University Press, 1994), 15–28.

3. James M. Harding and Cindy Rosenthal, "Between Characteristics, Continuities, and Change—Theorizing the Legacy of Radical Theatres," in *Restaging the Sixties: Radical Theaters and Their Legacies*, ed. Harding and Rosenthal (Ann Arbor: University of Michigan Press, 2006), 5.

4. Ibid., 7.

5. Ibid., 9.

6. Ibid.

7. Stanley Richards, introduction to *The Best Short Plays 1969*, ed. Stanley Richards (Philadelphia: Chilton Book Company, 1969), xii.

8. David Harvey, *A Brief History of Neoliberalism* (New York: Oxford University Press, 2007), 23. Harvey also points out that, according to neoliberal theory, "while individuals are supposedly free to choose, they are not supposed to choose to construct strong collective institutions" (69).

9. The most prominent theater history textbooks also tend to highlight the Open Theatre and particularly *The Serpent* as examples of collectivist theater. Oscar Brockett's *History of the Theatre* points to the Open Theatre as "one of the most important" innovative theaters specifically because of its collaborative approach, and then names *The Serpent* as one of the group's great successes. Oscar G. Brockett and Franklin J. Hildy, *History of the Theatre,* tenth edition (Boston: Pearson Education, 2008), 520–21. *Theatre Histories: An Introduction* greatly overstates the collaboration and completely erases van Itallie's authorial role by suggesting that the serpent was "created by . . . Joseph Chaikin . . . with his Open Theatre company." Phillip B. Zarrilli, Bruce McConachie, Gary Jay Williams, and Carol Fisher Sorgenfrei, *Theatre Histories: An Introduction,* second edition (New York: Routledge, 2010), 518.

10. William Coco, Gordon Rogoff, Jean-Claude van Itallie, Joyce Aaron, Susan Yankowitz, Paul Zimet, Richard Gilman, and Joseph Chaikin, "The Open Theatre [1963-1973]: Looking Back," *Performing Arts Journal* 7, no. 3 (1983): 25.

11. Robert Passoli, *A Book on the Open Theatre* (New York: Bobbs-Merrill, 1970), 110.

12. Ibid.

13. Van Itallie claims that *America Hurrah* was not an Open Theatre production, largely to underscore his independent creation of the play, though Chaikin directed and the actors were all Open Theatre members. See Coco et al., "Looking Back," 31.

14. Gene A. Plunka, *Jean-Claude van Itallie and the Off-Broadway Theater* (Newark: University of Delaware Press, 1999), 104.

15. Ibid., 104–5.

16. Passoli, *A Book on the Open Theatre*, 118.

17. Hans-Thies Lehmann, *Postdramatic Theatre*, trans. Karen Jurs-Munby (New York: Routledge, 2006), 21.

18. *The Serpent: A Ceremony*, James Barbosa, Joseph Chaikin, et al. (1970; New York, NY: Educational Broadcasting Corporation), video.

19. *The Serpent*, video.

20. Coco et al., "Looking Back," 34.

21. Plunka, *Van Itallie and the Off-Broadway Theater*, 112–13.

22. Ibid., 113.

23. Ibid. The inclusion of the material about van Itallie's mother especially highlights his insertion of himself as the individual author. Not only is this material unrelated to the group's explorations and entirely outside of anyone's experience but van Itallie's, it also plays into tropes of authorial intention. The autobiography links the unique, unnetworked self with the work, suggesting that one is an extension of the other. Van Itallie erases his would-be collaborators' contributions not only by including work to which they have no connection but also by suggesting that the work itself is fundamentally and inseparably tied to his identity.

24. Ibid.

25. Passoli, *A Book on the Open Theatre*, 121.

26. Joseph Chaikin, *The Presence of the Actor* (New York: Atheneum, 1980), 106.

27. Terry Eagleton, *Criticism and Ideology: A Study in Marxist Literary Theory* (London: NLB, 1976). Of particular interest at present is the chapter "Categories for a Materialist Criticism," 44–63.

28. Eagleton, *Criticism and Ideology*, 45. It is important to note there that by "distinguishing" these two forces Eagleton is in no way suggesting a clear delineation between their ideologies. They may, of course, overlap or mutually influence one another. He's simply distinguishing between foci. In fact, he argues that "the forces of production of the [Literary Mode of Production] are naturally provided by the [General Mode of Production] itself, of which the [Literary Mode of Production] is a particular substructure" (*Criticism*, 49).

29. Ibid., 54.

30. Ibid.

31. Ibid., 46.

32. To clarify and avoid any potential slippage, I am in this instance following Eagleton's use of the word "drama," by which I take it he means theatrical performance and production and not just the literary genre.

33. Eagleton, 49.

34. Antonio Gramsci, *Selections from Cultural Writings*, ed. David Forgacs and Geoffrey Nowell-Smith, trans. William Boelhower (Cambridge, MA: Harvard University Press, 1985), 420–21.

35. Passoli, *A Book on the Open Theatre*, 122. The published text includes several pieces that, according to narratives of the developmental process, were almost certainly based on the actors' improvisations and contributions to the workshop.

36. Jean-Claude van Itallie, *The Serpent*, in *America Hurrah and Other Plays* (New York: Grove Press, 1978), 11. The letter and van Itallie's explanation of its exegesis appear as prefatory material to the play.

37. Ibid.

38. Van Itallie's specific dismissive reference to Second City further suggests that his comments attempt to discredit the members of the Open Theatre because Chaikin based many of the group's exercises on his work with both Second City and Viola Spolin. See Passoli, *A Book on the Open Theatre*, 16.

39. Van Itallie, *The Serpent*, 11.

40. Ibid.

41. Coco et al., "Looking Back."

42. Richards, introduction, xii (emphasis original).

43. Van Itallie, *The Serpent*, 12.

44. Ibid.

45. Even when van Itallie dismisses the primacy of the word, he still clings tightly to the notion of the necessity of authorial intention in constructing the audience's experience. "At each point in constructing the ceremony the playwright must say to himself: 'what is the audience experiencing now? . . .' The 'trip' for the audience must be . . . carefully structured" (*The Serpent*, 6).

46. See the Sex Pistols.

47. Harvey, 42.

48. Ibid.

49. See Louis Althusser, "Ideology and Ideological State Apparatuses (Notes towards an Investigation)," in *Lenin and Philosophy and Other Essays*, trans. Ben Brewster (New York: Monthly Review Press, 1971): 127–86, especially 182. Althusser argues that many ideological state apparatuses interpellate subjects as free so that they will freely submit to larger cultural structures. In other words, where repressive state apparatuses interpellate subjects through force, ideological state apparatuses often interpellate subjects by creating appealing subject positions that nevertheless serve the function of reproducing structures of power that uphold the state and hegemon.

50. W. B. Worthen similarly investigates the copyright page as a site of authorship claims regarding Moisés Kaufman, the Tectonic Theater Project, and *The Laramie Project*. Worthen points out that while the cover and the author's note go to great lengths to stress the collaborative nature of the writing process, Kaufman claims the copyright as a single author. See W. B. Worthen, *Print and the Poetics of Modern Drama* (Cambridge: Cambridge University Press, 2005), 85–97.

51. The "copyright trust" of *The Serpent* does, however, also include several consultants outside the ensemble. The San Francisco Mime Troup, Joseph Campbell, Ellen Steward, and Susan Sontag all visited the early Bible workshop meetings to discuss the mythology of Genesis and methods of exploratory performance with the ensemble. Plunka, *Van Itallie and the Off-Broadway Theater*, 106.

52. Again, Worthen's work on *The Laramie Project* bears mentioning here. Whereas I focus on copyright culture's role in facilitating, even encouraging single authorship claims over collaboratively created works, Worthen focuses on the ways print culture and the form of the book itself encourage such claims. "Although *The Laramie Project* has its roots in the de-authorizing practices of contemporary performance—notably in the rise of performance eth-

nography—the book form of the play is revealing of our contemporary concern for the proprieties of print, its ability to stabilize and transmit not merely the work of art but a certain understanding of *authorized* writing, even at the moment that print seems to be on the wane as the defining means of creating and transmitting writing." Worthen, *Print and the Poetics of Modern Drama*, 13–14.

53. Siva Vaidhyanathan, *Copyrights and Copywrongs: The Rise of Intellectual Property and How It Threatens Creativity* (New York: NYU Press, 2001), 4.

54. Lawrence Lessig, *Free Culture: The Nature and Future of Creativity* (New York: Penguin, 2004).

55. Ibid., 10.

56. Oren Bracha, "The Ideology of Authorship Revisited: Authors, Markets, and Liberal Values in Early American Copyright," *Yale Law Journal* 118, no. 2 (2008): 265.

57. Harding and Rosenthal, "Between . . .": 10.

58. David Savran, "The Death of the Avantgarde," *TDR* 49, no. 3 (2005): 12.

59. "Career Guides: The Musical Book Writer," American Theatre Wing website, http://americantheatrewing.org/careerguides/detail/the_musical_book_writer.

60. See Mark N. Grant, *The Rise and Fall of the Broadway Musical* (Boston: Northeastern University Press, 2004), 51–54. Grant suggests that the rise of collaborative practice contributed more than any other factor to the success of the American musical.

61. Bruce Kirle, *Unfinished Show Business: Broadway Musicals as Works-in-Process* (Carbondale: Southern Illinois University Press, 2005), 1.

62. The controversy surrounding *A Chorus Line* and its shares of credit and compensation also suggests a move toward individualistic authorship in the musical, but the cases differ in several ways. Michael Bennett, whose estate owned the rights to *A Chorus Line*, did originally share credit and compensation with the actors on whose real-life stories he based characters and plots from the play. And following lawsuits, some of those actors received continuing shares of credit and compensation beyond their original contract. The significant difference here is that the actors involved were seeking credit and compensation for their life stories, not their creative input toward authoring a work. They essentially sought licensing fees for their life rights rather than credit as joint authors, so the case relates to a different set of legal and ideological questions altogether. For more information on the controversy, see Campbell Robertson, "Those First in 'Chorus Line' Gain a Continuing Stake," *New York Times*, February 2, 2008.

63. Faye Buckalew, "Joint Authorship in the Second Circuit: A Critique of the Law in the Second Circuit Following Childress v. Taylor and as Exemplified in Thomson v Larson," *Brooklyn Law Review* 64 (1998): 549.

64. Paulette S. Fox, "Preserving the Collaborative Spirit of American Theater: The Need for a 'Joint Authorship Default Rule' in Light of the Rent Decision's Unanswered Question," *Cardozo Arts and Entertainment Law Journal* 19 (2001): 503.

65. Ibid.

66. "Recent Cases: Copyright—Joint Authorship—Second Circuit Holds That Dramaturg's Contributions to the Musical Rent Did Not Establish Joint Authorship with Playwright-Composer," *Harvard Law Review* 112 (1999): 966.

67. Ibid. See also Fox, "Preserving the Collaborative Spirit," 503, and Buckalew, "Joint Authorship," 550–51. An alternative view might suggest that the perceived weaknesses of the script resulted from a bias among musical theater industry professionals toward the clear division of the roles of composer, lyricist, and librettist. In other words, the fact that Larson did *not* collaborate may have influenced judgments of his work in a field where collaboration is the norm. Ironically, it seems possible that collaboration in musicals is in fact a reification of individualism in the form of specialization. However, none of this changes Larson's adoption of the individual-genius model of authorship or the institutional and ideological defaults to that model that emerged so strongly in the trial.

68. Jonathan Larson, *tick, tick . . . Boom!: The Complete Book and Lyrics* (New York: Applause, 2009), 51. That *Hair* was in fact collaboratively and collectively developed bears mentioning here. Larson's autobiographical narrator throughout seems much more interested in obtaining the identity of the voice of a generation than in the process of creating that work.

69. *Harvard Law Review* 112: 966.

70. Ibid. See also Buckalew, "Joint Authorship," 551.
71. Brief for Appellant at 7, Thomson v. Larson, 147 F.3d 195 (2d Cir. 1998).
72. Buckalew, "Joint Authorship," 552.
73. For another example of the writer's private room becoming a site for collaboration, consider the possibly apocryphal story of the writing of *Cowboy Mouth*. Sam Shepard and Patti Smith allegedly wrote the play over the course of two nights by physically passing a typewriter back and forth across a table. See Don Shewey, *Sam Shepard: The Life, The Loves, Behind the Legend of a True American Original* (New York: Dell, 1985), 79.
74. Ibid. See also Fox, "Preserving the Collaborative Spirit," 504.
75. Appellant's Brief at 13, Thomson v. Larson. See also Buckalew, "Joint Authorship," 553, and Fox, "Preserving the Collaborative Spirit," 505.
76. Ibid.
77. Buckalew, "Joint Authorship," 554.
78. *Harvard Law Review* 112, 967.
79. Ibid.
80. U.S. Court of Appeals for the Second Circuit, 147 F.3d 195.
81. J. David Yarbrough Jr., "What's Mine Might Be Yours: Why We Should Rethink the Default Rule for Copyright Co-ownership in Joint Works," *Tulane Law Review* 76 (2001): 501.
82. Buckalew, "Joint Authorship," 559.
83. Ibid. See also Yarbrough, "What's Mine Might Be Yours," 501.
84. Ibid.
85. Yarbrough, "What's Mine Might Be Yours," 502.
86. Ibid.
87. Ibid.
88. Ibid.
89. 17 U.S.C. § 101 (1997).
90. No. 87 Civ. 6924, 1990 WL 196013 (S.D.N.Y. Nov. 28, 1990), aff'd 945 F. 2d 500 (2d Cir. 1991). 1900 WL 196013, at *4-6. See also Buckalew, "Joint Authorship," 567. A separate but parallel discussion about the difficulty of determining the status of joint authorship is also currently ongoing in the field of aesthetics. These arguments focus not on the legal status of joint authorship claims but on the theoretical, philosophical, and ontological conditions of such claims as well as their implications along those same vectors. I'm more interested in the practical dimensions of authorship for the purposes of the current study, but this discourse has certainly influenced some of my thinking. See Darren Hudson Hick, "Authorship, Co-Authorship, and Multiple Authorship," *Journal of Aesthetics and Art Criticism* 72 (2014): 147–56; Paisley Livingston, "On Authorship and Collaboration," *Journal of Aesthetics and Art Criticism* 69 (2011): 221–25; C. Paul Sellors, "Collective Authorship in Film," *Journal of Aesthetics and Art Criticism* 65 (2007): 263–71; and Sondra Bacharach and Debora Tollefsen, "*We* Did It: From Mere Contributors to Coauthors," *Journal of Aesthetics and Art Criticism* 68 (2010): 23–32.
91. Buckalew, "Joint Authorship," 573.
92. Ibid., 568.
93. Jesse McKinley, "Family of *Rent* Creator Settles Suit over Authorship," *New York Times*, September 10, 1998.
94. Buckalew, "Joint Authorship," 572.
95. Ibid. Buckalew's source here is the unpublished transcript of the judge's decision.
96. Ibid., 569.
97. Steven S. Kan, "Court Standards on Joint Inventorship and Authorship," *DePaul Journal of Art, Technology, and Intellectual Property Law* 267 (2009): 308.
98. Jane C. Lee, "Upstaging the Playwright: The Joint Authorship Entanglement Between Dramaturgs and Playwrights," *Loyola of Los Angeles Entertainment Law Journal* 19 (1998): 75–107.
99. *Harvard Law Review* 112, 966–67.
100. Fox, 519.
101. Even had Larson made the promises Thomson claimed—and the court to some extent believed—he made, the assumption that he would have credited Thomson is somewhat shaky.

First, Larson had reneged on his promise to Billy Aronson to credit him with the concept and some writing in every official document and playbill for *Rent*. See Kan, 307. Larson also faced posthumous copyright infringement accusations from Sarah Schulman, who claims that major plotlines and themes in *Rent* were lifted from her novel *People in Trouble*. See Sarah Schulman, *Stagestruck: Theater, AIDS, and the Marketing of Gay America* (Durham, NC: Duke University Press, 1998).

102. Peter Jaszi, "On the Author Effect: Contemporary Copyright and Collective Creativity," in *The Construction of Authorship: Textual Appropriation in Law and Literature*, ed. Woodmansee and Jaszi, 55.

103. Rachel Shteir, "The Dramaturg's Progress," *Theatre Topics* 13, no. 1 (March 2003): 165–68.

104. For an illustrative though certainly not exhaustive list of cases in which a collaborative creative process led to a joint copyright claim either by multiple playwrights and dramaturgs or an entire ensemble, see Worthen, *Print and the Poetics of Modern Drama*, 97.

105. Douglas M. Nevin, "Comment: No Business Like Show Business: Copyright Law, the Theatre Industry, and the Dilemma of Rewarding Collaboration," *Emory Law Journal* 53 (2004): 1534. Nevin also advocates considering productions as derivative works where all involved artists receive credit as joint authors, allowing everyone to benefit equally without taking away the playwright's ability to benefit from future productions. While on the one hand this argument may seem to offer new rights and powers to directors, actors, and designers, it also cements the position of those roles as secondary to the text.

106. Ryan J. Richardson, "The Art of Making Art: A Narrative of Collaboration in American Theatre and a Response to Calls for Change to the Copyright Act of 1976," *Cumberland Law Review* 42 (2011): 521.

107. Richardson, "The Art of Making Art," 522.

Chapter Three

Whose Joke Is It, Anyway? The Author as Originator

Ask any comedian who Carlos Mencia is, and she is likely to respond, "a joke thief." Mencia has been accused of stealing jokes from comedy legends, his contemporaries, and even up-and-coming comedians whose work he happened to see. The evidence of such acts of theft is readily available. Below, I will quote two stand-up comedy routines. The first is Bill Cosby's from the 1983 special "Himself" and the second is from Carlos Mencia's 2006 special "No Strings Attached."[1]

> You grab the boy when he's like this, see, and you say, "come here boy"—two years old—you say, "get down, Dad'll show you how to do it. Now you come at me, run through me. Boom! There, see, get back up—see you didn't do it right now came at me. Boom!" See, now we teach them—see now you say, "go attack that tree, bite it, come on back bite it again." You teach them all that: "tackle me!" And then soon he's bigger and stronger and he can hit you and you don't want him to hit you anymore, and you say, "alright son." Turn him loose on high school and he's running up and down the field in high school and touchdowns, he's a hundred touchdowns per game and you say, "yeah, that's my son!" and he goes to the big college, playing for a big school, three million students and eight hundred thousand people in the stands—national TV—and he catches the ball and he doesn't even bother to get out of the way. He just runs over everybody for a TD and he turns around and the camera's on him and you're looking and he says, "hi *mom*!" But you don't mind that. You know who taught him.

And now, Mencia's:

> He gives him a football and he shows him how to pass it. He shows him every day how to pass that football, how to three step, five step, seven step drop. He

> shows him how to throw the bomb, how to throw the out, how to throw the hook, how to throw the corner, he shows this little kid everything he needs to know about how to be a great quarterback, he even moves from one city to the other, so that kid can be in a better high school. Then that kid goes to college and that man is still [at] every single game, that dad is right there and he's in college getting better, he wins the Heisman trophy. He ends up in the NFL. Five years later, he ends up in the Super Bowl. He gets the MVP of the Super Bowl, and when the cameras come up to him and say, "you got anything to say to the camera?" "I love you *mom*." Ah! That bitch never played catch with you.

Many comedians (and I imagine many artists in general) would see Mencia's joke as an instance of stealing, of violating sacred originality. In this chapter, I will argue that such a response to the undeniable similarities of the jokes above reproduces neoliberal ideologies by, once again, treating authorship as the default mode of production. Because comedians occupy dual roles as writers and performers, comedy offers the clearest examples of the relationships among authorship, performance practices, and cultural attitudes about intellectual property. Comedy also throws into sharp relief the way authorship's position as default becomes normalized for nonliterary art forms in the second half of the twentieth century, as a notion of the comedian as a hybrid writer-performer only emerges with the rise of "persona" comedy in the late 1950s and early 1960s. At the same time that directors were beginning to reject authorial intent and theaters were experimenting with collectivity, comedy was replacing its teams of writers with individual authors whose unique points of view not only drove the performance but were its point. In many ways, then, the developments in this chapter occur along an opposite vector of the developments in the first two chapters. While authorship functioned in those cases as a reactionary response to the cutting-edge innovations in theatrical practice, the case of persona-era comedy sees artists openly embrace authorship as the means to give them a valid, countercultural voice. The irony is that late twentieth-century authorship itself and its demands for originality function precisely as a means of reproducing neoliberal ideology and capitalist assumptions about production and exchange. Whereas the first two chapters saw members of the theater world retreating to performance practices that went against their revolutionary rhetoric, here the revolution itself was deeply authorial and therefore intrinsically contradictory. In all these cases, authorship serves as the means of allowing space for revolutionary rhetoric within dominant modes of production without ever allowing that rhetoric to actually threaten those modes or their attendant ideologies. For comedy, the demand for originality paradoxically functions as both a vehicle for celebrating countercultural thinkers while simultaneously reproducing the very competitiveness and proprietorship of the culture those same thinkers critique.

As I mentioned in the preface, I made a go at a career as a professional stand-up comedian between 2007 and 2009 with some moderate success, but found I did not have a taste for the business to match my enjoyment of the craft. One of my small successes—being chosen as a finalist for Comedy Central's Open Mic Fight in 2007—threw comedy's deeply contradictory attitudes toward originality into sharp relief. The rules to which I had to agree in order to compete contained a clause that I found (and still find) intriguing regarding contestants' ownership of their own materials and the potential future use of such materials by Comedy Central and its parent company Comedy Partners, referred to in the contract and throughout as CP.

> 8. Ownership Rights; Rights to Use Entries and Performances. Past experience has shown that contests and promotions generate similar submissions or entries which closely resemble concepts and ideas developed by CP, whether before, during or after the contest. Entrants may see a presentation which seemingly incorporates an idea or concept or includes materials similar to that contained in their entry (e.g., VHS/DVD or online uploaded submission). Any similarity may be purely coincidental and is always unavoidable in light of the volume of ideas which CP routinely considers in the course of its program development. Consequently, . . . entrants hereby agree to the following terms and conditions (i) CP may use any and all ideas, concepts, material, or expression, in whole or in part, contained in an entry, or videotaped or recorded at a public performance in the regional competitions or semi-final competition (collectively, the "Materials") . . . [2]

Basically, this contract requires comedians to grant Comedy Partners a non-exclusive right to use any material from the competition. While this release is, on one hand, a means for CP to protect itself from copyright suits from any of the hundreds of entrants who do, inevitably, submit similar material, it also means that comedians must give CP the right to use any of their work without any credit or compensation in order to participate in the contest. CP's defense of this requirement rests on the assumption that conventions are so strong and so narrow in stand-up comedy as to render the notion of originality moot, at least in legal terms. If a comedian sees her material being performed by another comedian on television, CP argues, the apparent duplication is just as likely due to the "unavoidable" similarity of content generated by writers working under the same set of conventions as to the intentional use of her material without credit or compensation, although the contract also protects such uses. And while a high-volume submission process will certainly yield similar submissions, the release of rights here depends on and exposes an assumption that all material counts as equally unoriginal. In other words, comedians wanting to participate must sign a document denying both the possibility and the significance of their originality.

The same document from which comes the above dismissal of originality, however, also stresses the importance of originality in evaluating contestants. A comedian at the regional level of the contest can earn a maximum of forty-five points for his performance, broken down as follows: fifteen for "judge's impression," ten for the quality of the writing, ten for style and delivery, and, finally, ten for "originality," defined as "originality of premises for jokes, unique point of view, interesting stage persona." Also, a tie in scores will be broken by prioritizing these scoring areas, with originality being labeled the second most important after the catch-all "judge's impression."[3] The scoring section of the rules, then, suggests a valuation of originality contradictory to the release. Here, originality not only exists, but determines the quality of a performance more than any other specific element. Comedy Partners simultaneously values and denies the concept of originality as it applies to the creation and performance of stand-up comedy routines. Comedy Partners has obvious practical motivations to present such contradictory views. They want to be able to market the winner as a new and exciting product, hence the emphasis on originality in scoring, and want to protect themselves from an onslaught of lawsuits, hence the denial of originality in the intellectual property section. But CP is not alone among industry forces operating under a seemingly contradictory dual concept of originality. Gene Perret's *Successful Stand-Up Comedy: Advice from a Comedy Writer*, a how-to guide for aspiring comedians, offers similarly conflicting advice about originality.[4] One of the chapters, "Be Original," stresses the importance of standing out from the crowd by offering a unique style. In this chapter, Perret explicitly discourages emulating other performers. However, another chapter, "Learn from Others," encourages comedians not to feel as though they need to completely reinvent the wheel, and suggests identifying and emulating what works for more experienced comics. Distinguishing between two forms of originality clarifies this apparent contradiction. Perret advocates originality of performance style. He simultaneously acknowledges that in any given moment a relatively narrow set of topics will predominate and suggests that young comedians should learn joke construction from both their predecessors and contemporaries.

These apparently paradoxical constructions of originality point to an important question: what does originality mean in stand-up comedy and in performance-based art forms in general? The answer I will propose, as suggested above, is that stand-up comedy operates simultaneously under two constructions of originality that are both irreconcilable and inseparable: literary originality or originality of content on one hand and performance originality or originality of style on the other. Literary originality, because it is an aspect of authorship, often serves as the default mode of originality, rendering performance style vulnerable by obscuring its importance. The CP contract's argument that strong conventions in stand-up comedy nullify claims to originality and therefore ownership leads to my second guiding question: since issues of originality often arise in response to questions of appropriation or piracy, how does the cultural construct of intellectual property define both kinds of originality? Separating performance and literary originality can reframe questions about ownership and piracy as questions about iteration and imitation. Such separation also illuminates a complex relationship between the two types of originality and offers possibilities for new ways of thinking about performance style and originality in broader terms outside the scope of stand-up comedy. Earlier, I said that comedy represents a case where artists actively pursue the model of authorship rather than a case where they passively default to it. To highlight the choice of authorship and the implications it has for the kinds of ideologies comedy, as an industry, reproduces, I will point to other legal frameworks through which the comedy industry could potentially conceptualize originality and suggest that those frameworks undercut the seeming inevitability of authorship as the model for all cultural production. Comedy represents a space where the default to authorship is not embedded in either the legal code itself or in court decisions, but in cultural assumptions held even by comedians and legal scholars about how the law and cultural production work.

THE LEGAL BARK AND BITE OF ORIGINALITY

A familiar story: copyright protects a creator's exclusive rights to use and distribute his original artistic invention so that he can reap the financial rewards. The law offers this protection in order to provide financial incentive for creators to create, fulfilling the Constitution's authorization to create laws to "promote the Progress of Science and useful Arts, by securing for limited Times to Authors and Inventors the exclusive Right to their respective Writings and Discoveries."[5] Copyright maintains a strong originality requirement for protection in order to entice artists to push the progress of art in new directions by dangling the carrot of exclusive control of their unique shares of the market. It may be a familiar story, but almost every point of it is oversimplified if not completely inaccurate.

The story is so familiar, in fact, that it seeps into scholarship. Even Woodmansee, coeditor of and major contributor to perhaps the definitive volume on authorship and the law, falls for it. Woodmansee asserts that a work "may claim legal protection only insofar as it is determined to be a unique, original product of the intellection of a unique individual."[6] But Bracha, responding to Woodmansee, points out that

> one would never catch a lawyer making that argument. Unless heavily qualified, [Woodmansee's claim] is simply dead wrong. No copyright regime whose border wars of copyrightability involve telephone directories or guides

> of cable television companies and whose default rules often vest initial copyright ownership in faceless business corporations could be plausibly described as extending protection only to "a unique, original product of the intellection of a unique individual."[7]

In other words, in a world where compilations of publicly available data meet minimum originality requirements, arguments assuming originality as an essential defining element of copyright law become untenable. Bracha's response here forms part of his larger project of examining the complicated relationship between ideals central to the concept of authorship on one hand and the actual law on the other. He points to a long history of originality's gaining in rhetorical force even as it lost actual legal significance, resulting in "the paradoxical character of the modern originality requirement: the lower its practical bite as a substantive threshold for protection sank, the more dominant its status as a fundamental principle became."[8] Bracha goes on to call originality a "mechanism of mystification."[9] By this he means that originality, like many aspects of authorship, allows advocates of expanded copyright to claim support of Romantically idealistic concepts such as originality and individual genius while simultaneously pushing for policies and judgments that in fact diminish such concepts in practical terms. Bracha clarifies that

> The point . . . is not that anyone is being deceived. Rather, the curious and important quality of this conceptual field is the way in which it enables us to maintain deeply conflicting images, commitments, and modes of argument. [A] modern copyright lawyer . . . can move smoothly with very little sense of dissonance between arguments that assume and embody very different assumptions about authorship and about copyright protection. She can argue doctrinal questions of originality in terms that assume a cumulative process of creation and switch without blinking to arguing questions of infringement in terms that assume a sharp distinction between an original and a derivative. The mystification lies in the coexistence of those conflicting fundamental assumptions and in the mechanisms that allow us to maintain them.[10]

Originality, then, is less a substantive basis for copyright protection than a rhetorical screen used to make arguments about property and control look like arguments about authenticity and integrity. So while the demand for originality often does exert great practical force as seen in the cases in this chapter, it does so with ideological and not legal backing.

The other half of the familiar story that needs complication is the issue of incentive, an issue deeply tied to originality. The story goes that the law protects artists' abilities to make money from their original creations because without financial incentives protecting only new creations, the arts would not progress. Legal scholar Eric E. Johnson points to recent literature in behavioral science exploring nonfinancial motivations for creativity and innovation. Johnson suggests that such evidence should at the very least call the incentive theory into question and that even without copyright protection or financial motivations artists would still create.[11] More importantly, he argues that the incentive theory is "best understood as a post-hoc rationalization for a creature of pure politics."[12] By this, Johnson means that while the familiar story says the framers of early copyright laws designed those laws to provide incentives, the laws in fact arose from political and economic conflicts having nothing to do with individual incentives to create. Incentive theory appeared after the creation of the laws to justify them within a rhetoric of Romanticism so that copyright holders could keep their controlling interests intact despite the dissolution of the institutional and cultural foundations of early copyright law.

> The real history is not so much Adam Smith as Niccol [sic] Machiavelli: the monopolies now understood as copyrights and patents were originally created by royal decree, bestowed as a form of favoritism and control. As the power of the monarchy dwindled, these chartered monopolies were reformed, and essentially by default, they wound up in the hands of authors and inventors.[13]

Johnson overreaches a bit in characterizing modern copyrights as monopolies,[14] but his point—that exclusive rights to use certain materials have stronger historical roots in censorship and control than in providing financial rewards and motivation for individual artists and creators—remains salient. Johnson does not go so far as to advocate a total abandonment of copyright protection. Creative individuals' operating under nonfinancial motivations such as political or social advocacy or a personal sense of accomplishment should by no means invalidate their right to good protections against predatory creative and professional practices. His point, and mine, to an extent, is to expose the faulty logic underpinning many arguments about copyright and advocate a more honest conversation about modern exegeses, functions, and ideological implications of copyright law rather than to advocate particular changes to that law.

Comedy provides a great opportunity for examining these relationships among the ideal of authorship, the law, and actual creative practice because comedians straddle the line between two different art forms—writing and performance—with distinct sets of conventions and legal needs. As the CP contract suggests, the high likelihood of independent creation of similar material complicates the originality requirement for copyright, but originality's practical threshold remains low even while its rhetorical importance remains high. And the kind of originality that CP as well as many comedians and scholars focus on, the demand for original content, completely ignores style. When I talk about discussions of originality defaulting to authorship, then, I am really addressing two distinct problems. The first, as Bracha points to, is the disparity between the default view of originality contained in the construction of authorship and the actual legal standing of originality as a component of copyright law. The second is that by defaulting to authorship, the relative originality of the performance element of comedy gets overlooked, ever further entrenching the sense that originality always and only means the creation of totally new content over which its creator retains exclusive control.

As an aspect of our modern intellectual property regime, originality's bark is worse than its bite. The metaphor is especially apt here because the barking dog of its figure is still intimidating, and that intimidation can have practical consequences regardless of originality's actual toothlessness. The whole point of the metaphor, in fact, is to convey a sense that the perceived danger far outweighs the actual danger and thereby assuage trepidation. If that trepidation did not already exist or have consequence, the clarification would not be necessary. And originality, as Bracha points out, barks so loudly that many would not dream of testing its bite. Originality as an aspect of authorship, the default mode of cultural production, exercises both ideological and practical force in excess of its legal scope and standing, especially in stand-up comedy. Originality and the incentive fallacy mutually support one another to help maintain the cultural character of copyright law as a celebration and protection of creativity and individual accomplishment within a competitive marketplace. At the same time, copyright law moves more toward a protection of corporate interests such as CP, sometimes at the expense of individual creators. Originality functions similarly to individuality in maintaining authorship's position as the default mode of cultural production and in reproducing neoliberal ideology. Originality furthers the ideal of the Romantic individual, suggesting that an author's individual genius results in completely new works that are unlike any that came before because the individual who created them is unlike any who came before. At the same time, Romanticism and the originality it values promote capitalist market relationships by insisting that creativity must be neatly separated into distinct, discrete works. Originality becomes less about a celebration of the new and creative and more about the ability to meaningfully distinguish between products so that the exclusive rights to use those products can become commodities in a competitive marketplace. Before delving further into the rhetoric of originality, I first need to give a little bit of background about originality's standing in the context of stand-up comedy from the 1960s to the present, the time period I am calling the persona era of stand-up comedy.

THE PERSONA ERA: POINT-OF-VIEW-DRIVEN COMEDY

Comedians' competing identities as authors and performers take on special significance in the period from roughly the late 1950s to the present, a period dominated by "persona" or "point-of-view" comedy. As noted above, the CP contract even uses this language, defining the originality section of the scoring in terms of "unique point of view" and "interesting stage persona." The persona era breeds such a troublesome conflation of distinct concepts of originality partially because of how it departs from its predecessors in defining originality. In vaudeville, for example, many performers would use the same joke, and the notion of "stealing" rarely if ever came into play because the thing that distinguished performers, their career capital, was the manner and skill with which they delivered the content.[15] In vaudeville, then, literary originality mattered little in determining a comedian's success. A comic actor's performance originality, his ability to craft unique and easily distinguishable styles even within standard tropes and conventions, served as key career capital.[16] Comedian Milton Berle notes that it was common for performers to "borrow" jokes from one another during the time of vaudeville, and "etiquette demanded only that the borrower add to the joke and make it his own."[17] After the decline of vaudeville, stand-up comedy became a self-sustaining form rather than a portion of a variety show, and with the rise of the individual performer as headliner, "the basic unit of humor in the post-vaudeville period [became] the joke."[18] In many ways, the stand-up comedians of the mid-twentieth century operated under a valuation of originality similar to vaudeville. Stand-up comedians during this period often employed large teams of writers, a practice that might suggest a high threshold for literary originality, except for two factors: the jokes tended to focus on a very narrow set of topics, and these writers would shop the same joke around to many different comedians.[19] Again, then, these comedians relied on their performance originality to distinguish themselves. Good setup-punchline jokes plus a recognizable style or gimmick (Bob Hope's golf club and sly delivery, for example) could equal success, and the joke needed not come from or reflect the comedian's own thoughts or personality. Performance originality, then, both carried greater weight and, more importantly, was independent of literary originality. The ideal of the individual as both creator and performer of an act representing her own point of view was not yet the dominant model for a successful comedian. Such a hybrid writer-performer construct would become the norm with the beginning of the persona era in the late 1950s and reshape the relative importance of literary and performance originality in stand-up comedy.

Rather than attempt to pin down a specific starting moment for the persona era, I will point to some of the key figures in its development and entrenchment. Lenny Bruce is perhaps the most obvious choice as a revolutionary figure in stand-up comedy. Richard Zoglin argues that Lenny Bruce's obscenity trials and push for expanded freedom from censorship tend to overshadow his at least equally significant influence on a fundamental change in the formal conventions of stand-up comedy. In contrast to their immediate predecessors with their teams of joke writers, Bruce and other revolutionary comedians of the 1950s and 1960s "wrote their own material and used it to express their personal point of view about what was happening in the country, the culture, and their own lives."[20] Zoglin posits Bruce as the most influential of the new comics of the late 1950s and 1960s not because he was the funniest or even the most outrageous but because he represented the most complete marriage of material, performance, and self.[21] Bruce was not, of course, a one-man revolution, nor was he the first persona comic. Mort Sahl arrived on the scene earlier, creating an exasperated, professorial persona complete with his trademark bit of reading and commenting on headlines from the newspaper he held on stage, helping to inaugurate a brand of comedy based more on personal commentary and opinion than on crafting the best new iterations of generic topics filtered through the setup-punchline structure.[22] A recent piece on entertainment news site The AV Club puts Bob Newhart in the position of main visionary, citing the huge commercial success of his 1960 album *The Button-Down Mind of Bob Newhart* as the true moment of persona comedy's arrival.[23]

Regardless of who started the movement—Newhart, Sahl, Bruce, or anyone else—the key difference between persona-era comedy and its precedents came in the relationship between the performer, the material, and the audience. Where earlier comedians had basically been conduits or vehicles for jokes, the persona comics established a more direct relationship between themselves and the audience, expressing points of view for which they were personally responsible. These comedians' speaking directly, openly, and personally to the audience caused at least as much controversy as their taboo content. A 1959 *Time* magazine article labeling Bruce, Sahl, and other controversial comedians "sickniks" expresses almost as much distaste for Shelley Berman's "spelunking in his own psyche" as it does for the "social criticism laced with cyanide" and "jolly ghoulishness" dispensed by the likes of Bruce and Sahl, the "original sicknik."[24] And an op-ed by Robert Ruark from the *Saturday Evening Post* in 1963, pointedly titled "Let's Nix the Sickniks," offers a "shut up and sing" criticism against both comedians and musicians who put too much of their personality and commentary onto the stage, lamenting the fact that audiences are "being drowned in filth and philosophy by the comics."[25] Ruark links filth with philosophy, suggesting that the very presence of a clearly defined point of view on stage constituted a break with tradition just as radical as the free use of obscenities.

The work of Bruce, Sahl, Newhart, Berman, and other early persona comics taken together with criticisms such as Ruark's labeling them "sickniks" reveals an important perceived link between originality and identity in the United States. The criticism against these comics is not that their work is "sick," it's that they themselves are sick and are forcing their sickness on everyone else. In the persona era, audiences and critics often view the comedian's original persona as an extension of that comedian's personality.[26] This construct of originality cannot be separated from the individual, is in fact only original insofar as it extends from a unique individual. Authorship as the default mode of cultural production treats originality as the outward sign of individuality, the artistic reward for refusing to collaborate or adopt collective identities and for protecting one's self-reliant identity as a commodity in a competitive marketplace. Today, the idea that a comedian offers commentary from her own point of view is old hat, and the straightforward presentation of setup-punchline jokes would likely get a young comedian nowhere. The logic of the persona era is so ingrained as the dominant form of stand-up comedy, in fact, that comedians may draw censure for performing material that seems somehow inauthentic or not in keeping with their actual point of view. In a recent review of The Lonely Island's new comedy album, Marah Eakin criticizes the group for continuing to portray nerdy outsider characters when they have become successful pop icons with "cool lives" due to their work in television and movies, saying that it's "hard to believe" that such a stance really reflects their current point of view. Eakin's critique assumes that good comedy reflects a comedian's "true" point of view and that even things that are in themselves funny lose value as they cease to adhere to that truth.[27]

Performance style or personality in the persona era is more than just a way to differentiate between brands offering essentially the same product; it is the comedy itself. In other words, pre–persona era, stand-up comedy consisted of the jokes; in the persona era, a comedian's point of view itself constitutes the humor. This shift has enormous impact on the concept of originality within stand-up comedy. Performance originality remains as important as ever in the persona era, as a performer's distinct point of view must translate into performance elements: clothing, intonation, physicality, and so on. But the pressure for literary originality becomes greater than ever, with the demand for original jokes carried over from the comedians of the 1940s and early 1950s combined with the need for those jokes to express and cohere with the comedian's persona and the attendant assumption that the comedian's material is his own. Not only do jokes need to be new, they need to reflect a consistent point of view, meaning that the circulation of stock jokes or comedy writers trying to sell the same joke to different comedians no longer represent viable models. In this way, it may seem that literary originality should become subsumed under performance originality in the persona era, but this is not the case. The persona era idealizes and conflates both forms of originality. And even though performance originality has the longer history of significance within comedy, literary originality has recently caused the most anxiety, especially regarding the practice of joke stealing. In other words, where jokes once freely circulated, their ostensible inseparability from the writer-performer in the persona era has created a more guarded, even paranoid environment where literary originality must be protected at all costs. Authorship's position as the default mode of cultural production advances the equivalence of original material and original identity to the point that performance style becomes completely subsumed under literary originality. The rhetoric adopted by comedians and legal scholars suggests that ensuring comedians' exclusive rights to use material is a matter of securing comedians' very identities, not just shares in a competitive capitalist market.

LITERARY ORIGINALITY

For most comedians, developing routines is a long and painful process involving writing new material, trying it out in front of audiences, and then editing based on audience response. This process can stretch over several months or even years to create perhaps only thirty to sixty minutes of material with several times that amount left on the cutting-room floor. Investing so much time and effort into creating such precious career capital means that comedians are understandably upset when they perceive that their material has been stolen.[28] The amount of labor that goes into jokes also explains why joke stealing presents such temptation despite the social stigma and career risks associated with it.[29] Trevor Noah, recently picked to replace Jon Stewart as host of *The Daily Show* on Comedy Central, has faced accusations of joke stealing that have been treated as just as troubling for his career in his new post as the revelation of racist and sexist jokes on his Twitter account.[30] Despite the strong stigma against it, joke stealing remains an ongoing practice. In fact, one comedian speaking anonymously in an interview with attorneys and legal scholars Dotan Oliar and Christopher Sprigman expresses surprise that joke stealing does not occur more often because of the difficulty associated with the career necessity of creating new material. "There are a handful of guys [who] just have a reputation for being thieves and for the most part it's amazing to me, actually if you think about it, how rarely it happens because it's so professionally useful. A joke is such . . . a beautiful little gem. It comes along so rarely."[31] Perhaps the most infamous of "those guys" who have a reputation for joke stealing is Mencia. As a professional comedian on the Chicago comedy scene, I noticed that Mencia's name invariably came up whenever the topic of joke stealing arose. And it was a topic that came up quite a bit. I was once sitting at an open mic with the comedian and promoter who ran it, a friend I will refer to as "Bill." Another comedian whom I will dub "Steve" went on stage and told one of Bill's jokes word for word. I turned to Bill and said, "Did you hear that?"

"You mean the last joke Steve fucking Mencia ever told on my stage?" Bill said.

Mencia's name, then, had not just become synonymous with joke stealing. He had become a villainous figure, a symbol of all that ran counter to the standards of good, righteous comedy practices. Yet the comedy community also sensed that nothing could really be done about it, that people would continue stealing jokes in spite of such punitive actions as bans from comedy clubs. The Mencias of the world would go on stealing, and the righteous comedians would just have to keep pursuing the ideal of originality.

Comedians' sense of the elusiveness of justice for joke thieves reflects the actual legal situation accurately. Under current conventions of intellectual property law, Mencia may not have done anything actionable even with regard to the incredibly similar football jokes quoted above. First, Mencia did not take any phrases verbatim from Cosby.[32] Since copyright law covers only the expression and not the idea, Mencia's joke could be sufficiently different to avoid charges of stealing. Second, Mencia claims that he had never heard the Cosby version before writing his own, although that claim is so specious that it bears little consideration.[33] I argue that this potential lack of legal recourse against joke stealers only represents a crisis for comedy if one starts from the assumption that comedy functions as a particular version of authorship. Again, the comedy community's insistence that absolute originality must be maintained and that even the appearance of stealing must be stopped at all costs is not an idea forcibly imposed by the law but instead constitutes an expansion of the cultural assumptions underlying copyright law. Whatever the law might say, however, I find it hard to say that these two routines are not the same joke. Yes, there are differences. Mencia's mentions the NFL where Cosby's stops at college. Mencia's uses more technical terms and makes the misogyny much more explicit. But they share the same topic, the same structure, and the same punchline. They are both reducible, then, to the same underlying elements. Setup: father teaches son the basics of football and guides him through a successful career. Punchline: at the apex, the culmination of the boy's career and the father's hard work, the boy thanks his mother and neglects his father. The structure alone does not constitute the joke's identity. A joke made from that structure could then be reduced to a description with enough variations to be considered an entirely different structure. These variations largely come in terms of level of abstraction. For example, the joke might be reduced further. Setup: father devotes life to training son in some skill. Son succeeds in this skill. Punchline: after succeeding in said skill, son acknowledges mother and neglects father. Or even further. Setup: role model figure guides young person to success. Punchline: successful young person acknowledges someone other than role model figure. This outline would then cover a wide range of jokes that might not seem the same at all, for instance a joke about a mother driving a child to acting lessons every day. The child becomes a great actor, wins an Oscar, and thanks God, much to the chagrin of the mother. This joke is similar, but not the same as the football jokes. It is the combination of the structure with the topic that makes Cosby's and Mencia's jokes the same. In other words, the combination of structure and topic constitutes the minimum threshold for recognizing two jokes as the same. Literary originality depends on original combinations of structures and topics rather than jokes fixed in specific orderings of words.

I am making the case that comedians' looking to copyright for protection is an active and meaningful choice among comedians and not a function of copyright's offering the only viable means of protection. In the interest of making that case, it is important to examine what protections copyright might or might not offer comedians. Copyright law makes an important distinction between ideas and expression. Only expressions and not ideas can by protected under copyright. I can, in many cases, appropriate much of the plot of another novel, and as long as my new work is sufficiently different in expression and could not be considered an adaptation, there is nothing the original author can do. This may seem to pose a problem for copyright in comedy, as a comedian may express his same joke in several different ways, and under a strict interpretation of the idea-expression dichotomy something like the Cosby and Mencia jokes might seem like distinct enough expressions. However, copyright already protects other art forms in which expression may not consist of the exact final product but rather in the way an idea is expressed.[34] In fact, in his decision in the landmark case of *Nichols v. Universal Pictures*, Judge Learned Hand developed an "abstractions test" that acknowledged that locating the point where idea becomes expression might differ according to circumstances and conventions, and that it is at the point where someone has contributed something original in the means of expressing an idea that it becomes possible to protect it under copyright.[35] This means determining what is expression and what is idea varies not only from case to case but from art form to art form.

Legal scholars looking at comedy tend to assume that protecting comedians means protecting their literary originality, and that assumption leads them to frame all discussions of originality in comedy through the lens of copyright. Dotan Oliar and Christopher Sprigman point out that the law does not necessarily appreciate or adapt well to the complex, combinative identity of jokes. They argue that current intellectual property laws do not protect comedians effectively partly due to difficulties in determining ownership of jokes and partly due to the comedy community's preference—both culturally and economically motivated—for internal action against joke thieves. Oliar and Sprigman cite the distinction between idea and expression as one of the barriers to effective copyright enforcement.[36] Because much comedy is topical and even much nontopical comedy focuses on a narrow range of subjects—race, gender, dating, etc.—"comedians can in most instances lawfully appropriate the idea animating a joke simply by telling it in different words" whether that appropriation constitutes intentional stealing or not.[37] In other words, the law as practiced tends to protect only specific, fixed linguistic expressions. The free circulation of material and loose standards of ownership, they argue, represents a problem because "jokes are literary works, which constitute a protected category under copyright law."[38] Oliar and Sprigman also argue that other forms of intellectual property law such as trademark or patent law cannot protect comedians because only copyright could protect against joke stealing.[39] According to their argument, protecting comedians' original creation can only mean protecting their written material, their jokes. Oliar and Sprigman only consider comedians' protection under the law in terms of literary originality, and they find that protection lacking. The delivery, the performance of the joke, is irrelevant to questions of originality under this model except insofar as the performance contains or instantiates the "literary" content of the joke.

Legal scholar and former comedian Elizabeth Bolles takes issue with Oliar and Sprigman's claims that current copyright law offers insufficient protection to comedians.[40] She argues that stand-up comedy already meets all the criteria for protection and defends the concept of originality, stating that "it grows ever more difficult to propagate the canard that jokes as a class are so uncreative as to be unworthy of standard legal protections."[41] Bolles contends that the lack of consistent fixed expression and conventional nature of joke writing do not create barriers to protection because other forms of copyrightable material also have variable expression and strong conventions. She also argues that copyright law can actually deal well with the differing needs of protection for the respective varieties of comedy. Different kinds of jokes, according to Bolles, might have different levels of protection. Bolles points out that even a one-liner meets the basic thresholds for originality and fixedness required for protection. A long-form monologue, such as those performed by Eddie Izzard, merits even stronger protection because of the higher degree of complexity in expression. The independent creation of a monologue identical to one of Izzard's is less likely than the independent creation of identical one-liners because the Izzard monologue is more complex and filtered through Izzard's idiom.[42] Therefore, his particular way of expressing these ideas meets copyright standards. She goes on to reject Oliar and Sprigman's endorsement of self-enforcement of intellectual property norms within the stand-up community, arguing instead that "increased copyright protection for jokes will bring positive social change by creating parity among comics, . . . affording comics an opportunity to enforce author rights."[43] I agree with Bolles's assessment of the copyrightability of jokes on a technical, legal level. In all of these arguments, however, Bolles operates under the assumption that more protection is inherently better, that protection functions as an ideologically neutral, benevolent force. But protection in fact constitutes part of a process of valuation, of saying what is important about a work by saying what should be protected. The originality that Bolles wants protected, and here she agrees with Oliar and Sprigman, is originality of the joke, the "literary content." Even in arguing for the importance of protection, Bolles acknowledges that style animates content when she points out that Izzard's material is not "inherently funny," and that it is only his style that makes the content valuable in a commodity sense. But Bolles understands Izzard's style as his literary style, his rhetorical and linguistic strategies for dealing with his subject matter. She does not even consider the importance of his performance style, his cross-dressing, his odd mannerisms, his particular mumbling way of speaking. Izzard's performance style is irrelevant to Bolles. All that matters is ensuring that Izzard, and only Izzard, is allowed to use the jokes he comes up with. Her argument is as much about protecting comedians as it is about reproducing textual primacy in capitalist models of ownership and exchange.

While Bolles and Oliar and Sprigman disagree in their assessments of the law's ability to protect comedians' exclusive ownership of original material, they share the assumption that exclusive use of original material by the originator should be protected, leaving no room for circulation of material or a repertoire. But how does this valuation of originality mesh with CP's contention that conventions of stand-up comedy exert such force that independent creation of similar if not identical material is not only likely but inevitable? Dismissing CP's claim as a corporate entity's overreaching or simply attempting to cover its interests undercuts the complexity of the issues of originality and ownership. The strong conventions in stand-up comedy do present a challenge to protecting originality in both the legal and extralegal senses. Take for example the following four jokes. I will give the comedian's name and the date of the performance before each one.[44]

> Ari Shaffir, 2004:
> [Schwarzenegger] wants to build a brick wall all the way down the California/Mexico border . . . so no Mexicans can get in, but I'm like, "Dude, Arnold, who do you think is going to build that wall?"
>
> Carlos Mencia (striking again?), January 2006:
> I propose that we kick all the illegal aliens out of this country, then we build a super-fence so they can't get back in and I went, um, "Who's gonna build it?"
>
> D. L. Hughley, October 2006:
> Now they want to build a wall to keep the Mexicans out of the United States of America, I'm like, "Who gonna build the motherfucker?"
>
> George Lopez, November 2006:

> The republican answer to illegal immigration is they want to build a wall seven hundred miles long and twenty feet wide. Ok, but who you gonna get to build the wall?

I would argue that these are all the same joke. Same structure, same setup, same punchline, same topic. All reducible to the same iterable skeleton. And yet it is not at all clear that any stealing happened. The joke is simple enough, dealing with a topic that looms large in the popular consciousness (illegal immigration) and using well-known stereotypes (Mexicans as cheap labor and Republican xenophobia). These cases may very well fall under independent creation, and if legal action was taken it would be left to judges and juries "to infer copying based on the relative likelihood of independent invention. The level of proof required to establish copying requires, as with every element of a copyright claim, only that the evidence suggests that copying is more likely than not."[45] Comedians, then, may have to prove that they had never heard the joke before they performed it, and if they cannot, they may be in legal trouble. Norms within the comedy community go even further. Even in cases of independent creation, convention generally dictates that the comedian who performed the joke first has the more legitimate claim to it.[46] Under both the law and comedy community norms, comedians risk censure for simply employing the conventions of their field. Independent creation receives insufficient protection in both systems.[47] The point is that people have to prove independent creation. The law and comedy norms functionally assume copying in cases of sufficient similarity.

In fact, given the second set of similar jokes above, the notion that appropriation or unintentional copying of another comedian's work constitutes a necessarily negative act of theft becomes difficult to maintain. Among comedians at a lower level, say touring or within a major market but not nationally known, such instances of independent creation are often resolved when one comedian agrees not to tell the joke.[48] I personally encountered such a situation in Chicago. A mutual friend alerted me and another comedian to the fact that we were telling the same joke. We discussed it and determined that we could not have copied from one another based on when and where we had each performed it, and he agreed, graciously, to drop the joke from his act. In retrospect, however, I do not believe he needed to. Nor do I believe there is any reason that any of the comedians telling the fence jokes need be labeled thieves. Comedy is so driven by convention that genuine copies of jokes, equivalent instantiations of the same structure-content combinations, are bound to happen. CP, ultimately, is right about the unavoidable similarity of some jokes. Its claim for the inevitability of independent creation of similar material, however, ironically works against capitalist assumptions about production and ownership. If such independent creation is inevitable and renders content originality moot, then CP cannot claim to own a joke, although they may own, say, the recording of a particular comedian performing that joke. In other words, they may not own the fence-joke type, but they may own the token of a comedian performing the fence joke on one of their programs. Still, this admission of inevitability could create a system for the free circulation of jokes outside of a market. It is the stand-up comedy community, in a reversal of its own traditions of free circulation of material, and not the corporate entity in this case that reproduces the ideological assumptions underpinning neoliberalism and authorship's privileged position as the default mode of cultural production. This reversal reveals the force the default to authorship exerts as stand-up comedy as a mode of cultural production adjusts its own conventions to align with authorship's demand for originality. The fence jokes may be copies of one another, but copying did not necessarily take place. The jokes were written around the same time and dealt with an issue contemporaneous with the time of composition. Mencia's football joke, on the other hand, was written years after Cosby's and is less topical. The similarities between the football jokes, the time between composition, and the fact that Cosby's joke circulated in a widely distributed stand-up comedy recording all strongly suggest copying. Even if one or more of the comedians telling the fence joke did steal from one of the others, the temporal proximity and topical nature of the jokes complicates claims of originality or theft. I say this not to argue that comedians should or should not be anxious about joke stealing, but instead to argue that this anxiety is a symptom of authorship's position as the default mode of cultural production. Stand-up comedians buying into assumptions about the necessity of originality and about the need for exclusive rights to use new material to protect originality ultimately help reproduce neoliberal ideals about the universal virtue of individualistic competition.

The cases of the fence jokes and the football jokes suggest the need for considering two distinct senses in which jokes can be considered the same joke: identical jokes and copied jokes.[49] I will refer to two jokes that follow the same structure-topic combination as identical.[50] I will refer to a joke whose composition consists of an intentional act of copying from an earlier joke as a copy of that earlier joke. Therefore two independently created jokes might be identical despite history of production, while the authenticity of their ownership may depend completely upon such a history. The fence jokes are identical to one another, as are the football jokes, in the same way that all performances of Beethoven's Fifth are identical: though such elements as dynamics or tonality may change between performances of Beethoven's Fifth, the arrangements of notes and rhythms remain identical, which is what enables the labeling of a performance as an example of Beethoven's Fifth. With the jokes, the identity relies on the structure-topic combination while the elements that change among iterations—particular wordings, performance style, and so on—are irrelevant to the jokes' identity according to convention. The question of historical authenticity helps determine ownership. The fence jokes, despite being identical, do not seem to result from a historical act of copying whereas the evidence in the football jokes does suggest a historical act of copying. The fence joke and football joke in and of themselves, then, are like pieces of music that can be iterated or copied without losing their identity. The question of whether those iterations or copies are illicit is separate from their shared identity. Authorship's position as the default mode of cultural production conflates these two forms of authenticity and puts comedians at risk of censure for acts of independent creation. Focusing only on preventing historical copying not only fails to account for the many cases of independent creation of identical jokes in which none of the parties involved act in bad faith but also, perhaps more importantly, frames the field of stand-up comedy as an industry primarily focused on producing original, discrete units called jokes for dissemination in the marketplace. Separating out the two types of similarity also helps illuminate the problems with conflating the two kinds of originality. The anxiety over copying the joke comes down to an issue of licensing the rights to use a discrete work whose identity remains unchanged through its uses. The anxiety over copying performance instead focuses on the problem of imitation. The default to authorship creates the mistaken impression that without protections for literary originality, comedians would be indistinguishable and interchangeable and that the art form would therefore suffer because of a lack of incentive to innovate. Performance style, however, can distinguish comedians from one another and push the art form forward, and arguments such as Johnson's suggest that comedians would continue to innovate even without the motivation to control jokes as protected interests in a marketplace. In the next section, I look at the ways in which the law understands performance style as distinguishable and protectable without considering it property in order to show an alternative legal framework to the default mode of cultural production, an alternative that ironically challenges the reproduction of neoliberal ideologies by pulling structures from the same state apparatuses that elsewhere bolster capitalism.

PERFORMANCE ORIGINALITY

A few problems arise when considering originality solely in terms of jokes. Legal scholar Jane C. Lee points to one major problem that arises when attempting to apply copyright to any performance form. Lee specifically deals with performance art, but her arguments easily apply to other performance genres.

> Copyright law's notion of "fixed" may not be part of an artist's vocabulary. In addition, fixation of a performance may be a foreign concept to performance artists. These artists do not work from a written script and often improvise their work during their actual performance. Performance art also emphasizes

> audience participation so each show is unique depending on the audience's reaction. Therefore, performance artists cannot fix their movements or spontaneous ideas in any script or other tangible medium. Because they cannot fix their work, it is not copyrightable.[51]

Comedians often follow such a formula, creating structures for jokes but not necessarily repeating the jokes verbatim night after night. The need to divide comedy, or any form of performance, into discrete, fixable units such as jokes serves as one of the main means by which performance is interpellated as a derivative of authorship. Jokes, as Oliar and Sprigman assert, may be literary compositions, but jokes are not necessarily the defining unit of stand-up comedy. The few cases of joke stealing involving stand-up comedians to make it into a courtroom all involve some entity outside of stand-up comedy (such as a T-shirt printing company) appropriating comedians' jokes, but this legal focus on limiting the uses of written content does not mean that comedians consider themselves simply joke writers.[52] Comedy routines are often more complex, involving a certain amount of improvisation or physicality in order to animate the joke, if one even exists.[53]

A narrow focus on copyright as the only available framework for understanding comedy—a focus Oliar and Sprigman and Bolles suggest the law necessitates—also invalidates intentional attempts to reactivate material in new styles. Performance originality often thrives by rejecting literary originality. An original performance style can sometimes come through most clearly when the content is not original. A good example of performance originality's occasionally inverse relationship to literary originality comes from Morgan Murphy and again deals with Carlos Mencia. Murphy posted a video on her YouTube page of her doing one of Mencia's stand-up routines at one of her shows.[54] In the video, she cuts between her performance of the routine and Mencia's original performance. Murphy makes no attempt to defraud her audience into believing that she is Mencia or that the material is hers. She is a tall, thin, white woman with an enormous mass of curly hair dropping past her shoulders and partially obscuring her face, clearly not Carlos Mencia. She repeatedly refers to herself as Carlos or discusses her "sweaty balls," so that even in the live performance, without the cuts of Mencia's routine, she foregrounds the "stealing" as an integral part of the act. The performance's originality is directly related to the appropriation of the material. She playfully sets the conflicting notions of originality against one another. Part of the humor in her performance comes from the bold theft as a critique of Mencia's bad practices, reinforced by the text at the beginning of the video claiming she first performed the routine in 1923. The humor also comes from the ill fit between the content of the joke—usually performed in Mencia's intense, energetic, brash style—and Murphy's deadpan, understated delivery. Murphy's performance of Mencia's material not only mocks

Mencia, but also those who fret excessively over content originality by downplaying the gravity of joke stealing. Claims that Mencia steals, she seems to suggest, miss the point that he's just not very funny.

Mencia is certainly aware of his reputation as a joke thief, and he, too, rejects the almost sacred status of literary originality within stand-up comedy.

> Listen to me, and look at me when I tell you this with all honesty. If you think I steal jokes, fuck yeah you're right. Of course I fucking steal jokes. Are you out of your fucking mind? When I come to a comedy club, you better run, bitch. You better get the fuck off stage. Because if anything you say is even remotely funny, I'm going to make it mine. And all I'm going to do is say "Mexican" in the front. I'm like a rapper. I just sample shit and make it my own. Is that really my song? I don't know, but it sounds like mine. But it kind of sounds like somebody else's. It's a hit, bitch![55]

On one hand, this can be read as Mencia's petulance in response to being caught violating the rules. But this incendiary defense also suggests his deep sense of the contradictory concepts of originality at work in the current conventions of stand-up comedy. Although Mencia compares his actions to sampling, where rap musicians, for instance, take a piece of melody or a beat from another song and construct a new song around it, a more apt analogy, at least in terms of the football routine, may be to covering, where one band performs a song originally done by another band but in the new band's style.[56] In this light, appropriation of jokes, the creation of genuine copies of jokes in different styles, might be seen as a productive practice, a way of paying homage to influences or as a way of reanimating content in a completely different tone, as in Murphy's appropriation of Mencia's material. Authorship's position as the default mode of cultural production and its attendant demands for originality, then, potentially stymie creative practices.

Outside the United States, such playful and productive copying does occur. Mike Ward, a francophone comedian from Montreal who tours throughout Canada and France but also occasionally performs in English-speaking circuits, points out that not all markets express such concerns about preserving literary originality. "In France," Ward says, "'doing Cosby' in stand-up is no different than performing Moliere or Shakespeare on stage."[57] While international copyright law might disagree with Ward's statement, the fact that cultural conventions differ in their treatment of copying suggests that the importance placed on literary originality is culturally and historically bound. In 2012, one of London's premier comedy clubs started a show entirely centered on joke stealing called *Joke Thieves*.[58] In this format, comedians are paired off. In the first half of the show, each comedian does her own set. In the second half, the comedians perform their own versions of the set the other performed earlier in the evening. In this way, the U.K. comedy community has repurposed stealing as a productive act. The show has been successful and is being developed for television and for performances outside the United Kingdom, although no plans exist for any U.S. productions yet. Literary originality in stand-up comedy is at most half the picture, and despite the premium on original content in the persona era, performance originality still distinguishes comedians from one another.

Again, if I'm making the case that seeking copyright protection is an ideologically significant choice and not a necessity for the comedy community, then I need to demonstrate not only the existence of other legal or institutional frameworks for performance but also that these alternative frameworks operate under or reproduce different ideological assumptions and value systems. One possibility for framing a comedian's performance originality comes from a branch of law known as right of publicity. J. Thomas McCarthy, author of the standard treatise on right of publicity, defines it as the right "of every human being to control the commercial use of his or her identity." It often deals with such issues as the use of celebrity likenesses for endorsement without consent, although fame is not a prerequisite for this protection.[59] As I mentioned above, Oliar and Sprigman dismiss the importance of protecting performance style. They suggest that right of publicity could "protect a comedian against an appropriation of his looks or voice, but not against joke stealing."[60] By suggesting that right of publicity's inability to protect content renders this right irrelevant to protecting comedians, Oliar and Sprigman privilege literary originality. They further point out that while right of publicity could protect "unique performative elements" of a comedian's performance, such elements do not vary significantly enough, according to them, among comedians to warrant consideration for protection.[61] Oliar and Sprigman's narrow focus echoes Bolles's contention that style only animates the content that constitutes a comedian's identity. While Bolles argues against accepting "the canard that jokes as a class are so uncreative as to be unworthy of standard legal protections," she implies that canard is true when applied to performance.[62] Bolles and Oliar and Sprigman agree that conventionality and lack of concrete fixedness should not impede copyright protection for content, yet they claim that these same issues render protection of style either impossible or insignificant. Not only can performance style distinguish between comedians, certain branches of the law—completely separate from copyright—could frame comedy and originality in a way that protects comedians from fraud, values performance style, and reproduces ideologies other than neoliberalism instead of maintaining a strict insistence on a market-like exchange of individually owned commodities.

Though none deals explicitly with comedy, a number of important U.S. intellectual property cases and law review articles suggest other possible frameworks for conceptualizing performance style. One key case for acknowledging performance style's vulnerability to imitation and right to protection is the case of *Chaplin v. Amador* in which Charlie Chaplin successfully sought an injunction against Charles Amador, another actor performing Chaplin's tramp character and calling himself "Charlie Aplin."[63] The issue in *Chaplin* was not Amador's use of Chaplin's mannerisms per se, but his deceiving the public into believing he was Chaplin and therefore creating "unfair competition in business."[64] The *Chaplin* court further takes care to make explicit the fact that a plaintiff's right of action in a case such as *Chaplin v. Amador* does not arise from intellectual property law.

> The case of plaintiff does not depend on his right to the exclusive use of the role, garb, and mannerisms, etc.; it is based upon *fraud and deception.* The right of action in such a case arises from the *fraudulent purpose and conduct of appellant and injury caused to the plaintiff thereby, and the deception to the public*, and it exists independently of the law regulating trademarks.[65]

In other words, Chaplin's style itself did not qualify, in the court's opinion, as copyrightable material or as a protected trademark, but he did have the right to protect himself from unfair competition in the form of fraud. His style was not property, but he could still be protected from others pretending to be him, a nuance that challenges many of Oliar and Sprigman's and Bolles's arguments about the need for performers to frame themselves as authors in order to validate their artistry.

In the case of *West v. Lind*, the court maintained that the *Chaplin* decision only applies in cases involving "fraud and deception."[66] The issue in this case was Marie Lind's use of the mannerisms, style, and name of "Diamond Lil," a character frequently portrayed by Mae West. The court upheld a previous denial of West's request for an injunction against Lind because, according to the court, Lind made no attempt to deceive the public into believing she was West or even a substitute for West. The *West* decision further exemplifies the court's unwillingness to view performance style—defined as consistent patterns of mannerisms, gestures, tones, etc., fixed in a pattern of performance—as either a protected form of "writing" under copyright or as a viable form of trademark. At first glance, West's inability to obtain an injunction against Lind may seem to be evidence against my argument that style can be legally protected as West's style was not in this case. But it's important to note here that West's case was framed as an issue of copyright and trademark, of intellectual property. West's failure functions less as evidence of a general vulnerability and more as proof that style cannot be treated legally as *property*. West only would have had a case if she could have convinced the court that Lind had been working as an impostor, trying to defraud the public into believing she was West. More to the point, considerations of style have the potential to move conversations away from ubiquitous market metaphors framing artists solely as content-producing authors and their work as exchangeable commodities. Critics such as Bolles presume and reproduce the inherit rightness of market-based models for creativity and artistic production by suggesting that total anarchy and vulnerability would result from reframing the way we think about originality and protection. Taken together, though, the West and Chaplin cases suggest an already extant model under which material can circulate that recognizes performers' rights to protection against fraud without framing them as author-owners of discrete units of content. The court decisions framed them as performers instead of defaulting to an understanding of all kinds of creative production as different versions of authorship.

Two more recent decisions regarding singers with distinctive voices have further cemented the tenet that performance styles can differ enough to be legally distinct. The first of these cases is *Midler v. Ford Motor Company*, in which Bette Midler sued Ford for using a sound-alike singer in a commercial. The case was complicated because Ford and its advertising firm had secured the rights to the song in the commercial from the songwriters. The advertising company, however, had been unable to procure Midler's version, so they hired someone specifically to sound like Midler to sing for the commercial. Midler's suit was successful, and she received damages. John T. Noonan, the circuit judge writing the opinion for *Midler v. Ford Motor Company*, again reasserts that performance style merits legal protections. He very clearly states that "when a distinctive voice of a professional singer is widely known and is deliberately imitated in order to sell a product, the sellers have appropriated what is not theirs."[67] Noonan also takes care in his decision to point out that not all imitations of a voice necessitate or even warrant legal action. Part of the issue here is whether an imitation shows itself to be an imitation or purports to be the original. Midler might not have received damages had Ford used a parody or self-aware imitation; the problem was in deceiving the public into thinking that Midler was singing the song in the commercial. Noonan asks why the defendants would have sought out Midler and then gone to great lengths to copy her voice as closely as possible if Midler's voice were not valuable. Noonan says that "what they sought was an attribute of Midler's identity. Its value was what the market would have paid for Midler to have sung the commercial in person."[68] Effectively, then, Noonan and the court recognized that Midler's performance style was recognizable, valuable, and therefore protectable.

This tenet was extended in the case of *Waits v. Frito-Lay, Inc.*, in which an advertiser working for Frito-Lay, Inc., frustrated by Tom Waits's long-standing policy of not singing for or allowing his music to appear in commercials, hired a Waits impersonator for a TV ad. Again, Waits sued and won the case, receiving compensation and damages. In his decision, Judge Boochever reaffirms that style must not be property in order to be protected against misappropriation in cases such as *Waits* and *Midler*, as otherwise it would be preempted by federal copyright law because the advertisers in both cases had secured the rights to the songs. Style, in these cases, was protected specifically because it was not property but was instead considered a recognizable element of the performer's identity and the performers had the right to be protected from fraudulent impostors, a right considered separately from property rights. Framing performance as performance rather than as property under an author-owner model opens up the possibility for understanding cultural production in modes other than the default of authorship. That the courts can handle such framing suggests that comedy's internal insistence on an authorship model and its market logic results not from a unilateral imposition of values from outside institutions.[69] Instead, the deep cultural logic of authorship and neoliberalism encourages comedians to presume both their roles as authors and their positioning as commodity producers and therefore to seek out institutional spaces, such as copyright law, where those definitions most readily obtain.

Even legal scholarship tends toward framing performance as property when such framing is not necessary. Legal scholar Cheryl Hodgson, discussing *Chaplin v. Amador* and a few related cases, argues that a performer's style, insofar as it instantiates an idea in a specific expression, could and should function as a kind of protected "writing" under statutory law, but that the courts have impeded such interpretation.[70] Hodgson points out that in cases involving artistic property, the courts have used the following question for a standard to determine whether or not infringement has occurred: would the average person, upon seeing the allegedly derivative work, mistake it for an instantiation of the original or product of the same originator?[71] She then goes on to argue that this same standard could easily apply to performance style: "if an ordinary viewer would mistake the style or voice for that of its true creator, then passing-off is present."[72] Whereas Hodgson argues that the issue of protecting style calls for legislative action to specify performance style's protection under copyright law, Jill A. Phillips argues that "a legal remedy for the simulation of a recorded performance is more appropriately fashioned from legal theories outside federal copyright law."[73] In addition to the barriers to copyrighting style presented by the difficulty in fixing it, Phillips argues that style should not be considered property because it is almost never truly original or unique, instead drawing on influences and participating in discourse with other artists. She points out that treating style as property under copyright law "would be tantamount to granting Picasso exclusive rights in cubism simply because his works were the first to popularly incorporate that style."[74] Though Phillips and Hodgson disagree about whether style should be considered property, they share certain assumptions about what kind of cultural producers that comedians and performers, more broadly, are. While Phillips is certainly right that style is a matter of influence, trends, and conventions, she perhaps underestimates the differences among imitation, influence, and fraudulent misappropriation. By locating style at the level of a movement such as cubism, she undersells the importance of individual variations within larger stylistic trends, variations that in many cases depend intimately on a performer's physical body and voice and are therefore better understood through the legal and cultural framework of performance itself rather than resorting to comparisons to property, theft, and commodity production. Arguments such as Hodgson's that try to fit performance style into a framework of property rights rely on the default to authorship as the ideal mode of cultural production and support neoliberal ideologies by commodifying even performers' identities, personas, or bodies.

Taken together, the *Waits*, *Midler*, *West*, and *Chaplin* cases show that the legal institutions in the United States can frame and understand performance as something other than property. In fact, protection for artists in these cases frequently depends upon these institutions avoiding such framing. So the notion put forth by Bolles, Oliar and Sprigman, and others that comedians, if they want protection, have to conceptualize their creative roles as authors within a production model predicated on commodity exchange simply does not hold up. In that light, reliance on copyright becomes an ideologically loaded choice. I am trying to show how not only legal systems but also artists' and artistic communities' ideas *about* legal systems privilege authorship. Comedians have other legal options for protection and have even exercised those options in the past. The law does not force the model of authorship on the comedy community. Instead, the comedy community chooses authorship and the particular means of protection it offers. By turning to copyright, the comedy community adopts a model of authorship with a strong literary originality component and a neoliberal ideological underpinning that frames all cultural production as necessarily individualistic and competitive. The distrust of a model of free circulation of material reflects neoliberalism's suspicion of any system not guided by a profit motive.

CONCLUSIONS

In a genre with a history of reusing material and a present so entrenched in convention that independent creation of nearly identical content seems inevitable, the institutional emphasis on literary originality and relative lacuna regarding performance originality creates anxiety as seen in Mencia's angry rant, the physical and public verbal attacks on perceived joke thieves, and even Murphy's playful, intentionally weak attempt to "steal" Mencia's material. Framing comedy exclusively through the lens of copyright creates the mistaken impression that the reuse of content necessarily constitutes stealing. Comedians even occasionally acknowledge this complexity of originality. One example of a more playful attitude toward comedians' using similar material appears at the beginning of *The Comedians of Comedy: Live at the*

El Rey, a filmed performance of the eponymous "Comedians of Comedy" tour featuring several of the most successful alternative comics working in America today. To start the show, alternative comedy legend Bob Odenkirk lays out the rules for the evening and explains the standards for judging that the comedians will face. He labels the fictitious rubric for the ersatz judging the Garofalo-Bennett alternative comic standards scale, and it has, Odenkirk says, a very specific and scientific method for distributing points to the comedians.

> Referring to your notes will get you three-point-five points. Talking about how you are referring to your notes while you refer to your notes: five-point-three points. And reading directly from your notes: eight-point-two points. References are scored as follows: Hong Kong Filmmakers: five points. French Filmmakers: three points. Seventies Blaxploitation filmmakers: twelve points. Michel Gondry: automatic win. Referring to your deeply ingrained antisocial behavior: eight points. Referring to your Zoloft or Xanax prescription: six points. . . . Impersonations are an automatic disqualification, except impersonations of your Korean grandmother, automatic win. And you get a TV special.[75] Anti-Bush comments, two points. . . . Pro-Kerry comments: irrelevant, never come into play. . . . Anti-Don Rumsfeld comments four points, pro-Don Rumsfeld comment, that's . . . never happened. Use of the phrase "who's with me?" in an arch manner: twelve points. Use of the phrase "who's with me?" in an honest, straightforward manner: automatic disqualification. Lastly, dropping microphone at the end of the act, seven points.[76]

Odenkirk then drops the microphone and leaves the stage before the core members of the tour do their routines.

Rhetorically, Odenkirk both calls for and challenges the notion of originality. By laying bare the conventions of stand-up, he invites the audience in on the joke that stand-up comedians often trade on certain stock structures and materials in their jokes. The well-informed audience member is rewarded with references to the shtick of specific comics such as Janeane Garofalo's well-known propensity for referring to her iconic notebook. Simultaneously, he gives viewers less steeped in stand-up comedy guides or cues for reading the acts that follow: when you see an iteration of *x*, that's comedy. Laugh. His bit is something of a challenge to the following comedians, almost daring them, albeit playfully, to fall into those categories. And they often do just that. Patton Oswalt devotes the last third of his set to jokes based on his deep knowledge of Hollywood trivia and pop culture, earning several dubiously rewarding points on Odenkirk's scale of predictability, yet he keeps the audience on his side. Odenkirk's rules reveal an understanding of the force convention exerts on creating original content. Odenkirk calls the other comedians out for repeatedly following the same formulas, but he does so in a way that acknowledges the essential nature of this practice.

In fact, performance often maintains originality by repurposing existing content. Andrew Davis, for instance, points out that burlesque comedians in the early twentieth century pulled from a common pool of freely circulating material. While "nobody 'owned' these routines," comedians would distinguish their performance from others through their original, unique styles.[77] Davis stresses the importance of understanding burlesque comedy as an oral tradition in which performers openly borrowed routines they had seen and that "a comic's originality lay not in coming up with new scenes, but in the way he put the scene over."[78] Persona-era comedy places the same pressure on a comedian to develop an original performance style, but discourages the circulation of material by demanding a simultaneous literary originality backed up by the stigma against stealing and the arguments over copyrightability. Commentators such as Oliar and Sprigman and especially Bolles assume that the appropriation of material represents stealing or a state of career and financial insecurity for comedians. Within comedy's own history, however, are plenty of examples where the free circulation of material in fact benefited comedians as a class. Comedians and legal scholars alike rely on assumptions about the importance of originality and thereby reproduce ideologically loaded "common sense" about commodity exchange and competition as the models on which all social and cultural interactions are based.

Part of the reason literary and performance originality come into conflict is that the latter often thrives by appropriating elements from the former. These dual notions of originality recall Diana Taylor's model of the archive and the repertoire as distinct and equally valid epistemological systems. Taylor argues that while the archive stores knowledge through fixed media or documents, the repertoire maintains itself through acts of transfer, where one social actor learns some piece of embodied knowledge by copying it from another: "Performances function as vital acts of transfer, transmitting social knowledge, memory, and a sense of identity."[79] The repertoire not only allows for but depends upon copying to circulate and thereby store knowledge even though the practices change slightly when transferred.[80] In the archive, however, at least in the United States in the twentieth century, one performer's copying another is presumed to be stealing unless proven otherwise, and the possibility of copying as a means of preserving cultural knowledge is seen as aberrant at best. So a performer could, in many cases, violate literary originality in exercising performance originality. The problem of separating originality of content and originality of style is not unique to stand-up comedy. Anthea Kraut, for instance, argues that throughout the twentieth century, copyright law failed to account for the intricacies of borrowing, appropriation, and other means of circulating steps among what she calls "black vernacular dancers" and that intellectual property's protection favors white mainstream constructions of authorship in its definitions of "fixed" expressions. Kraut also argues that performance's ephemerality neither renders it impervious to theft nor allows it to "escape circulation within a capitalist economy" because, even before copyright law made moves toward greater protections for dance, dancers created norms for self-regulation just as comedians did.[81] Just because copyright law—with its demand of fixed expressions and constructions of ownership based in literary models of authorship—does not always account well for performance does not mean that performance should be thought of as intangible and somehow free from market forces.[82] The idea of performance's ephemerality and naturally free circulation potentially renders performers vulnerable by overlooking a piece of career capital at least as important as content (be it choreography or written jokes): a performer's original style. The law's ability to recognize and protect style even while stressing its difference from copyrightable property suggests that conflating literary and performance originality offers no extra protection and could, in fact, place unnecessarily narrow limits on performance as a valid mode of cultural production separate from authorship. Authorship as the default mode of cultural production is archival and leads to institutional and cultural privileging of archival conventions storage, transfer, and ownership. This default neither protects comedians' performance styles nor frees them from market relationships. Instead, the ideological dominance of authorship rejects the repertoire as a valid episteme and favors those models of cultural production that adhere most closely to neoliberal assumptions about ownership and competition.

Perhaps the clearest example of an inverse relationship between performance originality and literary originality comes from *The Aristocrats*.[83] This film documents one hundred different comedians all telling the same legendary joke. The joke follows a basic structure: the comedian says that a man walks into a talent agent's office and says his family has a great act. The agent asks to see the act. The comedian then goes on to describe the most vile, offensive, disgusting act he can think of, combining scatological, sexual, and extremely violent elements. At the end of the act, the talent agent asks what they call the act, and the father proudly says, "The Aristocrats!" The intentionally anticlimactic punchline, based on the dissonance between the propriety suggested by the word "aristocrats" and the depravity described in the act, does not constitute the humor of the joke. The humor comes from the individual performance. *The Aristocrats* allegedly goes back at least to vaudeville, has become something of a contest among comedians to see who can be the filthiest, and was Johnny Carson's favorite joke. The documentary, however, shows that the joke not only pushes comedians' abilities to test the boundaries of good taste but also exhibits their individual performance styles. The comedians not only follow the same structure, but also rely on a relatively small set of topics to shock. Nevertheless, the takes on the joke vary wildly, from Bob Saget's grinning schoolboy glee to Steven Wright's deadpan and Drew Carey's genial joviality. Carey's style in telling the joke even extends to a flourish of his hands, a flourish apparently so tied to his style that other comedians ask the documentarians if Carey did it for them. Perhaps the most distinctive performance comes from Steven Banks, also known as Billy the Mime, who "tells" the joke by miming the most disgusting acts he can think of while maintaining a big smile on his black-and-white-painted face. The variety of the performances suggests that the constraint to use the same content forces these performers to rely on their unique performance styles to differentiate themselves from one another. Much of the anxiety expressed by both comedians and legal scholars regarding literary originality in comedy rests on the assumption that comedians live and die on their ability to create new material. Protecting comedians' exclusive right to use that material, such arguments run, provides comedians with the only means of maintaining their livelihood or promoting the art form. But *The Aristocrats* suggests not only that performance style can distinguish comedians at least as effectively, but also that suspending demands for literary originality can actually help throw into sharper contrast the things that distinguish comedians from one another.

Patton Oswalt recently posted a piece on his website addressing the issue of joke stealing.[84] Oswalt has been the victim of joke stealing by thieves both within and outside the stand-up community. In his letter, Oswalt claims that his real targets in his vocal, direct attacks on such thieves are not the thieves themselves. Instead, he claims such attacks actually target the critics and commentators who defend or excuse such thieves. He also targets arguments like CP's that suggest conventions render the very concept of originality moot. The problem, he says, is not with the thieves, but with the "goddamned *theorizing*." According to Oswalt, this theorizing stems from envy and devalues the hard work that comedians must do to generate new material. Because everyone wants to be funny and most people are not, those who are not use theorizing to trivialize stealing, thus denying the talent and hard work that go into creating comedy. Oswalt, in other words, suggests that any downplaying of literary originality is at its heart an attempt to validate the critic's own inability to be funny. Whatever my theorizing might or might not say about my insecurities as a performer, I do not think it denies other performers' originality or the importance of their originality. In fact, I part with the arguments of both CP and Oswalt precisely because they occupy extreme ends of an unnecessary dichotomy in ways that deny the importance of either literary or performance originality. CP, on one hand, totally dismisses original content. Oswalt, on the other, suggests that even questioning the universal importance of content originality is a petty and demeaning act of envy, an argument that renders performance originality secondary at best, aberrant at worst. Both, however, frame comedy in authorship's terms: discrete units of original content to be exchanged in a market. By trying to frame comedy through other legal, social, and cultural apparatuses, I seek to expose that the framework of authorship—appealing as it may be for the validity it seems to bestow—carries with it ideological assumptions that run counter to many comedians' professed beliefs. Further, the question of what apparatuses can frame comedy need not be a choice between ideals and pragmatism; other frameworks can also create environments where comedians can engage in a creative economy. In fact, given copyright's general move toward vesting control of intellectual property in corporations rather than individuals, comedians' pursuit of protection and validation through copyright might have unintended negative effects. Part of the allure of authorship lies in its seemingly privileged status among modes of cultural production, but inhabiting its structures may mean, ironically, exposing artists to greater exploitation by corporate interests such as CP.

In the cases in my first two chapters, authorship's position as the default mode of cultural production was reinforced by the law. Cultural assumptions about the law, ownership, and control continue to allow the Becketts, Albees, and Millers to limit the use of and even references to their texts. The courts in *Childress v. Taylor* and *Thomson v. Larson* assume individual authorship as the base case and require an extremely high burden of proof for collaboration. The cultural producers in these cases, even those who claim to resist capitalist structures, were also complicit in reproducing the ideologies supporting these structures, but a reading that is more sympathetic to the artists and perhaps slightly more paranoid might suggest that the law and cultural assumptions even force artists to reproduce these ideologies. The difference between the cases in the first two chapters and the comedians discussed in this chapter is that law and capitalist interests such as the megacorporation Comedy Partners actually create space for a model of exchange that does not depend on ownership or property rights yet still offers protection to artists. It is the legal scholars and the comedians themselves who insist on couching their cultural production within capitalist models of exchange. The default to authorship, then, is not simply a matter of law or powerful institutions imposing onto artists the assumptions that best maintain the hegemon. Comedians often default to the assumption that individuality, ownership, and originality just are the natural conditions of cultural production even when social institutions allow space for other models, including models proven viable by comedy's own history. The demand for originality unnecessarily problematizes the independent creation of similar material. The assumption that the only viable model for the production of stand-up comedy is one in which comedians are authors and in which jokes are discrete, meaningfully distinguishable units of capital to be protected ignores stand-up comedy's roots of a repertoire of shared material. The assumption that performance style cannot be protected rests on the assumption that only property can be protected, and this assumption, too, is factually inaccurate. Both assumptions serve to reproduce the self-obscuring ideological link between the celebration and protection of original creativity on one hand and the neoliberal assumption that profit motives and a competitive marketplace serve the greater good on the other. Proponents of the importance of demanding originality often resort to one of two major arguments. One is the need for a profit-incentive backed up by exclusive rights to use original content in order to ensure the promotion of the arts. The other argument suggests that the reuse of material necessarily constitutes copying and copying is, by common sense definition, wrong. Both arguments rhetorically embrace the Romantic celebration of the unique, original spirit of individual genius and simultaneously reproduce the arguably more cynical assumption that a profit incentive is a prerequisite for productivity. That stand-up comedians default to authorship in spite of their field's own tradition of a different mode of cultural production and in spite of legal and institutional space allowing for such a mode shows how deeply the default to authorship is entrenched as common sense and how effectively it reproduces neoliberal ideology.

NOTES

1. Carlos Mencia, *No Strings Attached: Live, Extended, and Uncensored*, directed by David Steinberg (2006; USA: Paramount), DVD; Bill Cosby, *Himself*, directed by Bill Cosby (2004; USA: 20th Century Fox), DVD. To watch the performances back to back, see nomencia, "Mencia Steals from Cosby?" March 20, 2007, available at http://www.youtube.com/watch?v=lCixAktGPlg (accessed October 16, 2013). See Dotan Oliar and Christopher Sprigman, "There's No Free Laugh (Anymore): The Emergence of Intellectual Property Norms and the Transformation of Stand-Up Comedy," *Virginia Law Review* 94, no. 8 (2008): 1795–96.
2. Comedy Partners, "Open Mic Fight" official rules, e-mail to George Pate, June 21, 2007.
3. Ibid.
4. Gene Perret, *Successful Stand-Up Comedy: Advice from a Comedy Writer* (New York: Samuel French, 1993).
5. U.S. Constitution, Section 1, Article 8.
6. Martha Woodmansee, "On the Author Effect: Recovering Collectivity," in *The Construction of Authorship: Textual Appropriation in Law and Literature*, ed. Woodmansee and Peter Jaszi (Durham, NC: Duke University Press, 1994), 27–28, quoted in Bracha, "The Ideology of Authorship Revisited: Authors, Markets, and Liberal Values in Early American Copyright," *Yale Law Journal* 118, no. 2 (2008): 195.
7. Bracha, "The Ideology of Authorship," 195.
8. Ibid., 190.
9. Ibid., 269. Bracha here draws on Eagleton's terminology of Ideology as a "motivated mystification." Calling originality a "mechanism of mystification" rather than an ideological apparatus has some advantages. For one, it suggests a less deterministic outcome. An ideological apparatus always produces the same result—the unilateral interpellation of the subject into the dominant ideology—whereas a mechanism of mystification suggests a means by which ideological assumptions are couched in the language of "common sense" or obscured in other ways that allow them to influence the direction of a discourse and a culture even when not being explicitly talked about. I have elected throughout to stick with ideological apparatus, however, because I also think the term "mystification" risks suggesting that individual agency and intention are behind ideological reproduction; ideological assumptions, I think, circulate in much more nuanced, complicated, and reciprocal ways than one party "mystifying" another.
10. Ibid., 267–68.

11. Eric E. Johnson, "Intellectual Property and the Incentive Fallacy," *Florida State University Law Review* 39 (2012): 623–79.
12. Ibid., 627.
13. Ibid., 625.
14. Even though the case of *Chaplin v. Amador* ultimately did not rest on intellectual property law, Judge Preston, who wrote the opinion, makes an important distinction between monopoly and protecting originality. As I'll discuss later, Amador had been ordered to stop copying Chaplin's performance style. Amador claimed that Chaplin was effectively being given an unlawful monopoly by having exclusive rights to perform the tramp character. In his decision, Preston counters that "the question of monopoly is in no way involved in this action. Plaintiff is not seeking to prevent the appellant, Charles Amador, from appearing in motion pictures, but only seeks to prevent him from imitating the plaintiff in such a way as to deceive the public and work a fraud upon the public and plaintiff." In other words, protection against imitation of an original performance style is less like a monopoly than it is like protection of the use of a brand. Just because Coca-Cola can stop me from bottling a product and selling it as "Coke" does not mean that Coca-Cola has a monopoly on making sodas. This makes protection of style more akin to trademark law, but as I argue here, it actually arises more out of laws against fraud. See 93 Cal. App. 362–63.
15. Dotan Oliar and Christopher Sprigman, "There's No Free Laugh (Anymore): The Emergence of Intellectual Property Norms and the Transformation of Stand-Up Comedy," *Virginia Law Review* 94, no. 8 (2008): 1787–1867, especially 1844.
16. For a good discussion of the ways in which comic material circulated with relative freedom among comedians in the late nineteenth and early twentieth centuries, see Andrew Davis, *Baggy Pants Comedy: Burlesque and the Oral Tradition* (New York: Palgrave, 2011).
17. Milton Berle, *Milton Berle's Private Joke File: Over 10,000 of His Best Gags, Anecdotes, and One-Liners* (New York: Three Rivers Press, 1989), xxiii. Berle may, however, be doing a little bit of self-justification here. Berle has often joked that he took material from others so often that he came to be known as "The Thief of Bad Gag." That the term "thief" would apply in a friendly, joking manner to a comedian who used that material other comedians had already used suggests a transitional moment between the attitudes of free circulation in the vaudeville and burlesque eras and of ownership and control in the persona era.
18. Oliar and Sprigman, "There's No Free Laugh," 1847.
19. Ibid., 1848. Perret also discusses this practice throughout his book, including his time working on writing teams for such comedians as Bob Hope.
20. Richard Zoglin, *Comedy at the Edge: How Stand-Up in the 1970s Changed America* (New York: Bloomsbury, 2008), 4. See also Oliar and Sprigman, 1848–50.
21. Zoglin, *Comedy at the Edge*, 13. John Limon offers another take on the reasons for Bruce's success. Limon's examination of stand-up comedy since the 1960s is based largely on psychoanalysis, so he suggests that Bruce tapped into a uniquely American version of phallic aggression and the Oedipal complex. See John Limon, *Stand-Up Comedy in Theory, or, Abjection in America* (Durham, NC: Duke University Press, 2000), 11–27. Elizabeth Bolles also points out that Bruce played a pivotal role in a formal revolution in solo comedy, a movement from a norm where comedians fired off a string of relatively short jokes to a norm where comedians delivered long monologues that often caused laughs to be more spaced out. Elizabeth Moranian Bolles, "Stand-Up Comedy, Joke Theft, and Copyright Law," *Tulane Journal of Technology and Intellectual Property* 14 (2011): 237–61, 249.
22. See Gerald Nachman, *Seriously Funny: The Rebel Comedians of the 1950s and 1960s* (New York: Pantheon, 2003), 6–7. Nachman firmly asserts that Sahl was the progenitor of the new movement in comedy.
23. Kyle Ryan, "The Surprisingly Subversive Album That Changed Stand-Up Comedy Forever," The AV Club, May 14, 2013, available at http://www.avclub.com/articles/the-surprisingly-subversive-album-that-changed-sta,97686/ (accessed May 16, 2013).
24. "The Sickniks," *Time*, July 13, 1959, Vol. 74, Issue 2, 44–45.
25. Robert Ruark, "Let's Nix the Sickniks," *Saturday Evening Post*, June 29, 1963: 38–39.

26. Of course, comedians' personas do not always match their identities in daily life, but audiences have largely come to expect that comedians on stage are espousing their "authentic" points of view.

27. Marah Eakin, review of "The Wack Album," The Lonely Island, The AV Club, June 11, 2013, available at http://www.avclub.com/articles/the-lonely-island-the-wack-album,98811/ (accessed June 11, 2013). The Lonely Island's early fame for their musical sketch comedy videos on the Internet pushed member Andy Samberg to stardom on *Saturday Night Live* and, more recently, *Brooklyn Nine-Nine*. The group often portrays themselves as nerds with a false sheen of hip. The album Eakin reviewed came out after Samberg and the group had become entrenched in pop culture.

28. In this chapter, I focus more on instances of stealing within the comedy community, that is, instances where one comedian steals a joke from another comedian to use on stage. A number of cases also exist in which some outside force appropriates a comedian's jokes without permission or compensation. Such suits include Jeff Foxworthy's suing T-shirt manufacturers using "You might be a redneck" jokes and Jay Leno and NBC's suing joke book publishers. For a good summary of such cases, see Bolles, "Stand-Up Comedy, Joke Theft, and Copyright Law," 239–41.

29. Oliar and Sprigman, "There's No Free Laugh," 1812–17.

30. One of the many news outlets reporting on accusations that Noah was a joke thief put it this way: "As if newly announced *Daily Show* host Trevor Noah didn't have enough bad press to deflect with the internet digging up his old tweets, yesterday Canadian comedian Russell Peters told a Singapore news outlet that Noah is also a joke thief, and had stolen his material in the past." This report, like many others, suggests that stealing jokes stands shoulder to shoulder with racism and sexism in terms of bad practices. It's worth noting that Peters later revealed his accusations were a prank although another comedian, David Kau, has also accused Noah of joke theft. Stacey Ritzen, "Russell Peters Admitted His Comments about Trevor Noah Stealing His Jokes Were 'A Prank,'" *Uproxx*, April 8, 2015.

31. Oliar and Sprigman, "There's No Free Laugh," 1817, from an interview with an anonymous comedian.

32. Oliar and Sprigman, "There's No Free Laugh," 1796.

33. Ibid.

34. See Bolles, "Stand-Up Comedy, Joke Theft, and Copyright Law," 244–52.

35. *Nichols v. Universal Pictures Corp.*, 45 F.2d 119, 121 (2d Cir. 1930).

36. Oliar and Sprigman, "There's No Free Laugh," 1802–4.

37. Ibid., 1803.

38. Ibid., 1798.

39. Ibid., 1808–9.

40. Bolles, "Stand-Up Comedy, Joke Theft, and Copyright Law."

41. Ibid., 239.

42. Ibid., 251. Bolles's arguments all presume the correctness of the incentive argument, the idea that without rules to protect their exclusive financial incentives, comedians would not create new material. Such an argument clearly reproduces authorship as the default mode of cultural production.

43. Ibid., 258.

44. deadfrogcomedy, "Whose Joke Is It? Carlos Mencia? D.L Hughley? George Lopez?" February 19, 2007, http://www.youtube.com/watch?v=kPuu_VE7KOA (accessed October 16, 2013). See Oliar and Sprigman, "There's No Free Laugh," 1804–5.

45. Oliar and Sprigman, "There's No Free Laugh," 1805.

46. Ibid., 1826.

47. One of the landmark cases in independent creation is *Selle v. Gibb* in which Ronald Selle, a part-time musician, accused Maurice, Robin, and Barry Gibb, better known as the Bee Gees, of stealing his song "Let It End" in creating their hit "How Deep Is Your Love." Selle brought in musicologists and provided analytics to try to prove that the songs were so similar that copying was the only possible reason despite his lack of evidence that the Bee Gees had access to the song. The Bee Gees provided testimony, corroborated by others and unchallenged by Selle, that they had not only never heard Selle's song but would have had no way to access it

considering they had never before heard of him and his song was not distributed or played on the radio. The jury in this case found in favor of the plaintiff, suggesting that the default to authorship and its attendant demands for originality ideologically permeate the culture as "common sense." The Bee Gees made a motion for the court to offer a judgment notwithstanding the jury verdict in their favor, a motion which the court granted. The court decision heavily implies that Selle's lack of evidence of access might not have been sufficient if not for the Bee Gees' "uncontradicted and corroborated testimony of non-access." Essentially, then, the Bee Gees had to create a positive case for their not having heard it. Selle's inability to offer proof of anything beyond inference of access in the face of Gibb's arguments toward proving nonaccess ultimately led the courts to consider this a case of independent creation. The appeals court decision which upheld the district court's finding explicitly states that similarity alone is necessary but not sufficient circumstantial evidence for inference of access and establishes a threshold that the works must be at least sufficiently similar and that the original work must have at least been *available* to the alleged infringer. In *Selle v. Gibb*, Selle could not prove the availability of his song to the Bee Gees. In comedy, given the nature of the open-mic circuits and especially the ubiquity of camera-phones and YouTube, proving availability of the similar content to the alleged copier becomes so easy that inferences of access are almost a given in many cases of similarity, leaving comedians accused of copying in genuine cases of independent creation in the nearly impossible position of positively proving nonaccess. See 741 F.2d 896 and 567 F. Supp. 1173.

48. Ibid., 1814.

49. My thinking on this issue of different kinds of replication is deeply indebted to Nelson Goodman's *Languages of Art*. Goodman separates all art forms into two categories based on whether or not the distinction between a copy and an original is significant within a given form. Nelson Goodman, *Languages of Art* (London: Oxford University Press, 1968). See also Jerrold Levinson, "Autographic and Allographic Art Revisited," in *Music, Art, and Metaphysics: Essays in Philosophical Aesthetics* (Ithaca, NY: Cornell University Press, 1990), 89–106. Levinson points out that if someone played the notes of Beethoven's Fifth before Beethoven wrote it, then, according to Goodman, he would have played Beethoven's Fifth even though it had not been written. Where Levinson sees this paradox as a problem for Goodman's argument, I take it as evidence of two distinct modes of sameness. The pre-Beethoven Fifth is identical to Beethoven's Fifth but not a historical copy of it.

50. Saying two jokes are identical is not the same as saying they are tokens of the same type. Types are sortal concepts and sort members into classes according, in part, to a production history. Saying jokes are identical means they share an identity. This shared identity is still governed by convention but operates independently of production history. When I say two jokes share an identity or are identical, then, I mean that there exists a set of conventions for identifying jokes (the structure-topic combination) under which two jokes share all of their defining elements. In determining identity, the production history of the joke is irrelevant. In other words, the pre-Beethoven Fifth in my note above would not have been a token of the Fifth-type at the time of its performance because the Fifth-type did yet not exist as a category into which one could sort that performance, even though the thing performed would have shared an identity with all tokens of the Fifth-type according to the conventions of musical notation. The pre-Beethoven Fifth and performances of Beethoven's Fifth could then be said to be identical but not copies of one another in the same way that two jokes could be identical but not copies.

51. Jane C. Lee, "Upstaging the Playwright: The Joint Authorship Entanglement between Dramaturgs and Playwrights," *Loyola of Los Angeles Entertainment Law Journal* 75 (1998): 101–2.

52. See n.27.

53. See the career of Andy Kaufman.

54. veryplain, "Mencia Steals Yet Again," May 21, 2007, available at https://www.youtube.com/watch?v=YFCy1syW8Nc (accessed June 7, 2013).

55. *I Am Comic*, directed by Jordan Brady (2010; USA: Monterey Video and IFC Films), DVD.

56. Section 115 of the 1976 Copyright Act requires copyright holders of nondramatic musical works to license others to record and distribute covers of the holder's works after the holder has distributed the original work and provided the covering artist notifies the holder in advance, pays a fee, and does not change the "fundamental character" of the work. Such a license is called a statutory or compulsory license. Though comedy obviously does not qualify as a "nondramatic musical composition," the statute here at least points to the law's recognition that some limitations on copyright holders' ability to limit content circulation and reuse might be counterproductive. Title 17 of the U.S. code covers copyright law and can be found in its entirety at http://www.copyright.gov/title17/ . For an in-depth examination of the complicated relationship between copyright law, constructions of ownership, and hip-hop, see Richard Schur, *Parodies of Ownership: Hip-Hop Aesthetics and Intellectual Property Law* (Ann Arbor: University of Michigan Press, 2009).

57. Quoted in John St. Godard, "Stealing Jokes Isn't Funny, Unless Your Audience Doesn't Care," *The Gazette (Montreal)*, July 22, 2011, available at http://www2.canada.com/montrealgazette/news/movies/story.html?id=cd84aa6c-9de8-45e8-bf3c-7283d7ee4b10&p=1 (accessed October 16, 2013).

58. www.jokethieves.com. While this model does suggest the potential of copying as a generative, productive, or creative act, the show's choice to call itself *Joke Thieves* still suggests that copying or circulating materials is somehow invalid or deviant unless wryly authorized in this way. The show's title reproduces the very assumptions about originality and authorship that its format potentially resists.

59. J. Thomas McCarthy, *The Rights of Publicity and Privacy*, Vol. 1 (St. Paul, MN: West Group, 1999), vii. For an account of the development of right of publicity from a cultural studies lens, more grounded in its impact on cultural production than the technical intricacies of the law, see Jane M. Gaines, *Contested Culture: The Image, the Voice, and the Law* (Chapel Hill: University of North Carolina Press, 1991).

60. Oliar and Sprigman, "There's No Free Laugh," 1809.

61. Ibid.

62. Bolles, "Stand-Up Comedy, Joke Theft, and Copyright Law," 239.

63. 93 Cal. App. 358. See also Cheryl Hodgson, "Intellectual Property—Performer's Style—A Quest for Ascertainment, Recognition and Protection [notes]," *Denver Law Journal* 52, no. 2 (1975): 561–94, especially 569–70; and Gaines, *Contested Culture*, 105–43.

64. 93 Cal. App. 363.

65. Ibid. Emphasis original.

66. 186 Cal. App. 2d 563. The *West* court's interpretation that style is only protected in cases of fraud was further upheld in 1980 in the case of *KGB, Inc. v. Giannoulas* 101 Cal. App. 3d 323.

67. 849 F. 2d 460. See also Jill A. Phillips, "Performance Rights: Protecting a Performer's Style [notes]," *Wayne Law Review* 37, no. 3 (1991): 1683–98.

68. 849 F. 2d 460.

69. 978 F. 2d at 1100. See also Auslander, *Liveness*, 142–44, including n. 50.

70. Supra n. 57.

71. Hodgson, "Performer's Style," 573.

72. Ibid., 583.

73. Jill A. Phillips, "Performance Rights: Protecting a Performer's Style [notes]," *Wayne Law Review* 37, no. 3 (1991): 1685.

74. Phillips, "Performance Rights," 1694. The same could be applied to content. If I write in short, pared-down sentences, I shouldn't have to pay the Hemingway estate.

75. Here Odenkirk is referring to Margaret Cho, who achieved great commercial success with a stand-up act which prominently featured impersonations of her Korean grandmother. I read this as a move to distance the Comedians of Comedy from mainstream, popular comedy while getting a laugh at its expense. As in rock music, nothing is less hip in the stand-up comedy world than success.

76. *The Comedians of Comedy: Live at the El Rey*, starring Patton Oswalt, Brian Posehn, and Maria Bamford (Starz, 2007), DVD.

77. Davis, *Baggy Pants Comedy*, ix.

78. Ibid., 10.
79. Diana Taylor, *The Archive and the Repertoire: Performing Cultural Memory in the Americas* (Durham, NC: Duke University Press, 2003), 2.
80. Ibid., 20.
81. Kraut, "Stealing Steps," 188.
82. Oliver Gerland argues that even if performance is ephemeral, this fact only makes it more attractive to capitalist interests because continual disappearance renders piracy more difficult; Gerland, "From Playhouse to P2P Network," 94. For a broader look at the relationship between authorship, ideology, and copyright law, see Oren Bracha, "The Ideology of Authorship Revisited."
83. *The Aristocrats*, dir. Penn Jillette and Paul Provenza (2005; Santa Monica, CA: Lionsgate, 2005), DVD. I feel obligated, even in this context, to mention that this film is extremely offensive in almost any way one could imagine. The jokes are by most standards disgusting, disturbing, racist, sexist, and push the line even for comedians who, as a group, tend to get a good deal out of mileage out of pushing boundaries.
84. Patton Oswalt, "A Closed Letter to Myself," Patton Oswalt Official Website, June 14, 2013, available at http://www.pattonoswalt.com/index.cfm?page=spew&id=167 (accessed June 14, 2013).

Conclusion

The Return of the Author

Authorship's role as the default mode of cultural production continues to expand and deepen, even for nonliterary modes of production. The regulation of cultural production, carried out ever more by ideology and "common sense" than by actual codes and laws, continues to move toward the ideal of total ownership. Even as the idea of the death of the author becomes a kind of common sense itself in academic discourse, the author's power and control continue to expand and apply not just to traditional authors but to all creators of cultural products. The late twentieth-century ideology of authorship normalizes cultural production toward reproducing capitalist means of production, and those artists who claim their roles as authors, even when they do so in order to assert their aesthetic power and its attendant ability to critique the status quo, necessarily reproduce capitalism's underlying assumptions and structures.

As seen in Miller's actual power to limit the Wooster Group's ability to produce a response to his play and in the community norms governing originality demands in stand-up comedy, this is more than an issue of theory. The ideology of authorship imposes real consequences, often in excess of the law even while it cites the law as its source of validity. As the set of extralegal powers that artists, critics, and even some legal scholars associate with copyright continue to expand and authorship becomes more and more entrenched as the default mode of cultural production, areas of theater and performance that have traditionally posited themselves as revolutionary or resistant to dominant ideologies are starting to embrace copyright and authorship. Performance art has long been seen as a form particularly suited to revolutionary or resistant politics. But Marina Abramović now even sells the rights to reperform her pieces based on detailed, prescriptive instructions.[1] Given that many of her pieces at their base simply involve certain configurations of bodies and spaces, what effects might the logic of total ownership and authorship have, especially when coupled with increasingly broad similarity standards? In what circumstances could one person sitting across from another violate Abramović's rights to *The Artist Is Present*?[2] Jay-Z recently approached Abramović for permission to adapt this seminal piece, in which she sits opposite the viewer, for a video shoot for his song "Picasso Baby."[3] But Jay-Z's video bears very little resemblance to *The Artist Is Present*. He simply performs the song directly to a seated audience member in an art gallery. Why does he need Abramović's permission for this? Does she own, even in an extralegal sense, the action of being opposite someone in a physical space? She's certainly not the first to do such a thing. Is Abramović not violating Samuel Beckett's intellectual property in *Ohio Impromptu*, a play featuring two characters sitting opposite? Entering into the logic of total ownership might mean accepting such consequences. If I'm eating dinner across from my wife in a restaurant, is that considered too similar a public performance? This might seem a slippery slope argument of the most fallacious kind, but I use it to make a point. Performance art, which has always shared and tested blurred-at-best borders with the "real world" and everyday life, is starting to enter into the discourse of authorship and ownership. A genre whose history is largely based on resisting control and hegemonic ideologies threatens to extend the scope of those very ideologies and their attendant power structures further than ever before. Furthermore, framing lived, embodied experience as a work of performance in a predominantly neoliberal ideological environment frames our daily performances of self as commodities subject to ownership that is, by its nature, open to exchange. Amelia Jones, discussing the recent practice of reperforming pieces of performance art and the questions that practice raises about performance and commodification, points to those "younger-generation artists" who "[resist] the simplistic notion of any commodification as necessarily damaging to progressive political goals" and who "have recognized and begun to negotiate the structures of capital and the related structures of repetition and reiteration that underlie any performance project."[4] Commodification may not damage all progressive political goals, but commodification does beget commodification. Commodification is inextricable from capitalist ideological assumptions about labor, markets, competition. Artists may put politically progressive messages into commodified performances, but by buying into commodification, even questioning it from within, they help reproduce its ideological underpinnings. And "[negotiating] the structures of capital" always necessarily reproduces and props up those structures. Jones in particular admires work that, "in its self-reflexive acknowledgement of the art world as a marketplace, at least proposes possible ways of navigating these structures without fully succumbing to the political evacuations of the full-blown spectacle."[5] While such work may call attention to and allow critique of the marketplace, it also functions within the marketplace and therefore inevitably helps the marketplace continue to function. I do not mean to suggest that artists have a responsibility to shun the marketplace or even that the marketplace is antithetical to art; I only mean to point out that anticapitalist commodities, by functioning as commodities, support the reproduction of capitalism and its attendant ideologies.

Abramović's willful adoption of the role of author has consequences beyond her personal shock of being treated like a broker rather than an artist after intentionally entering a competitive marketplace. More broadly, her taking on this role reveals the deep, inextricable relationship between the logic of commodities and the marketplace and capitalism. It is impossible to have an efficaciously anticapitalist commodity, because commodities themselves support the functioning of capitalism. Even if a commodity has a revolutionary or radically anticapitalist message, such a message is only a brand, a marketing tool to recommend it to a particular sector of buyers. Its functioning as a commodity renders its content moot; by entering into the competition and exchange of capitalism, it supports capitalism's functioning, even implicitly argues for capitalism's natural rightness as the mode for all cultural production, social interaction, and political discourse. Slavoj Žižek argues that "today, authentic emancipatory politics has to define itself through its active opposition to the universe of the capital."[6] The point of this study is not—as Žižek's is—to advocate for such an emancipatory politics, nor is it to suggest that artists such as Abramović have some kind of responsibility to participate in such politics. But Žižek's argument suggests a corollary that sums up one of my major conclusions: the absolute inseparability of participating in commodity exchange and supporting capitalist structures and ideologies. No amount of rhetoric or anticapitalist content will change the fact that treating all cultural production as some outgrowth of the model of authorship supports the reproduction of capitalism and further ingrains its ideology as "common sense." The adoption of the role of author is always an argument in favor of capitalism and neoliberalism.

Copyright law, the constitutional justification for which is the promotion of the arts and sciences, does actually come to limit artists' ability to create as proponents of reform such as Lessig and Vaidhyanathan say it does. This limitation, however, comes not only from the vesting of a control over a great amount of content in the hands of a relatively small number of powerful parties, but also from assumptions, fully adopted by even many of those artists not in these positions of power, that creativity means isolated, ex nihilo creation of something and that the most important outcomes of creation are ownership and control. In the United States, starting around 1960, just when revolutionary and radically anticapitalist practices and rhetorics start to take off again, these assumptions lead to a number of reactionary reassertions of neoliberal ideology as common sense. They lead to playwrights shutting down productions of their own plays, even acting against their own political views, out of a sense of responsibility to maintain ownership. They lead to the mistrust of collaboration and the continual reassertion that real art only emanates from a single, unique consciousness. They lead to prohibitions against freely circulating material, even when that material is revitalized at each iteration by addition or translation into a new style. And they always lead to the reproduction of neoliberal ideology as a kind of "common sense," an assumption that erases itself as an assumption. Artists have internalized the logic of the market and its controls so fully that they self-impose limitations far beyond those imposed by official institutional structures. And all of this limiting and controlling is done in the name of protecting a Romantic version of artistry even as it interpellates works as commodities and artists as brands. A world without such limitations on art is not necessarily an intrinsically better or more desirable world. My point here is not to advocate for a dismantling of any structures or to criticize laws or artists' attitudes. Instead, my point is to show the deep contradiction built into the rhetoric of authorship, the ways in which it uses promises of protection and artistic freedom to limit those very things in the name of reproducing neoliberal ideology through all modes of cultural production.

My point has been to expose the dissonance between attempts to decentralize the author on one hand and the return to authorship on the other. This return to authorship is not a return to the way things were. Instead, the return to authorship involves adapting rhetorically or superficially antiauthorial modes of production to fit within the structure of authorship. Playwrights exhort anticommercial rhetoric while simultaneously going to great lengths to maintain and even expand their exclusive commercial interests in the uses of their plays. Collaboration and communal living become marketing tools for an individually authored, fixed text commodity rather than an authentically new mode of production. Stand-up comedy's traditions and practices come to be seen as aberrant in the name of incentivizing originality of content and promoting competition in a marketplace over circulation within a repertoire.

Institutions and cultural conventions create roles that support market-based models of cultural production but appeal to artists on their own terms. An artist such as Beckett or Albee may preach against commodification and commercialism but embrace a role of ownership in the name of protecting the integrity of his works. This embrace and vehement defense of ownership in turn supports the cultural hegemony of capitalism, inscribing capitalist structures as ostensibly neutral common sense assumptions. Capitalist structures make room for dissenting voices by placing them in positions that seem powerful, but ultimately artists' accepting these positions goes much further toward supporting dominant hierarchies and structures than their rhetoric goes toward resisting them. The collaborative theater groups of the '60s understood that resistant rhetorics could easily become co-opted by capitalist structures and lose efficacy and therefore tried to create new modes of production fundamentally separate from capitalism. Ironically, *The Serpent* became a perfect example of such appropriation, reducing revolutionary, countercultural rhetoric to a marketing tool supporting an individually authored commodity competing in a capitalist marketplace. Stand-up comedians default to assumptions about individuality, originality, and ownership even when not pressured to do so by the law or other cultural institutions and even when that default leads to an invalidation of almost a century of comedy's own traditional practices and even when the law offers other avenues for protection. The dominant structures and ideologies seem to invite artists into superficially resistant positions for which those systems can account. "You can say whatever you like about capitalism," these structures say. "In fact, the capitalist system will even reward you for decrying capitalism by giving you exclusive control over your anticapitalist sentiments. You can then use that exclusive control to treat your ideas as commodity on a competitive marketplace with other radically anticapitalist thinkers like yourself."

The three elements of authorship work in concert to suit neoliberal ideology to the anticommercial rhetoric of Romanticism. The model of authorship suggests that a cultural producer needs to be an individual genius, meaning her genius is a direct result of her unique identity. Because the creator is a unique individual genius, she creates wholly original works. The works are like no other works because the creator is like no other creator. Derivative works are necessarily lesser according to this model because they are not truly expressions of the artist's unique individuality and therefore, by definition, not art. Because a truly original and worthwhile work of art can be created by one and only one individual and the identity of the artwork is intimately tied to the artist's identity, the creator possesses intrinsic rights of ownership and control over the works that can only be hers. At each point, this model fits with Romantic celebration of individualism, but it also supports the underlying assumptions of neoliberalism, namely that a competitive marketplace that incentivizes individuals to create new products by ensuring their exclusive control over products they create is the most effective means of ensuring productivity and promoting economic growth. The Romantic ideal of authorship necessarily promotes ownership based on property rights rather than labor. Performance and theater artists in the late twentieth century often adopt the ideals of Romanticism while simultaneously claiming to resist capitalism, but one cannot have one's cake and eat it too, in this case, because the very underpinnings of Romantic authorship as the default mode of cultural production are the same as the underpinnings of capitalism. Supporting authorship necessarily means reproducing neoliberal ideologies.

In no way is anything I've written throughout this work meant to suggest that authorship is intrinsically "bad" or that postdramatic or performance-centric modes of cultural production are naturally and universally "good" or even more desirable. When I say that one attempt or another to resist authorship or to foreground radically different modes of production and consumption has "failed" I do not mean that in any kind of global way, as though the dismantling or dethroning of authorship is the *telos* of performance and theater history's progress. These attempts at resistance or reinvention fail locally and according to their own terms, relative to the goals they set for themselves in terms of their revolutionary practices or anticapitalist rhetoric. I also do not mean to suggest that all attempts to resist dominant ideologies always end up fully reproducing authorship and the dominant, hegemonic ideologies authorship supports. Instead, I have tried to expose the difficulties of activating resistant ideologies through practices of cultural production. I also wanted to examine the stakes involved when revolutionary or radical reinventions of cultural production end up reproducing the very hierarchies and ideologies their work seeks to resist. The consequences of these failures are more complex than simple unfulfilled intentions. *The Serpent*, for instance, not only fails to accomplish its goal of modeling radical or revolutionary structures of production and consumption but also interpellates a superficially radical, revolutionary cultural object within a capitalist system. Anticapitalist rhetoric itself becomes commodified. The revolutionary form becomes a part of and therefore ensures the continuation of the very structures it was resisting. This ability of capitalist structures to reappropriate and market their own resistance makes activating truly new structures or hierarchies of production incredibly difficult. For now, at least, authorship maintains its place as the goal toward which theatrical and performance-based modes of production strive by emulating its practices and making claims to their own validity relative to it.

NOTES

1. Amelia Jones, "'The Artist Is Present': Artistic Re-enactments and the Impossibility of Presence," *TDR* 55 (2011): 35.

2. Abramović has not yet registered any of her performance pieces with the U.S. Copyright Office. That she licenses the rights to use them anyway is a perfect example of how the logic of authorship and the ideal of total ownership grants powerful players in artistic fields abilities, often extralegal but no less real and powerful, to limit others' ability to create.

3. The coverage of this story alternated between celebrating a renewed relationship between high art and pop and claiming that this marked the end of performance art's legitimacy, with plenty of references to Ai Weiwei and Yoko Ono. For an illustrative though far from exhaustive sampling of this coverage, see Jonathan Jones, "Jay-Z and Marina Abramović Rekindle Art's Relationship with Pop," *The Guardian*, July 11, 2013, http://www.theguardian.com/artanddesign/jonathanjonesblog/2013/jul/11/jay-z-marina-abramovic-art-pop; and, on the other side, Jillian Steinhauer, "Jay-Z Raps at Marina Abramović, or the Day Performance Art Died," *Hyperallergic*, July 10, 2013, http://hyperallergic.com/75293/. Another wrinkle in this

story came when Abramović stated in an interview that she was extremely dissatisfied with her working relationship with Jay-Z and that she felt she had been used for a quick branding gimmick, which may be one of the unforeseen consequences of entering into the logic of the marketplace: if you seek commodity status to protect yourself you may find yourself treated as a commodity. See Kolja Reichert, "'I Will Never Do It Again': Marina Abramovic Is Disappointed by Jay-Z," *Spike Art Magazine*, May 18, 2015, http://www.spikeartmagazine.com/en/articles/i-will-never-do-it-again.

4. Jones, "The Artist Is Present," 36.
5. Ibid., 37.
6. Slavoj Žižek, *First as Tragedy, Then as Farce* (New York: Verso, 2009), 131, n. 35.

Bibliography

Albee, Edward. *Stretching My Mind* (New York: Carroll and Graf, 2005).

Althusser, Louis. *Lenin and Philosophy and Other Essays*. Trans. Ben Brewster (New York: Monthly Review Press, 1971).

The Aristocrats. Directed by Penn Jillette and Paul Provenza. Santa Monica: Lionsgate, 2005.

Artaud, Antonin. *The Theater and Its Double*. Trans. Mary Caroline Richards (New York: Grove Press, 1958).

Auslander, Philip. *Liveness: Performance in a Mediatized Culture* (New York: Routledge, 1999).

Barthes, Roland. *Image-Music-Text*. Trans. Stephen Heath (New York: Hill and Wang, 1977).

Beckett, Samuel. *Collected Shorter Plays* (New York: Grove Press, 1984).

———. *Endgame and Act Without Words* (New York: Grove Press, 1958).

Berle, Milton. *Milton Berle's Private Joke File: Over 10,000 of His Best Gags, Anecdotes, and One-Liners* (New York: Three Rivers Press, 1989).

Bigsby, Christopher, ed. *The Cambridge Companion to Arthur Miller*, second edition (Cambridge: Cambridge University Press, 2010).

Bolles, Elizabeth Moranian. "Stand-Up Comedy, Joke Theft, and Copyright Law." *Tulane Journal of Technology and Intellectual Property* 14 (2011).

Bottoms, Stephen, ed. *The Cambridge Companion to Edward Albee* (Cambridge: Cambridge University Press, 2005).

Bracha, Oren. "The Ideology of Authorship Revisited: Authors, Markets, and Liberal Values in Early American Copyright." *Yale Law Journal* 118, no. 2 (2008).

Bradshaw, James. "Plumbing a Beckett Play, Finding It Flush with Obstacles." *Globe and Mail* 29.

Buckalew, Faye. "Joint Authorship in the Second Circuit: A Critique of the Law in the Second Circuit Following Childress v. Taylor and as Exemplified in Thomson v Larson." *Brooklyn Law Review* 64 (1998).

Byron, Mark, ed. *Samuel Beckett's Endgame* (New York: Rodopi, 2007).

Chaikin, Joseph. *The Presence of the Actor* (New York: Atheneum, 1980).

Coco, William, et al. "The Open Theatre [1963-1973]: Looking Back." *Performing Arts Journal* 7, no. 3 (1983).

Cody, Gabrielle and Rebecca Schneider, eds. *Re:direction: A Theoretical and Practical Guide* (New York: Routledge, 2002).

The Comedians of Comedy: Live at the El Rey. Starring Patton Oswalt, Brian Posehn, and Maria Bamford. Starz, 2007.

Davis, Andrew. *Baggy Pants Comedy: Burlesque and the Oral Tradition* (New York: Palgrave, 2011).

Davis, J. Madison and Philip C. Kolin, eds. *Critical Essays on Edward Albee* (Boston: G.K. Hall and Co., 1986).

Derrida, Jacques. *Limited Inc.* Trans. Samuel Weber (Evanston, IL: Northwestern University Press, 1988).

Dilks, Stephen John. "Portraits of Beckett as a Famous Writer." *Journal of Modern Literature* 29, no. 4 (2006).

———. *Samuel Beckett in the Literary Marketplace* (Syracuse, NY: Syracuse University Press, 2011).

Duncan, Raymond. "Waiting for No Woman." *The Herald*, July 27, 1998.

Eagleton, Terry. *Criticism and Ideology: A Study in Marxist Literary Theory* (London: NLB, 1976).

———. *Ideology: An Introduction* (New York: Verso, 1991).

———. *Literary Theory: An Introduction* (Minneapolis: University of Minnesota Press, 1996).

Foucault, Michel. *Aesthetics, Methods, and Epistemology*. Ed. James Faubion (New York: The New Press, 1998).

Fox, Paulette S. "Preserving the Collaborative Spirit of American Theater: The Need for a 'Joint Authorship Default Rule' in Light of the Rent Decision's Unanswered Question." *Cardozo Arts and Entertainment Law Journal* 19 (2001).

Gaines, Jane M. *Contested Culture: The Image, the Voice, and the Law* (Chapel Hill: The University of North Carolina Press, 1991).

Gerland, Oliver. "From Playhouse to P2P Network: The History and Theory of Performance under Copyright Law in the United States." *Theatre Journal* 59 (2007).

Gontarski, S. E. "Reinventing Beckett." *Modern Drama* 49, no. 4 (2006).

———. "Editing Beckett." *Twentieth Century Literature* 41, no. 2 (1995).

Goodman, Nelson. *Languages of Art* (London: Oxford University Press, 1968).

Gramsci, Antonio. *Selections from Cultural Writings*. Ed. David Forgacs and Geoffrey Nowell-Smith. Trans. William Boelhower (Cambridge, MA: Harvard University Press, 1985).

Grant, Mark N. *The Rise and Fall of the Broadway Musical* (Boston: Northeastern University Press, 2004).

Gussow, Mel. "Critic's Notebook; Enter Fearless Director, Pursued by Playwright." *New York Times*, January 3, 1985.

Harding, James M. and Cindy Rosenthal, eds. *Restaging the Sixties: Radical Theaters and Their Legacies* (Ann Arbor: University of Michigan Press, 2006).

Harmon, Maurice, ed. *No Author Better Served: The Correspondence of Samuel Beckett and Alan Schneider* (Cambridge, MA: Harvard University Press, 1998).

Harvey, David. *A Brief History of Neoliberalism* (New York: Oxford University Press, 2007).

———. *The Enigma of Capital* (New York: Oxford University Press, 2010).

Himself. Directed by Bill Cosby. USA: 20th Century Fox, 2004.

Hodgson, Cheryl. "Intellectual Property—Performer's Style—A Quest for Ascertainment, Recognition and Protection [notes]." *Denver Law Journal* 52, no. 2 (1975).

Hood, Woodrow. "Please, Steal My Art: Does Intellectual Property Law Hinder Creativity? Or, Can We Stop Talking about Intellectual Property Law and Talk about Creative Practice Rights?" *Wake Forest Journal of Business and Intellectual Property Law* 12 (2012).

I Am Comic. Directed by Jordan Brady. USA: Monterey Video and IFC Films, 2010.

Jameson, Frederic. *Postmodernism, Or, The Cultural Logic of Late Capitalism* (Durham, NC: Duke University Press, 1991).

Jaszi, Peter and Martha Woodmansee, eds. *The Construction of Authorship: Textual Appropriation in Law and Literature* (Durham, NC: Duke University Press, 1994).

Johnson, Eric E. "Intellectual Property and the Incentive Fallacy." *Florida State University Law Review* 29 (2012).

Jones, Amelia. "'The Artist Is Present': Artistic Re-enactments and the Impossibility of Presence." *TDR* 55 (2011).

Jury, Louise. "Death and the Artist." *The Independent*, August 2, 1998.

Kalb, Jonathan. *Beckett in Performance* (Cambridge: Cambridge University Press, 1989).

Kan, Steven S. "Court Standards on Joint Inventorship and Authorship." *DePaul Journal of Art, Technology, and Intellectual Property Law* 267 (2009).

Kirle, Bruce. *Unfinished Show Business: Broadway Musicals as Works-in-Process* (Carbondale: Southern Illinois University Press, 2005).

Kolin, Philip C., ed. *Conversations with Edward Albee* (Jackson: University of Mississippi Press, 1988).

Kraut, Anthea. "'Stealing Steps' and Signature Moves: Embodied Theories of Dance as Intellectual Property." *Theatre Journal* 62 (2010).

Larson, Jonathan. *tick, tick . . . Boom!: The Complete Book and Lyrics* (New York: Applause, 2009).

Lee, Jane C. "Upstaging the Playwright: The Joint Authorship Entanglement Between Dramaturgs and Playwrights." *Loyola of Los Angeles Entertainment Law Journal* 19 (1998).

Lehmann, Hans-Thies. *Postdramatic Theatre*. Trans. Karen Jurs-Munby (New York: Routledge, 2006).

Lemley, Mark. "Romantic Authorship and Rhetoric of Property." *Texas Law Review* 75 (1997).

Lessig, Lawrence. *Free Culture: The Nature and Future of Creativity* (New York: Penguin, 2004).

Levinson, Jerrold. *Music, Art, and Metaphysics: Essays in Philosophical Aesthetics* (Ithaca, NY: Cornell University Press, 1990).

Limon, John. *Stand-Up Comedy in Theory, or, Abjection in America* (Durham, NC: Duke University Press, 2000).

Mann, Bruce J. *Edward Albee: A Casebook* (New York: Routledge, 2003).

McCarthy, J. Thomas. *The Rights of Publicity and Privacy* (St. Paul, MN: West Group, 1999).

McCarthy, Philip. "The Man Who Cried Woolf." *The Age*, August 18, 2007.

McLeod, Kembrew. *Owning Culture: Authorship, Ownership, and Intellectual Property Law* (New York: Peter Lang, 2001).

McMahon, Barbara. "Beckett Estate Fails to Stop Women Waiting for Godot." *The Guardian* 3, February 2006.

Mee, Erin B. "Shattered and Fucked Up and Full of Wreckage: The Words and Works of Charles L. Mee." *TDR* 46 (2002).

Miller, Derek. "Performative Performances: A History and Theory of the 'Copyright Performance.'" *Theatre Journal* 64 (2012).

Nachman, Gerald. *Seriously Funny: The Rebel Comedians of the 1950s and 1960s* (New York: Pantheon, 2003).

Nevin, Douglas M. "Comment: No Business Like Show Business: Copyright Law, the Theatre Industry, and the Dilemma of Rewarding Collaboration." *Emory Law Journal* 53 (2004).

No Strings Attached: Live, Extended, and Uncensored. Directed by David Steinberg. USA: Paramount, 2006.

Oliar, Dotan and Christopher Sprigman. "There's No Free Laugh (Anymore): The Emergence of Intellectual Property Norms and the Transformation of Stand-Up Comedy." *Virginia Law Review* 94, no. 8 (2008).

Pasolli, Robert. *A Book on the Open Theatre* (New York: Bobbs-Merrill, 1970).

Perret, Gene. *Successful Stand-Up Comedy: Advice from a Comedy Writer* (New York: Samuel French, 1993).

Phelan, Peggy. *Unmarked: The Politics of Performance* (London: Routledge, 1993).

Phelan, Peggy and Marquard Smith. "Performance, Live Culture and Things of the Heart." *Journal of Visual Culture* 2, no. 3 (2003).

Phillips, Jill A. "Performance Rights: Protecting a Performer's Style [notes]." *Wayne Law Review* 37, no. 3 (1991).

Plunka, Gene A. *Jean-Claude van Itallie and the Off-Broadway Theater* (Newark: University of Delaware Press, 1999).

Rabkin, Gerald. "Is There a Text on This Stage? Theatre/Authorship/Interpretation." *Performing Arts Journal* 9, no. 2/3 (1985).

Richards, Stanley, ed. *The Best Short Plays of 1969* (Philadelphia: Chilton Book Company, 1969).

Richardson, Ryan J. "The Art of Making Art: A Narrative of Collaboration in American Theatre and a Response to Calls for Change to the Copyright Act of 1976." *Cumberland Law Review* 42 (2011).

Robertson, Nan. "Dispute over 'L.S.D.' Appears Ended." *New York Times*, January 10, 1985.
Rose, Mark. *Authors and Owners: The Invention of Copyright* (Cambridge, MA: Harvard University Press, 1993).
Saltz, David Z. "What Theatrical Performance Is (Not): The Interpretation Fallacy." *Journal of Aesthetics and Art Criticism* 59, no. 3 (2001).
———. "When Is the Play the Thing?—Analytic Aesthetics and Dramatic Theory." *Theatre Research International* 20, no. 3 (2002).
Saunders, David. *Authorship and Copyright* (New York: Routledge, 1992).
Savran, David. *The Wooster Group, 1975-1985: Breaking the Rules* (Ann Arbor, MI: UMI Research Press, 1986).
Schroeder, Jonathan E. "The Artist and the Brand." *European Journal of Marketing* 39, no. 11/12 (2005).
Schulman, Sarah. *Stagestruck: Theater, AIDS, and the Marketing of Gay America* (Durham, NC: Duke University Press, 1998).
Schur, Richard. *Parodies of Ownership: Hip-Hop Aesthetics and Intellectual Property Law* (Ann Arbor: University of Michigan Press, 2009).
The Serpent: A Ceremony. Directed by James Barbosa, Joseph Chaikin, et al. New York: Educational Broadcasting Corporation, 1970.
Shewey, Don. *Sam Shepard: The Life, The Loves, Behind the Legend of a True American Original* (New York: Dell, 1985).
Shteir, Rachel. "The Dramaturg's Progress." *Theatre Topics* 13, no. 1 (March 2003).
Sidiropoulou, Avra. *Authoring Performance: The Director in Contemporary Theatre* (New York: Palgrave, 2011).
Solomon, Rakesh H. *Albee in Performance* (Bloomington: University of Indiana Press, 2010).
Taylor, Diana. *The Archive and the Repertoire: Performing Cultural Memory in the Americas* (Durham, NC: Duke University Press, 2003).
Templeton, Sara-Kate. "Beckett Estate Rules Out Female Version of Godot." *The Scotsman* 27, July 1998.
Vaidhyanathan, Siva. *Copyrights and Copywrongs: The Rise of Intellectual Property and How It Threatens Creativity* (New York: NYU Press, 2001).
Van Itallie, Jean-Claude. *America Hurrah and Other Plays* (New York: Grove Press, 1978).
Wade, Mike. "Plumbing the Depths? Actors Take to the Toilet." *London Times*, August 15, 2009.
Waiting for Beckett. Directed by John L. Reilly. New York: Global Village, 1994.
Wimsatt, W. K. and Monroe C. Beardsley. *The Verbal Icon* (Lexington: University Press of Kentucky, 1982).
Wollheim, Richard. *Art and Its Objects*, second edition with six supplementary essays (Cambridge: Cambridge University Press, 1980).
Woodmansee, Martha. "The Genius and the Copyright: Economic and Legal Conditions of the Emergence of the 'Author.'" *Eighteenth-Century Studies* 17, no. 4 (1984).
Worthen, W. B. *Print and the Poetics of Modern Drama* (Cambridge: Cambridge University Press, 2005).
Yarbrough Jr., J. David. "What's Mine Might Be Yours: Why We Should Rethink the Default Rule for Copyright Co-ownership in Joint Works." *Tulane Law Review* 76 (2001).
Žižek, Slavoj. *First as Tragedy, Then as Farce* (New York: Verso, 2009).
Zoglin, Richard. *Comedy at the Edge: How Stand-Up in the 1970s Changed America* (New York: Bloomsbury, 2008).

Index

About the Author

George Pate currently serves as assistant professor of theater and drama in the Department of English, Theater, and Liberal Studies at the University of South Carolina at Beaufort. His scholarship has appeared in *Theater Journal*, the *Journal of Dramatic Theory and Criticism*, the *Journal of American Drama and Theater*, and *Theater Symposium*. He is also an actor, director, and playwright. His play *Sanguine* recently underwent a two-year development process at the Barter Theatre in Abingdon, Virginia, culminating in a workshop production.

Lightning Source UK Ltd.
Milton Keynes UK
UKHW011022070620
364561UK00005B/205

9 781683 931584